AF739177

Historical Sociology

Historical Sociology

A Rokkanian Approach to Eastern European Development

Arne Kommisrud

LEXINGTON BOOKS

A division of
ROWMAN & LITTLEFIELD PUBLISHERS, INC.
Lanham • Boulder • New York • Toronto • Plymouth, UK

A division of Rowman & Littlefield Publishers, Inc.
A wholly owned subsidiary of The Rowman & Littlefield Publishing Group, Inc.
4501 Forbes Boulevard, Suite 200
Lanham, MD 20706

Estover Road
Plymouth PL6 7PY
United Kingdom

Copyright © 2009 by Lexington Books

All rights reserved. No part of this publication may be reproduced, stored in a retrieval system, or transmitted in any form or by any means, electronic, mechanical, photocopying, recording, or otherwise, without the prior permission of the publisher.

British Library Cataloguing in Publication Information Available

Library of Congress Cataloging-in-Publication Data

Kommisrud, Arne, 1952-
Historical sociology : a Rokkanian approach to Eastern European development / Arne Kommisrud.
p. cm.
Includes bibliographical references and index.
ISBN 978-0-7391-2871-8 (hardcover : alk. paper) —
ISBN 978-0-7391-3634-8 (electronic : alk. paper)
1. Europe, Eastern—Economic conditions. 2. Historical sociology.
3. Rokkan, Stein. I. Title.
HC244.K6336 2009
338.947—dc22 2008054835

Printed in the United States of America

♾™ The paper used in this publication meets the minimum requirements of American National Standard for Information Sciences—Permanence of Paper for Printed Library Materials, ANSI/NISO Z39.48–1992.

Contents

Chapter One

Stein Rokkan's European Macro Model and the Historical-Sociological Tradition

The purpose of this chapter is to attempt a clarification of the main outline, or the range of variation in research strategy, through a macro historical approach to the study of politics. This will be done by presenting Stein Rokkan's model of European history and by attempting to place his macro historical research strategy in relation to that applied by other scholars in this field.

In his later work—from the latter half of the 1960s until his death in 1979—Stein Rokkan returned to more basic issues in political science: the basis of political legitimacy and nation building in Europe, which had been his intellectual starting point, not through historical–philosophical speculation, but by formulating meta-theoretical models of variations in the speed and proliferation of the extension of rights in political history. He also wished to explain disparities in the party system in Continental Europe. In his work on these problems he also gradually turned away from the ahistorical, abstract development formulas that form the starting point of the postwar modernization theories, and adopted the view that all of the most important sets of variables in model building must be historically founded.[1] The result of this was his detailed conceptual maps of European development. The development of these coincided with a renaissance of macro historical works within, or rather on the periphery of, Western social sciences research.

Macro history makes relatively bold comparisons of structures and processes in various societies and historical periods.[2] Nevertheless the historical forms, from an analytical perspective, are relatively limited: The number of entities, such as states, empires and historical civilizations, are comparatively few; the number of dependent variables, such as political and economic systems, may be more numerous; but the empirically existing values that these may assume are far from indefinite in number. This, logically enough, establishes some constraints on the choice of strategies and theoretical postulates in this branch of social sciences. Stein Rokkan himself emphasized the astonishment he experienced on discovering the *morphology* between his own attempt at explaining the variations in the extension of suffrage in Western Europe and attempts by Barrington Moore Jr., Perry Anderson and Immanuel Wallerstein to explain in macro historical terms why different forms of political regime developed in the 20th century (Moore); why the only workers' revolution that succeeded in this century did so precisely in Russia (Anderson), and the emergence of dependence and exploitation structures at the global level in today's world (Wallerstein). This astonishment prompted the development of the conceptual maps that Rokkan proposed in the 1970s.[3] Although scholars who are Marxist or Marxist-inspired, such as Perry Anderson and Immanuel Wallerstein, have not developed their theoretical analyses in dialogue with Stein Rokkan, I feel that a comparison may be of value. It can help identify some common basic questions relating to the approach itself, and also, naturally, to reveal some special characteristics of Rokkan's thinking.

Macro history, as a genre in the social sciences, can be said in many ways to continue the classic tradition in sociology and political science. Names like Alexis de Toqueville, Max Weber and Karl Marx are associated with problems and tentative solutions that, in social science research in general, have often been overshadowed by more limited and frequently *technocratized* hyphenated disciplines. Specialization in itself is no evil, of course, but the kind of question the classics posed must often lead to an *interdisciplinary* fundamental attitude to elicit an answer.

Questions important to macro history concern the relationship between various social and economic processes of change which, at the transition from the middle ages to early modern times, gave Europe special characteristics and an advantage compared with other countries and continents. The unique thing in the European political experience, the preconditions and consequences of the European breakthrough, can be considered by looking at a number of mutually related topics: the transition from feudalism to capitalism in its various phases; cultural conditions (the Renaissance, the Reformation); state building and the superiority in military technology from the late 16th century; the formation of a European system of nation states; revolutions and nation-building processes; war and nationalism—and not least the fascism of the 20th century, which Rokkan, encouraged by his pupils, became concerned with toward the end of his life.[4]

Macro history, in grappling with such problems, finds itself in a field of tension between, on the one hand, concrete historical research emphasizing the characteristics of the sequences of development of certain countries and regions and, on the other hand, generalizing research in the social sciences. Elements from these two fields can be combined in a number of ways and constitutes different research strategies. The term *research strategies* is here taken to mean the relationship between theories and scientific findings, and differs from the methodical tools used to establish these findings, such as a comparative method and historical source criticism. What distinguishes different macro historical strategies from each other is how many of the units studied and to how many of the values on the dependent variable the researcher wishes to give a theoretically deduced explanation.[5]

At the *methodological* level there is no consistent opinion among various macro historical researchers, and may not even be possible or desirable. The debate on the basic issues will, however, have much in common with the discussion about such questions in social science research in general: the relationship between actor-based and structure-based categories of explanation; functionalism versus strategic thinking; independent empirical indicators as a test of higher-level systems, etc. These are issues that will have to be treated seriously to avoid the more speculative excrescences that macro history obviously invites. Concept development and abstraction, the conceptual homogenization of a highly heterogeneous empirical field, is the precondition of systematic research through comparative methods. This raises the question of the fruitfulness of different levels of generalization, and Rokkan's macro historical approach must be said to represent a rejection of the airiest theoretical strata. Macro historical analysis is related to the study of development problems in today's non-Western world. The empirical foundation of the research is, however, considerably wider and greater for macro history. This provides a better possibility for theoretical continuity and cumulative results, and thus also for avoiding the numerous crises and breakdown of paradigms that have characterized the rise and fall of various schools in development studies. In contrast, Weber, as one of the most prominent macro historical social scientists, worked with such a vast background of material that his works on Greece, Rome, Egypt, Mesopotamia, India and China are still basic books for anyone wishing to study the history and sociology of these societies even today.

Three sets of substantial questions will be highlighted in the following comparison: 1) the development of capitalism, 2) state development, and 3) nation building/nationalism. Each of the various authors emphasizes these three questions differently; in discussing these authors, this work will follow their individual focii.

STEIN ROKKAN AS MACRO HISTORIAN

As a starting point, however, I would like to dwell a little on Rokkan's 1960s comparative historical analyses. Two main phases in Rokkan's theoretical work can be distinguished. His discontent with his own analyses in the first phase leads to the second, that is, his central texts on the process of the structuring of mass politics in Western Europe, written in the 1960s, were later to be extended by means of his conceptual maps of Europe.

His continuous basic problem may be said to have been twofold: 1) What explains the variations in the possibilities of expressing protest, posing demands and mobilizing support in different countries, where there is everywhere a wide range of political opinions in electorates and the spectrum of political options accommodates these only to an imperfect degree? 2) What explains the variations in political alternatives (*institutional packages* or *profiles*) with which the different countries end up, and their prehistory?

One characteristic of Rokkan's research practice is the basically open attitude toward competing theories. His models and perspectives changed continuously as a consequence of the emergence along the way of an Albert Hirschmann, a Barrington Moore Jr. or an Immanuel Wallerstein.[6] New variables were added to the old, new perspectives were tentatively integrated in his project. Any type of reductionism, reducing development to the forms of manifesation of a single fundamental factor, was rejected in favor of an emphasis on the complex interaction between economic, political, cultural, religious and demographic factors. Other people's monocausal explanations were included in his work in a diverse totality, more often than not in a surprising manner.[7]

Rokkan's interest was oriented toward shifts in the alliances of power in states and among elites. He therefore proposed four "critical junctures" as the main turning points of splits and alliances in the historical development of Western Europe as the main organizing path through which all states and political entities had to pass. With a retrospective method he could "map" the alliance structures through a period of 400 years and reveal the present party system as an outcome.

Rokkan had as a point of departure that to "gain understanding of the processes of center formation and nation building, it was essential to analyze not only the conflicts or bargains between the landowners and merchants . . . but also the arrangements between secular and religious authorities, between majority and minority churches, and between religious hierarchies and the lower levels of priesthood."[8] A central core of nation builders will have to decide on alliances on two fronts: the religious (Roman Catholic, Protestant, or a secular posture) and the economic (landowners or urban commercial and industrial entrepreneurs). The nation-building core will everywhere have to face opposition from a dissident, nonconformist religious body and from a movement of resistance in the periphery. The first of the center's choices (the first critical juncture) will determine the next. At each juncture a political opposition arises depending on the nation builders' choice of alliance, thus reducing "the bewildering variety of empirical party systems to a set of ordered consequences of decisions and developments at three critical junctures in the history of each nation."[9] Rokkan's scheme of analysis posited four decisive dimensions of cleavage in Western polities:

> In fact it is not very difficult to translate the succession of "revolutionary junctures" into a straightforward account of events at four critical junctures in the political history of Western Europe:
>
> 1. The great upheavals of the *Reformation and the Thirty Years War*, that left Europe divided into three parts:
>   a. a wholly Protestant North (Denmark–Norway, Sweden–Finland, Prussia);
>   b. a broad belt of religiously mixed territories from Ireland toward the Alps (Britain–Ireland, the Low Countries; The Rhineland, large sections of France until 1685, the Swiss cantons);
>   c. the Counter-Reformation countries in the East and the South (the Habsburg territories, Spain and the Italian territories, France after 1685).
> 2. *The National Revolution* triggered off in territory after territory in the wake of the Napoleonic Wars caused very different sorts of cleavages in the three parts of Europe:
>   a. in the Protestant North the decisive cleavages tended to be territorial–cultural: the awakening peasantry and the defenders of ethnic peripheries allied themselves with outgroups within the urban elite and developed broad "Left" fronts against established administrative and religious bureaucracy;
>   b. in the broad "border belt" conflicts developed on two fronts: peripheral protest and Protestant dissent on the one side, movements for the defence of Catholic minorities on the other;
>   c. in Counter-Reformation Europe a deep division between Radical–Liberal secularizers and Catholic defenders of the privileges of the Church.
> 3. *The Industrial Revolution* added further dimensions to each national cleavage structure:
>   a. in the Protestant North and in the Protestant regions of the "border belt" the growth of industrial production generated increasing tension between rural and urban interests, but this cleavage did not always find expression in the organization of distinct agrarian parties;
>   i. in economies dominated by large estates (England, Scotland, Prussia) the rural interest tended to be aggregated within broader Establishment fronts;
>   b. in countries and regions with larger proportions of smaller, family-sized farms distinct agrarian parties were more likely to emerge;

i. in the Counter-Reformation countries the emerging Catholic mass parties found most of their support within the devout peasantry and were able to aggregate the agrarian interests without much difficulty;

4. The Industrial Revolution also generated within each country deepening cleavages between workers and salaried employees on the one hand, employers and owners on the other, but these cleavages did not always generate unified politcal movements: the leaders of the last stratum of the population to be given regular rights of political citizenship were torn between their commitment to the historical nation they were part of, and their commitment to the international solidarity of their class; this was an old-established line of cleavage in most working-class movements but the dilemma became particularly acute when one country, the Soviet Union, made itself the champion of international working-class solidarity and generated splits within each national movement.[10]

These four sources of conflict, center–periphery (conflicts between the national culture and assorted subordinate ones, such as ethnic, linguistic, or religious groups often located in the peripheries), state–church (struggles between the state seeking to dominate, and the church trying to maintain its historical corporate rights), land–industry (conflicts between the landed elite and the growing bourgeois class), and capitalist–worker (the struggles on which Marx focused) have continued into the contemporary world, and have provided a framework for the party systems of the stable liberal and social democratic polities of Western Europe. Class became the most salient source of conflict and voting, particularly after the extension of the suffrage to all adult males.

"The decisive contrast among the Western party systems clearly reflect differences in *the national histories of conflict and compromise across the first three of the four cleavage lines*: the 'center–periphery,' the state–church, and the land–industry cleavages generated national developments in *divergent* directions, while the owner–worker cleavage tended to bring the party systems *closer to each other* in their basic structure."[11]

However, taking traditional *positivist* psephology in the 1950s and early 1960s as his starting point, Rokkan in the 1970s developed his models ever further backward in time to explain the phenomena that originally interested him. Even if the elements in his initial analysis of cleavage structures "reappear unchanged in Rokkan's later publications," he introduced additional variables by linking the variations in democratizations with the earlier variations in state formation and nation building.[12] Here the evolution of language and the setting of cultural boundaries played a major role. Rokkan explained the new theoretical efforts in the following way:

> I was not very happy with the typology. . . . It treated every case in isolation, without taking into account the context of the surrounding world, or its geo-

> political position. I began by studying connections in space between the various countries, and I became convinced of the vital importance of inter-territorial connections, both in nation building processes and subsequently in the structuring of mass mobilization.[13]

The intention underlying his model, and its more precise formulation in his detailed conceptual maps of European history, was to establish a well-founded starting point for constructing substantial theories on the origins of specific political systems—to say something about the principles the scholar should consider when explaining a certain class phenomenon.[14] But while his explicanda was still the same, now "in principle every variable in this model could be at once a 'dependent' and an 'independent variable.'"[15]

The Norwegian sociologist Lars Mjøset was the first to sharply contrast the starting point of Rokkan's theory construction with a more actor-oriented one, as for instance expressed in the first Norwegian Survey of the country's power structures (*Maktutredningen*). Although it was hardly Rokkan's intention that his model be seen as an independent alternative, which could be set against and chosen instead of more traditional thinking and well-established tools in political science, a quotation from Mjøset's interpretation may be clarifying:

> The problem of the power model, then, is that without a link to rationality contexts and conditions of action it can only produce hypothetical calculations between rational actors. . . . As soon as a context and conditions are specified, the action rationality will conform to these specific conditions. A concise formalization of decision theory at this level would be far too complicated for calculations. . . . Depending on how the 'surroundings' and the actors' understanding of these are interpreted, one may, provided a rational action, produce various hypotheses and theories. . . . An alternative to such revaluation of formal decision-making theory would be to establish our theory immediately at the level of the action conditions and the rationality context.[16]

I think that such a view in historically oriented research may be of value. All social science research, in its explanations, must give constant attention to the complex interplay between actors' autonomy and the constraints inherent in the structures. In many cases, however, the historical situation, seen as a framework for action, will be beyond the actors' own horizon and field of overview. Rokkan's models and conceptual maps are interesting in terms of methodology in this connection, because they systematize the variations in the sociocultural and socioeconomic *constraints*, which various political actors have been faced with historically.[17]

The underlying thinking can in some cases help reformulate certain difficult questions for actor-oriented theories: Why do certain preferences arise in certain actors at certain times—and similarly: How do the limitations in options open to them at different times and places vary? How can we in specific contexts explain the paradox that history is apparently an endless chain of ideal projects that fail?

Rokkan's basic model, which steered the course backward in time, and his various conceptual maps, reduced the complexity of Europe's territorial history to a number of mutually connected constellations of variables over time. His declared program was to "develop and thoroughly try out explanations and models of a variety of sequences and assessments of implications of alternative sequences."[18]

The background of the model has the following conditions:

> The breakthrough toward merchant capitalism produced a world network of economic transactions and undermined established boundaries, while the emergence of nation-states tended to mark off clear-cut boundaries and accentuate territorial identity and citizenship. This is the great paradox of Western European development: The model was designed as a tool for systematic research on the sources and consequences of this paradox.[19]

Three big categories of variables are schematically distinguished in the following way:

1. *Precondition variables* identify the decisive differences in the initial conditions and the early processes of territorial organization, of state building and resource combination before the French Revolution.
2. *Intervening process variables* describe the interaction of the national revolution with the industrial 1789–1920s.
3. *Explicanda* describe variations in political response structures: the structuring of political alternatives and the decisive dimensions of mass alignments in each territorial system.[20]

Rokkan strongly emphasized the multidimensional character of the model. At any level of the construction of the model a distinction is made between three types of variables: economic, territorial, or political in a narrow sense, and cultural. In some cases the variables will coincide in the classification of the empirical units, in other cases they are combined in more or less complex typologies.

Rokkan's idea is that the model shall be capable of being applied so that it can be read both *en aval* (*downstream*) and *en amont* (*upstream*), that is, both forward looking and backward looking in time, using a distinction from the Annales historians. In the first case variables can be read as direct characteristics of historical regions, or they can characterize the regions contextually on the basis of the values of the larger units of which they are a part. One takes as one's starting point a given historical condition of the past and attempts to arrive at its future alternative outcomes. The latter retrospective diachronic way of reading the model, that is by explaining period-specific variations by a combination of variables in earlier periods, is, however, closer to Rokkan's own thinking.

As a result, historical sociologist Charles Tilly pointed out Rokkan's own perspective played a role in restricting the development of the models by viewing earlier periods too much through his own contemporary lens: "The distinction Rokkan introduced late in his career between 'upstream' and 'downstream' analyses was interesting and relevant, but in fact he never much enjoyed moving downstream from past to present."[21]

STATE AND NATION BUILDING

Rokkan saw the development of the state as the penetration of the periphery by the center, in which a tax-imposing military–administrative core area renders outlying districts passive and secures their external boundaries. The strategy employed in external boundary building determines the development of the internal political system (the nature and duration of the phases of democratization).

The possibilities and the type of external "Exit" determines, in Albert Hirschmann's terminology, the conditions of the emergence of an internal "Voice."[22] This interplay is developed in detail in several of Rokkan's most well-known conceptual maps of Europe. In Rokkan's own words: "The essential rationale for my 'typological–topological' model of Europe is that it generates hypotheses about *the interaction between external and internal boundary-building strategies* in the history of different territorial systems: the policies pursued in controlling external transactions also affected internal channelling of voice."[23]

Rokkan called attention to *systematic differences in the political experiences of peoples in various regions of Western Europe,* as a function of their relationships to two major *axes* of development. The South–North dimension received the name of *the state–culture axis* by Rokkan, while the East-West line was called the *state-economy axis*:

1) The state–culture axis: One must here remember that there was not the same degree of commercial unification that one would get later on—market connections were much less strongly developed than after the Renaissance—the cultural unity of the Western European space, however, was far greater in

the premodern era than after because of the peasantry, the universal Catholic church and the institutional unity where one feudal matrix covered the whole of Europe. In the study of transactions over distances, the state–culture axis refers to the differences in cultural conditions of communication: ethnic affinities or enmities, differences in language, in moral codes, in religion. In the North we find a band in which national Protestant churches early on marked off religious and linguistic areas within which the barriers to the state's cultural penetration were relatively low. "Gutenberg created an essential technology for the building of nations; the mass reproduction of books, tracts and broadsheets made it possible to confine communication within the limits of the particular vernacular. The Reformation reinforced this process in Northern Europe; it meant much more than a break with Rome in matters of theological doctrine; it strengthened the distinctiveness of each territorial culture by integrating the priesthood into the administrative machinery of the state and restricting priests to the confines of the given vernacular."[24] As we move to the South we encounter increasing degrees of religious *supraterritoriality*, with corresponding higher barriers to cultural integration, and ethnic particularities with a strong base for resistance to national integration.

2) The state–economy axis: In the West were states that extracted surplus from a highly monetized economy, long stimulated by their involvement in seaborne trade. In the center was a band of tightly linked trading cities extending from northern Italy up to Flanders, surrounded by areas of intensive agriculture: city–state Europe. In the East were states that ultimately extracted their surplus from coerced agricultural labor. It proved much easier to develop effective core areas at the edges of the city-studded territories of the Roman empire; in these regions, centers could be developed under less competitive conditions and could achieve command of the resources in peripheral areas. Rokkan's East–West axis provides three different conditions for the state builders: in the West one finds states that withdrew the earnings of a highly monetized economy, in the center the urban belt, and in the east commercialized country-estate farming. The difference in the character of the state-administrative center-formation is influenced by the balance between the agrarian economy and the urban economy along the fringes of the old empire.

With the concept of the *city belt* Rokkan pointed at two ideas: the balance of forces and the stability of territorial positions. After the breakup of the Roman Empire, the cities in the trade routes connecting Southern and Northern Europe continued their economic function. "This 'city belt' was at the same time the stronghold of the Roman Catholic Church; this territory had a high density of cathedrals, monasteries and ecclesiastical principalities."[25] They now achieved various forms of political independence in such a way that none of them totally dominated the others.

The city belt functioned as a channel for diffusion of law codes, alphabet, religion, demands from citizens, alliance positions, etc. The cities of the trade-route belt were for centuries strong enough to thwart all efforts at military–administration. On the other hand, access to the taxable trade organized by those cities gave crucial advantages to state makers whose territories lay adjacent to the dense trading networks.

The big paradox in European state development, according to Rokkan, is the fact that the German and Italian core areas, which were still the culturally and technologically most advanced, remained politically fragmented until the latter half of the 19th century, while at the same time strong and stable states emerged along the peripheries. The explanation is to be found in the urban belt, which was also confessionally divided (had problems with the anchorage of loyalty between a supra-national Roman Catholic church and a church organized by the state). A combination of autonomy based on overseas trade and economic strength provided such a highly fragmented *geographic space* at the same time as a national identity was developed early through a community of language.[26]

Nation building, defined as cultural boundary-drawing externally and corresponding standardization internally (the development of national institutions and the spread of a national consciousness), is thus the designation of the process whereby the geographical area of a state's authority also develops to define the boundaries of the shared feeling of identity and culture of a population. The nation-building analysis is, furthermore, based on Weber's distinction between state (monopoly on the legitimate use of violence) and nation (culture as the common basis of identity). To Rokkan, societies in the nation-building process are faced with a set of homogenous problems/crises that describe the process:

> Phase I . . . covers the initial *state-building process*: in Western Europe the period from the High Middle Ages to the French Revolution. This is typically a period of political, economic and cultural unification at the elite level: a series of bargains are struck and a variety of cultural bonds are established across networks of local power-holder and a number of institutions are built for the extraction of resources for common defence, for the maintenance of internal order and the adjudication of disputes, for the protection of established rights and privileges and for the elementary infrastructure requirements of the economy and polity.
>
> Phase II brings in larger sectors of the *masses* into the system: the conscript armies, the compulsory schools, the emerging mass media create channels for direct contact between the central elite and parochial populations of the peripheries and generate widespread feelings of identity with the total political system,

> frequently, but not necessarily, in protracted conflict with already established identities such as those built up through churches or sects or through peripheral linguistic elites.
>
> Phase III brings these subject masses into *active participation* in the workings of the territorial political system: typically through the establishments of privileges of opposition, the extension of the electorates for organs of representation, the formation of organized parties for the mobilization of support and the articulation and aggregation of demands.
>
> Phase IV finally represents the next series of steps in the expansion of the administrative apparatus of the territorial state: the growth of *agencies of redistribution,* the building of public welfare services, the development of nationwide policies for the equalization of economic conditions, negatively through progressive taxation, positively through transfers from the better-off strata to the poorer, from the richer to the backward regions.[27]

The order in which problems were confronted could vary, but the way in which they were solved created structures that set the frames of politics even today. The *crisis accumulation syndrome*, the simultaneous coincidence of a number of crises of development, which limit the time and the possibilities available for resolving them, is also used as a partial explanation of the victory of fascism in Germany and Italy by Rokkan and Hagtvet.[28]

Rokkan developed this four-stage model taken from Talcott Parsons by crossing each of the four subsystems with a center–periphery dimension. The political systems could thus be divided into four different types of domination and hierarchy, each with their specific potential for conflict and resistance that the analyst should observe if he or she wishes to account for certain classes of phenomena. This model (as well as Parsons') should be considered as formal and metatheoretical, which means that an analysis of social change based on it ought to be firmly situated in a specific time and in particular circumstances. It therefore needs to be filled out with complementary theoretical propositions and appropriate data of a *historical* kind, that means partial and local ones.[29] This is what Stein Rokkan does with the development of his conceptual maps.

Rokkan's point is that *nation building is a center vs. periphery conflict*; national consolidation is a stage in popular political participation, which at the same time leads to the erasure of periphery-based countercultures.[30] The distribution of both religious and linguistic affiliation determines the outcome. The Reformation represented the first step toward defining national territories in Europe. Both Lutherans and Calvinists broke away from the Roman Catholic supraterritoriality and integrated the ecclesiastic bureaucracies into a secular political–administrative organization. In Protestant countries the state churches became important instruments in the development of homogenous national cultures. The Catholic Church, which retained its supraterritorial character, delayed the development of a national identity. It was not until later, after the French Revolution, that it came to play a role in the development of periphery nationalisms in alliance with nationalist leaders who fought against a Protestant (Belgium prior to 1830, Ireland after 1820), Orthodox (Poland, Lithuania), or secularized center. In Rokkan's own words

> [The reformation] meant more than a break with Rome in matters of theological doctrine; it strengthened the distinctiveness of each territorial culture by integrating the priesthood into the administrative machinery of the state and by restricting priests to the confines of the given vernacular. In Hirschman's (1970) terms, the Reformation built up a wall against cultural "exits" into other territories. This wall was not only an important strategy in legitimizing the new territorial state, but in the longer run was also a crucial step in preparing the broader population for the use of "voice" within their system.[31]

A large proportion of the variations in state-building costs in Europe must, however, be ascribed to the distribution of ethnic groups, which are more clearly territorially rooted than religious groups. This distribution contributed to determining the degree and nature of political opposition and the groups and areas that were to become political peripheries. In Rokkan's opinion *language* is the most genuine expression of the citizens' cultural identity. *He therefore associates the modern concept of the nation very closely with the concept of language.* Accordingly, after the French Revolution the members of the French nation were those who inhabited the country's territory and who spoke the central vernacular, the vernacular of the *Île de France*. According to Rokkan, language now had a double significance: partly the totality of the vernaculars in use, partly the vernacular of the standardizing elite as the norm of written communication. The background of the fate of the various languages in institutional and political terms was that only a few had the possibility of being recognized as written languages. Three factors explain this different distribution of roles: territorial consolidation, the invention of printing, and industrialization. It was of decisive importance to the development of a language whether, prior to the development of mass-reproduction technology, it had become the relatively stable norm of a center. The chances of survival of peripheral languages, on the other hand, were slim unless they had developed their own institutionally rooted norms (in school systems and mass education) prior to the industrial revolution. The new geographical mobility in its wake exposed large proportions of the rural population to the dominant-language norm in industrial areas.[32]

To Rokkan, the territorial distribution of peripheries in Europe before *the era of nation building* is the outcome of a long historical process in which the state-builders, in many stages, created, consolidated and superimposed on each other linguistic and national boundaries. Rokkan distinguished between two main types of peripheries, the dissimilarities of which affect the form of opposition to the center. Among the first are

- the *pure peripheries*, the subjugated areas in the Celtic–Atlantic West and in the eastern border areas, which had no independent political organization in the Middle Ages,
- the failed centers, which for a period sustained their own state organizations, but which later were absorbed in greater territorial associations (Scotland, Catalonia, Bavaria).

Both the above-mentioned forms are termed *external peripheries*. In addition he used the term *buffer peripheries*, meaning the areas at intersecting points between dominant centers, but without being completely swallowed up by them. First and foremost on the fringes of the old empire there were *interface peripheries* (on the eastern side between Germans and Italians and Slavs or Hungarians, in the north between Germans on the one side and Danes or Dutch on the other, and between France and parts of the old realm, such as Flanders, Savoy, Alsace–Lorraine). These were the *raw materials* of nationalism in Europe prior to the French Revolution, according to Stein Rokkan.[33]

FROM BASIC MODEL TO AN EXPLANATION OF HISTORICAL VARIATION

Rokkan's research strategy in his late period—the relationship between his draft theories and the empirical findings to which they relate and seek to explain—must be characterized as highly demanding. He wanted no less than to explain all the values which a certain dependent variable (the modern party system) could assume for one single unit, the European or West European territorial system. In principle such a strategy can be carried out if one uses the territories' location in the system as a whole as the starting point of the explanation, a way of thinking also found in Fernand Braudel and Immanuel Wallerstein.

Was Rokkan successful in accomplishing this? As will become apparent, my answer to the question is ambiguous. On the one hand, it is on this issue that his most important and original contribution to historical sociology is made; on the other hand, his outline of European development approaches a point where the model-building ambition, from one point of view, seems to prevent the carrying out of a promising historical synthesis. I will not, however, anticipate this discussion here.

Rokkan's conceptual maps are a way of simplifying, or homogenizing, this enormously heterogeneous historical material, which is suitable for a wholly new and clear insight into the conditions of European politics. The main idea behind the development of his conceptual maps is that variations between today's political systems in Western Europe can be explained by the region's relations with the two most important differentiating processes in European history—in Rokkan summarized in two axis systems. These processes along two dimensions place considerable restraints on the political actors in the processes of state building and nation building. An economic east–west axis, where the distance from a central trade belt of free cities from Italy to Flanders (originating from the restoration of trade between the East, the Mediterranean and the North Sea after the defeat of the Muslims) and the degree of monetization were decisive. A cultural south–north axis (Catholic supranational ecclesiastical organization versus Protestant state churches) at the same time imposed varying constraints on the possibilities of nation building, that is culturally homogenous nation states.

The specific approach Rokkan employed to construct his conceptual maps was to combine three of the *initial variables* of the basic model: geopolitical position, strength/structure of the city network, and the result of the Reformation. The first two variables are given a five-step east–west typology, while the third divides the Europe previously dominated by the Catholic Church into three zones.

In the following points Rokkan gave a description of the paradox in European state building, which he attempted to explain through his conceptual maps:

1. The heartland of the old Western Empire was studded with cities in a broad trade-route belt stretching from the Mediterranean to the east as well as west of the Alps northward to the Rhine and the Danube;
2. This *city belt* was at the same time the stronghold of the Roman Catholic Church; this territory had a high density of cathedrals, monasteries, and ecclesiastical principalities;
3. The very density of established centers within this territory made it difficult to single out any one as superior to all others; there was no geography-given core area for the development of a strong territorial system;
4. The resurrection of the Holy Roman Empire under the leadership of the four German tribes did not help to unify the territory; the emperors were prey to shifting electoral alliances; many of them were mere figureheads and the best and the strongest of them expended their energies in quarrels with the pope and with the Italian cities;

5. By contrast, it proved much easier to develop effective core areas at the edges of the city-studded territories of the old Empire; in these regions, centers could be built up under less competition and could achieve command of the resources in peripheral areas too far from the cities in the central trade belt;
6. The earliest successes in such efforts of system building at the edges of the old Empire came in the west and in the north, in France, in England, in Scandinavia, later also in Spain; in all these cases the dynasties in the core areas were able to command resources from peripheral territories largely beyond the reach of the cities of the central trade belt;
7. The second wave of successful center building took place on the landward side: first the Habsburgs, with their core area in Austria; then the eastern march of the German Empire; next the Swedes; and finally, and decisively, the Prussians;
8. The fragmented middle belt of cities and petty states was the scene of endless onslaughts, counter-moves and efforts of reorganization during the long centuries from Charlemagne to Bismarck: first, the French monarchs gradually took over the old Lotharingian–Burgurdian buffer zone from Provence to Flanders and incorporated such typical trade cities as Avignon, Aix, and Lyons; second, the key cities to the north of the Alps managed to establish a defense league against all comers and gradually built up the Swiss confederation; similar leagues were established along the Rhine and across the Baltic and the North Sea but never managed to establish themselves as sovereign territorial formations; third, the Habsburgs made a number of encroachments both on the west and on the east of the belt and for some time controlled the crucial territories at the mouth of the Rhine, triggering the next successful effort of consociational confederation, the United Netherlands; finally, in the wake of the French Revolution, Napoleon moved across the middle belt both north and south of the Alps and set in motion a series of efforts at unification, which ended with the successes of the Prussians and the Piedmontese in 1870.[34]

According to Rokkan, three forms of dissolution took place in Europe after the fall of the Roman Empire: feudalization, the emergence of national languages, and center or state formation on the fringes of the old empire. The main point in reading Rokkan's model is that these processes did not coincide in time and that precisely this fact produced highly different conditions of state building and nation building in different places.

Rokkan gradually made his model more nuanced by placing a stronger emphasis on the fact that the dissolution processes, and the ensuing attempts at territory building in the north, west and east, were influenced by the great waves of migration and colonization (i.e., the large-scale removal of ethnically diverse peoples). One important consequence of this was increased assimilation of peripheral communities in one or more of the territorial-controlling networks (cities, church and peripheral centers). This also meant that there was potential for peripheral protest and politicizing of peripheries. The release of this potential explains a large part of the variation in the costs of state building and linguistic standardization between individual territorial structures, supplementing factors of an economic and cultural nature, as mentioned above.

Rokkan's model reflects a specific view of the course of political development: The first phase in the political unification of a territory is state formation, with taxation, army and civil service. Then the second phase follows national integration, with standardization of culture and language. The last phase is associated with the emergence of modern class conflicts, with the various types of division between interest groups in manufacturing and marketplace. Each phase of development creates differences deposited as archaeological layers in the political tradition, without the traces of the old divisions disappearing. The *contents of politics* at a certain time is therefore made up of a complicated interaction between intersecting lines of conflict, different in different countries in terms of geographical, economic and cultural–historical conditions, which either reinforce each other (where e.g., class struggle, religious strife and language strife coincide) or which moderate each other where the lines of conflict are crosswise. The classic unilinearity of modernization theory is thus dissolved, and the *variations* in political development become the subject of explanation.

Rokkan's dependent variable is defined in part as the dismantling of various institutional barriers or thresholds to political activity and political mobilization, and in part as variations in the party systems in recent times, and the differences in stability and instability for the modern political system. Institutional thresholds, which can also be seen as phases in the dismantling of absolutism, are 1) *the threshold of legitimacy*, that is, the barrier to freedom of association and discussion, the right of criticism and opposition; 2) *the threshold of incorporation*, the barrier to the right of political participation, the different stages in the extension of suffrage; 3) *the threshold of representation*, the barrier to eligibility and equality in the relationship between votes and gain in seats; and 4) *the threshold of the executive*, the government's accountability and the opposition's (new groups on the political arena) right to take over executive power.[35]

His conceptual maps mark the beginning of his model building in the narrower sense. By developing a region-specific and historically founded Western European model in the 1970s, Rokkan ultimately sought to predict the variations among Western democracies, although in principle, every variable could be at once a dependent and an independent variable.[36]

Historical development in Europe after the fall of the Roman Empire and the migrations can be seen in terms of three different types of periphery formation: political–administrative, military and economic. In total, they constitute a complex differentiating process from the simple to the diverse, visually and parsimoniously represented by Rokkan as a fan-shaped movement. Five main variables play a decisive role in the outcome of this formation of systems for territorial control:

1. the geopolitical distance northward from Rome, the fountainhead of the Old Empire, the focus of Western Christendom after the Schism of 1054, and the symbolic center for the effort of legal unification through the revival of Roman Law;
2. the geopolitical distance westward or eastward from the central belt of trade-route cities from Northern Italy to the areas once controlled by the Hanseatic League;
3. the outcome of the Reformation seen as a revolt against Latin, that is, the degree of resistance against using the national vernacular standards as languages of statecraft and worship;
4. the concentrations of land holdings and the consequent independence or dependence of the peasantry; and
5. the ethnic basis of the early efforts of center building and the linguistic conditions for early versus late consolidation, that is, the relationship of the region to the seven major waves of migration that left their residues across the European map and produced a complex distribution of ethnic/linguistic groups across Western Europe.[37]

STEIN ROKKAN AS A MODEL BUILDER: "THICK COMPARISONS"? [38]

The main principles underlying Stein Rokkan's various conceptual maps and the main features of his model of European development have been presented. Rokkan himself (until his untimely death at the age of 57) developed general models, developmental models and conceptual maps, specifying the main variables and important interrelationships. He was convinced that you need a view of the macro-situation(s) in order to specify more specific hypotheses. Rokkan's "model seeks to balance contextual totality against systematic parsimony. No single explanatory or intervening variable can be linked up with a dependent variable in isolation from the context, whether across systems or across stages."[39] An important characteristic of historical sociology is the use of cases analogically towards one another. This type of comparison is higly facilitated by Rokkan's conceptual maps. His typological maps of Western European party systems—a main contribution to comparative macro-sociology—started from the quantitative analysis of merely a couple of party systems: the other party systems were then integrated in Rokkan's analysis through a method of continued comparison, focusing on a qualitative delimitation (or determination) of contextual factors. The party systems were used as analogies towards one another. "And no variable can justify its position in the scheme simply because it helps to describe the conditions in one particular system at one particular stage: to qualify for inclusion in the analysis a variable must specify a necessary or a sufficient condition for a patent difference in later-stage outcomes between at least two distinct systems."[40] Although some of the variables were "universal," his models were Europe-specific, related to European institutions and organizations and cultural traits. In this sense, his models were not ideal types in the Weberian sense. They were intended as systematic attempts to develop general hypotheses, which then had to be specified in historical and regional contexts, and finally be tested empirically. Three issues are decisive to the outcome of state and nation building in Europe: the strength of the state building core area, the strength of the urban network, and the strength of the opposition against cultural standardization. Rokkan's maps locate constellations of factors that explain the political structuring of Rokkan's cases. They also trace various aspects of causal conjunctures that "structured" the political systems.

There is nevertheless a permanent underlying methodological problem related to his working method that need to be addressed: How are we to understand Rokkan's own unambiguous and step-by-step approach to empirical history research? What is the status of the increasingly more numerous statements of details in the development of specific countries—which is often possible to interpret as a derogation of the main pattern, summarized in the axis system—to his *theoretical* project: Are we still dealing with what, in Rokkan's own words, is a *hypothesis-generating model*, or does the project change in the course of its progress toward constructing an interpretive historical synthesis, in which the borders between the theoretical and the empirical level have been erased? This problem arises from a nomological-deductive point of view, that is, from the standard ideal of post-1945 social science that has aimed at explanation by means of universal laws as in the *covering law* notion.

Using this ideal which codifes the procedures of experimental natural science as our point of departure, we will be hard put to avoid ending up in a circular conclusion when Rokkan's model is used as the starting point of specific studies. Generalization does not necessarily mean establishing "rules without exceptions," but it does at least involve in the words of the Norwegian historian Francis Sejersted, "a disintegration of historical situations in order to isolate special mechanisms which shall be capable of isolation and identification in other historical situations."[41] Rokkan's work is distinguished by a constant search for the dimensions of Europe's diverse trajectories of political development, which made up his empirical data. The problematic point here is that we are eventually left with just as many theoretical developments as actual, historical developments. In other words, every theoretical development covers only the case that exemplifies it, while every case represents a specific development among numerous different combinations that, in principle, are possible among the given variables. The fact that Rokkan increasingly erases the difference between the theoretical and the empirical level in his expositions makes it very difficult to establish the analytical control of empirical diversity, which could prevent us from biting our own tails.[42] From a nomological-deductive perspective, his original model-building ambition collapses through extensive use of ad hoc hypotheses and ad hoc explanations.

However, the social science tradition also contains notions of theory that are not committed to the nomological-deductive ideal. Basically they refuse to compare and evaluate present theoretical knowledge with a utopian state of full knowledge. They claim instead that knowledge is and will always be imperfect. Thus it is very difficult to draw a more precise line between science and various forms of everyday knowledge. Such an understanding is at the roots of conceptions such as "grounded theory" and "thick description" and characterises Rokkan's later works as well. As the Norwegian sociologist Lars Mjøset argues:

> Despite the fact that Rokkan was strongly influenced by 1950–1960s variables-oriented sociology, his standing achievement was dense historical-sociological models and maps that can only be given solid methodological grounding through the alternatives currently being developed by the critics of the variables-based approach, in sociology, as well as by critics of explanation by laws in sociological discussions. One reason for this is certainly to be found in Rokkan's intellectual biography: he took up social science only after he had graduated in philosophy and language. In his mature phases he rediscovered his roots in this European humanist tradition. He took these roots seriously without forgetting his experience with American-style empirical studies based on huge data collections.[43]

Glaser and Strauss developed their ideas of grounded theory in opposition to the testing of "already established knowledge." Emphasizing the discovery of new knowledge, they even suggested that categories should "not be contaminated by concepts more suited to different areas. Similarities and convergences with the (theoretical) literature can be established after the analyrtical core of categories has emerged."[44] Later Strauss emphasized that one may well use existing theory to begin with, provided it was also created as grounded theory, that is in research within the same subject area.[45] He thereby confirmed that grounded theory can be accumulated into more concentrated knowledge. Grounded theory thus implies the discovery of theory from data. As for *thick description*, according to Clifford Geertz, its "major theoretical contributions . . . lie in specific studies. . . . Theoretical formulations hover so low over the interpretations that they don't make much sense or holds much interest apart from them. This is so, not because they are not general (if they are not general, they are not theoretical), but because, stated independently of their applications, they seem either commonplace or vacant."[46]

According to Glaser and Strauss, grounded theory is developed by going back and forth between conceptual clarification and fieldwork. Theory development is not based on deduction from universal laws, nor distinct from explanation. Where Rokkan is concerned, he alternated between conceptual constructions and historical-empirical information in his efforts at explaining European diversity: "We venture to believe that this step-by-step process of confrontation, recasting, and retesting models will eventually help us forward toward the construction of a unified theory of sociocultural, economic, and political change, at least for the territories of Europe."[47] His use of analogies help grounding the theory in context. I therefore agree with Lars Mjøset that Rokkan's later works should be placed within such a non-nomologcal-deductive tradition in social sciences research. It is much more difficult to apply obvious criteria of illegimate ad hoc arguments in this reading of social science than in experimental natural science. "Rokkan was not content with postulates about national exceptionalism. His point was rather that while all units may be seen as exceptional, the goal must be to find the dimensions defining all these exceptional cases. He was seeking patterned variety . . . Rokkan's work shows that . . . we find much accumulated knowledge in grounded theories discovered within specific fields of study . . . (G)eneral *explanatory* theory must be general summaries of contextual factors that may be of value to several local research frontiers."[48]

Rokkan himself had worked empirically mainly on two topics. The first was democratization: the varying cleavages emerging in the process of state- and nation building, and the differing party systems emerging from these cleavages in the process of extending the suffrage. The second topic was nation building in Europe from the 16th to the 20th century, related to the historically much longer process of ethnic-linguistic differentiation. From the emphasis on these two topics follows that Rokkan has neglected others. I will in the following attempt to delimit some other such subjects by discussing some other central models of, or approaches to, European historical macrosociology, and to discuss whether the factors highlighted by these models are consistent with and capable of integration into Rokkan's model.

PERRY ANDERSON'S APPROACH

Perry Anderson is found along quite a much-traveled path in the macro historical tradition. He therefore contrasts well with Rokkan, as he seeks to apply a comparative method to determine and precisely explain the value of the dependent variable for one single unit. As already indicated, the ultimate goal of Perry Anderson's project is, so to speak, to provide reasons for Antonio Gramsci's explanation of the Russian revolution and the success of the Leninist strategy in Russia. "In Russia the state was everything, and the civil society was primordial and gelatinous; in the West there was a proper relation between state and civil society, and when the state trembled a sturdy structure of civil society was at once revealed," Gramsci wrote.[49] In the West civil society, with its organizations and its social substructures between the citizens and the state, meant that the socialist strategy had to be different from that in Russia. Anderson pursued the difference in state organization (a structural dividing line between West and East Europe along the Elbe) backward in time. He attempted to explain historically the origin of this difference around the central problem of why capitalism arose first in West Europe and only there (West Europe's unique avenue to modernization, as it has been called).

His project becomes a slightly marxified version of Max Weber—something he seems rather unwilling to admit. As is well known, Weber defined his overarching project thus: "to what combination of circumstances the fact should be attributed that in Western civilization, and in Western civilization only, cultural phenomena have appeared which (as we like to think) lie in a line of development having universal significance and value."[50] The conceptual tools used by Anderson to solve the problem are also, in several important respects, so remarkably close to Weber's that the similarity cannot be accidental.[51]

He arrived at the explanation by means of a "genealogy of modes of production." There was nothing about feudalism *per se* which, based on some immanent logic, made capitalism necessary: "the one generated automatically and entirely from within the other by an organic internal succession, and therewith effacing it," according to Anderson.[52] The West European social formation was, however, characterized by the presence of both *Germanic* and antique modes of production as elements that could be reactivated. The antique elements were reactivated during the Renaissance, which represents a transitional phase before capitalism in West Europe and the decisive point in European history as a whole. In this period European societies inherited a number of decisive characteristics unknown to other feudal societies, such as Japan: a relatively sophisticated urban ferment; the rediscovery of Roman law which made possible the transition from a scaled to an absolute proprietary right; the reconquest of virtually the entire scientific heritage of antiquity; church independence, representation of the estates of the realm, and so forth:[53]

> The course towards capitalism reveals a *remanence* of the legacy of one mode of production within an epoch *dominated* by another, and a *reactivation* of its spell in the passage to a third. The "advantage" of Europe over Japan lay in its classical antecedence, which after the Dark Ages did not disappear "behind" it, but survived in certain respects "in front of it." In this sense, the concrete historical genesis of feudalism in Europe, far from vanishing like fire and vapour into the terrestrial solidity of its accomplished structure, had tangible effects on its final dissolution. The real historical temporality governing the three great historical modes of production that have dominated Europe up to the present century was thus radically distinct from the continuum of an evolutionary chronology. Contrary to all historicist assumptions, time was as if at certain levels inverted between the first two, to release the critical shift to the last. Contrary to all structuralist assumptions, there was no self-moving mechanism of displacement from the feudal mode of production, as contagious and closed systems. The concatenation of the ancient and the feudal modes of production was necessary to yield the capitalist mode of production in Europe—a relationship that was not merely of diachronic sequence, but also at a certain stage of synchronic articulation.[54]

The power of absolute rule plays a necessary role in this transitional period. Feudalism, according to Anderson, is characterized by fragmented political sovereignty and graduated proprietary rights (an extension and Weberian-inspired reformulation of the classic Marxist definition, which is based on the use of extra-economic coercion in the acquisition of the social surplus product.) The power of absolute rule represents, however, a relinquishment of both these characteristics. The latter follows from the former: The centralization of sovereignty at the top of society dissolves the feudal unity of politics and economy, which as a whole gives the feudal aristocracy two advantages: 1) control of the entire territory, and 2) absolute land possession. The power of absolute rule is, in Anderson's slightly vague Althusserian terms, "primarily determined" by the interests of the feudal aristocracy; it is a *feudal* reaction (regrouping the aristocracy at the level of the state) by concentrating power over society on one hand in order better to withstand the pressure of emerging capitalism. But at the same time it is "secondarily determined" by the interests of the bourgeoisie. This latter statement means that the *methods* employed by the absolute monarchs in their aristocratic defense struggle, indirectly contributed to the development of capitalism in Europe.

Apart from the fact that Anderson here used two different definitions of feudalism when defining absolutism as a feudal political form, his *general* model is somewhat off the mark where the problem is concerned. Anderson specified the model to explain the emergence of capitalism as the dominant mode of production. This capitalist breakthrough did not, however, occur in Europe *in general, but in England in particular.* There, the rebirth of antiquity was of little significance, and there was no strong monarch.[55]

What is interesting in Anderson's exposition, bearing in mind a discussion of Rokkan's model, is, however, his differing periodization and explanation of the state development in West and East Europe. For West Europe Anderson refers to a classic Marxist problem: What was the *class character* of absolutism? He here chooses one of three possible answers: 1) bourgeois, 2) aristocratic, 3) Bonapartist or balancing between the bourgeoisie and the aristocracy.[56] However, common to all three answers is the fact that the development of the form of the state is considered a political result of *internal* socio-economic processes of change. For East Europe, however, the periodization and the determination of the state structure are not linked to the development of the capitalist way of production in a suitable country, but to *external* conditions: warfare and the necessity of defending the country against more advanced West European countries, although East European absolutism was a "repressive machine of a feudal class that had just erased the traditional communal freedom of the poor," "a device for the consolidation of serfdom."[57] An attempt is made here to integrate a tradition from people like Otto Hintze in a Marxist history matrix.[58] Hintze emphasized the international system of states and the role it played in determining individual state building. In other words, in this tradition *an element of interaction comes into play*: Innovation in the art of warfare and the exercise of authority is communicated from one country to the others through warfare. Taxes, and consequently a unified national administration, are made necessary as a response to the demands made by the external state system on the operators in state politics. The political elite is in the field of tension between the international state system and the domestic class structure from which it has to withdraw resources in the merciless interstate rivalry. In this struggle, for the domestic surplus product, the state elite must compete with, and if necessary defeat, representatives of the agrarian upper class that maintains its privileges and rights. To meet the people's (i.e., the peasants') resistance to the tax burden, the centralization and power of the state machinery must be further increased and rationalized.

This perspective on state development, continued by people like Charles Tilly and Theda Skocpol, is important for a critique of Stein Rokkan.[59] Rokkan's conceptual maps tend to regard every individual country's political development as a result of a specific combination of the effect of a set of abstract variables. Although Rokkan himself was aware of this and wished to do something about it, it may here be a question of a weakness associated with his research strategy and his historiography in terms of maps as such. In his model, interaction among the states vanishes in an abstraction. The wars were precisely such an immensely important link in Europe's development between the various national histories before industrialism and capitalism created an economic world system. The apparatus political rulers built was oftentimes an unintended byproduct in a struggle to survive and defeat other pretenders claiming the leadership role in a geographic area. A myriad of state-building projects thus suffered defeat in Europe when present-day states emerged.

Perry Anderson's specific historical chapters can thus be read as a critique of Rokkan's model, as a possible clarification of a necessary, supplementing perspective on the phenomena that Rokkan tried to catch by his conceptual maps. A further interesting point in Anderson in this context is that *Russia*, which Rokkan does not discuss, lets itself become integrated into and be understood as part of Europe's general political development.

The relationship between state development and capitalism is also elaborated through such a highlighting of the international system of states. While capitalism, in the sense of the merchant capitalist trade belt, in Rokkan is a structural constraint (the cities represent a possibility of state building by means of taxation, while also showing political resistance to any attempt at being subjugated by the state builders), capitalism in Anderson in addition becomes a dependent variable. A capitalist development can be generated to meet the demands made by international rivalry. More of this later.

In terms of *methodology* Anderson's project is saddled with certain weaknesses, which, although originating far from Rokkan's "empiricism," paradoxically has the same non-falsifiability as a consequence when considered from a nomological-deductive point of view. This is, I believe, associated with certain assumptions of the theory of knowledge in more orthodox Marxism where Anderson is concerned: the idea that development of abstract theoretical concepts corresponds to a sort of reality's own "real processes of abstraction" of the same phenomena described by those concepts. He used two levels in his exposition: a general theoretical level where a general model is presented, which is then followed in detail and special characteristics in the subsequent nation studies, which represent his second "concrete level." The general level is here tendentially dissolved in favor of a good, but still the same more traditional historical synthesis, thus a dialectic ascent to the concrete has taken place. In practice, however, any theme may be adapted without contesting the implicit validity of the hypotheses of explanation. Skocpol and Somers refer to this, but without seeing it in the context of Anderson's declared wish to make a Marxist analysis.[60]

However, Anderson's specific nation studies overcome the weaknesses of the general model. Where England is concerned, for instance, he shows how the country's geopolitical position made it possible for the aristocracy to be exempted from their military functions and embark on commercial careers at an early stage in the country's history. This, in my opinion, is considerably more important to the breakthrough of capitalism than "the genealogy of the modes of production" he uses in his general model.

IMMANUEL WALLERSTEIN'S "MODERN WORLD SYSTEM"

Wallerstein followed the same research strategy as Rokkan. He sought to explain the values of all units of the dependent variable through their location in an overall structure or system. However, the way he shaped this thinking, in terms of concepts, was different from Rokkan's. The character of Wallerstein's "world system" is one of a radical reformulation of the Marxist debate on the transition from feudalism to capitalism. According to Wallerstein, the development of capitalism must be understood as a development both within and across conventional frames the nation-states constituted for the analysis of the problem. The distinction between external and internal factors is annulled. The capitalist mode of production is equalled to the world system, where development and underdevelopment are two sides of the same coin. First some remarks about Wallerstein's general model and then about the place of the state and of politics in it.

Wallerstein's historical model contains two types of social system: the micro system and the world system. The criterion for distinguishing between them is the existence of division of labor and trade. The closed self-sufficient micro society with no important economic exchanges (as exemplified by a tribe of hunters) constitutes (in a term taken from Karl Polanyi) a "reciprocal mini-system." In a *world system*, an ensemble of several such micro systems are placed into a context with each other and are transformed into subsystems with a mutual division of labor and exchange. One characteristic of world systems, to Wallerstein, is that they either dissolve or are transformed into empires, where the boundaries of economic interaction coincided with political state boundaries. However, attempts at transforming the European world system into a political empire failed. The dynamism was thus to develop freely, independent of great, unproductive expenses. This made the European world system quite unique in world history. A systematic economic division of labor between central areas, semi-peripheries (buffer zones) and peripheral areas can now be developed. In this system, central areas are developed at the expense of peripheral areas. A complex business community characterizes the center, while a commercial and export-oriented mono-production is the main feature of the periphery. The forms of labor control and the ways to meet the need for labor are different. In the center a "free" labor market emerges, while in the periphery the so-called second serfdom is developed (i.e., peasants are tied to the manor and are owned by the lord, as is the land they cultivate). The semi-periphery is based on mixed forms, with so-called sharecropping. *Why* some areas developed into center and others into periphery cannot be deduced from the model, however. An attempt at explaining the differences between East and West in terms of economic system will probably, in my opinion, have to change the order of Wallerstein's form: The type of labor at hand *predisposed* Eastern Europe to the type of export-oriented landed proprietorship that developed, not vice versa.[61] The important thing therefore becomes, as pointed out by Robert Brenner, to explain *how* different class structures could emerge in the West and the East.[62]

What, then, is the role of the state in Wallerstein's picture? The state has an ambiguous role. On the one hand it is seen only as a reflection of position in the international division of labor: The status of center automatically creates strong states, while the status of periphery create weak. On the other hand at the same time this hierarchy of states of different strengths is of decisive importance to the continued existence of the system. Independent operational indicators of the strength of a state (independent of the definitional connections in Wallerstein's general model) are *not* provided. The whole thing therefore becomes tautological.[63] The political development as a conceptually independent field, with an intrinsic causal weight, was not problematized by Wallerstein. If, in keeping with Rokkan's own open-minded attitude toward other people's contributions, we were to imagine the possibility of combining Rokkan's and Wallerstein's two clarifications of the same strategic approach to macro historical theory building, the conclusion would be something like this: Wallerstein's emphasis on the significance of the division of labor to regional differences will probably be easily integrated into Rokkan's model as yet another "systemic constraint," while Rokkan's model, on its part, cannot be reconciled with Wallerstein's, if Wallerstein's model is to form the starting point of a combination of the two.

Like Anderson, Wallerstein pointed to the significance of the international system to domestic political development. While Anderson emphasized the international system of states, Wallerstein highlighted the international division of labor.[64] One central point in Wallerstein is the fact that politically nondemocratic regimes and states can prolong their existence in peripheral areas by adapting to the needs of the core area. This happens at the expense of all-round national development. However, there may be doubt as to whether the international economic system had a sufficiently strong dynamism to mark peripheral nations' internal economic and political development to any degree before the definitive breakthrough of industrial capitalism. This breakthrough happened at a far later stage than the date Wallerstein applied for the origin of his world system.

In fact, one could turn the whole thing around and say that the political processes emphasized by Rokkan (and Anderson) played a part in developing and shaping capitalism in a way that made it very different from what could have been expected, based on a system analysis alone. There is nothing in the nature of capitalism to indicate that we were to have a capitalism that was fragmented into a series of national capitalisms or an international class structure that was nationally segmented. Basically, the situation was the opposite of what Wallerstein described: the power that capitalism gained was dependent on the nation-state's own power, the nation-states structured the geographical space of capitalism and became an important impulse in the development of the capitalist system. *Rokkan's* model can thus help us explain why we have got a *historically really existing capitalism,* which is every bit as different from an ideal-typical capitalist model as *the really existing socialism* was from a socialist ideal type (insofar as such a comparison is permissible).

BACKWARDNESS AND COMBINED UNEVEN DEVELOPMENT

The angle of approach to this way of thinking is an important problem that Barrington Moore Jr. addressed in his now classic work, *Social Origins of Dictatorship and Democracy.* Moore here proposed "a model of 'polity-building' options and seeks to substantiate a set of propositions about the consequences of such options for the structuring of the central institutions in each territory."[65] The compromises made between various social classes and groups, the degree of popular participation, the basis of recruitment of political elite groups, in short "the forms of regime"—these were his broader political–sociological *explicanda.* He sought to explain the diversity of values on this dependent variable among all the units he analyzed. This strategy is in itself another turn to the macro-historical approach, deviating from Rokkan's, Anderson's and Wallerstein's. The explanation of the variations between the modern political systems is sought in the class alliances that emerged during the agrarian society's encounter with the commercial and capitalist impulse.

In his own words, Moore "seek[s] to understand the role of the landed upper classes and the peasants in the bourgeois revolutions leading to capitalist democracy, the abortive bourgeois revolutions leading to fascism, and the peasant revolutions leading to communism. The ways in which the landed upper classes and the peasants reacted to the challenge of commercial agriculture were decisive factors in creating the political outcome."[66]

According to Rokkan's interpretation, Moore's thesis might be formulated as two propositions: "the closer the ties of interaction and cooperation between the rural and the urban economic elites, the greater the chances for a successful transition to a full-scale competitive democracy; the greater the distance between the urban and the landed economies, the greater the likelihood for an unchecked and unbalanced growth of the state, the greater, in fact, the chances for a cumulation of crises in the transition to mass politics."[67] Rokkan himself extended and incorporated this approach into his own when developing his conceptual maps.

However, Moore later went on to consider political systems as phases of the same global process of modernization. The three different ways to modernity (the democratic way, exemplified by England; the authoritarian, exemplified by Germany; and the agrarian–revolutionary, exemplified by Russia) should then, according to Moore, be seen as successive phases rather than options to choose between.

> To a very limited extent these three types—bourgeois revolutions culminating in the Western form of democracy, conservative revolutions from above ending in fascism, and peasant revolutions leading to communism—may constitute alternative routes and choices. They are much more clearly successive stages. As such, they display a limited determinate relation to each other. The methods of modernization chosen in one country change the dimensions of the problem for the next countries who take the step, as Veblen recognized when he coined the now fashionable term, "the advantages of backwardness." Without the prior democratic modernization of England, the reactionary methods adopted in Germany and Japan would scarcely have been possible. Without the capitalist and reactionary experiences, the communist method would have been something entirely different.[68]

This breaks with the other aspects of his presentation. But Moore himself did not go any further along this road: Here the question of interaction and mediating links between various regional histories was raised again. We are here in the midst of the "intervening" variables in Rokkan's basic model, that is, the interplay between the industrial and the national revolution in the period between the French revolution and First World War.

Various forms of explanation will have to be applied to explain the Industrial Revolution in England and on the continent. In England the industrial breakthrough in its early phase was a spontaneous process at the social macro level, based on the principle of trial and error at the micro level in the economy. The fact that an industrial nation existed already, however, provided an altered context for the thinking around other European countries' own economic development. The tension between one's own situation and the reality already in existence elsewhere (and therefore also, in principle, realizable in one's own country) could trigger an industrial development in "relatively backward countries." It will be based on the *mechanisms* of loan (transfers of physical objects and personnel) and learning (which assumes a transfer of information). Development through backwardness therefore assumes the presence of awareness of one's own backwardness and the existence of interaction between the backward and the advanced country. Initial backwardness may be an advantage to the further development of a "follower country"; it can be a disadvantage or give rise to differences in the course of development in relation to the "pioneering country." Among the writers who have analyzed various aspects and consequences of backwardness are Thorstein Veblen, Alexander Gerschenkron and Leon Trotsky.[69]

At this point I would refer to Trotsky's analysis of Russia at the start of the 20th century, just before the 1917 revolution.[70] He attempted to prove how backwardness is a disadvantage to the bourgeoisie as regards the possibility of asserting their interests vis-à-vis the absolute state, and a corresponding advantage to the working class. He also stressed that learning takes place at the political level, not just at the economic-organizational level. Thus, according to Leon Trotsky, in Russia an economically speaking sophisticated capitalist class was created, associated with the most modern large-scale industry. But this happened "immediately" without a preindustrial bourgeoisie having existed before. Thus, the Russian State, erected on the basis of Russian economic conditions, was pushed forward by the friendly, and even more by the hostile pressure of neighboring state organizations, which had grown up on a higher economic basis. From a certain moment—especially from the end of the 17th century—the state strove with all its power to accelerate the country's natural economic development. New branches of handicraft, machinery, factories, big industry, and capital, were, so to speak, artificially grafted on the natural economic stem. Capitalism seemed to be an offspring of the state. Society as a whole is characterized by an asymmetrical development with a high bourgeoisie in the economic sense, but no bourgeoisie in the social sense. Industrial economic interests are created, but no bourgeois class interest or solidarity exists. There was upper-class luxury, but no middle-class structure or ethos. The bourgeoisie owed its weakness to the absence of mediating groups between the top and the bottom of society, and of a hierarchy of social transitional stratum. This caused the bourgeoisie, which was without a broader social basis for its support vis-à-vis the state, to become fundamentally weak and dependent. The state had created it, because of outside demands, and processed the flow of foreign capital on which this bourgeoisie depended for its existence.

With his description of the industrial breakthrough, Trotsky did not intend to show that Russia was drawing closer to capitalism and that the process would soon culminate, but to place the increased industrial capacity in a context of dynamic interaction with more primitive forces. This is a vicious circle causing society to disintegrate:

> The more profound it is, the more contradictions it creates and the more it makes necessary their solution; politics and society lag behind economics but the latter is continually undermining the old character of the former, sooner or later the vicious circle will be broken the contradictions will become untolerable. The antagonisms aggravated, the incompatibilities unresolvable within the existing framework. . . . Backwardness, once the characteristic of a stagnant but relatively stable society, will have become the source of instability, change, and finally, revolution.[71]

The disproportion in development between different sectors leads to accumulation of tensions predisposing society to political revolution, without the country having undergone a capitalist phase, as assumed in classic Marxism. The subject of the revolution is the modern proletariat, which is the sheer opposite of the weak bourgeoisie. It has been created at an earlier stage than the bourgeoisie. Russian backwardness provides two advantages in the creation of the working class: 1) its concentration in enormous factories, which makes it easier for it to become welded together, strengthens its class consciousness, and represents a strategic striking force; 2) the possibility of borrowing theories and of learning from the most advanced experiences of struggle in Western Europe:

> Moreover, in Russia the proletariat did not arise gradually through the ages, carrying with itself the burden of the past as in England, but in leaps involving sharp changes of environment, ties, relations, and a sharp break with the past. It is just this fact—combined with the concentrated oppression of czarism—that made the Russian workers hospitable to the boldest conclusions of revolutionary thought—just as the backward industries were hospitable to the last word in capitalist organization.[72]

Marxists, however, have often tended to disregard the fact that that not only oppositionist and revolutionaries but also rulers and absolutist regimes were able to learn from political struggles and political-institutional solutions of the more advanced countries. A main point for the political regimes will be that English economic equipment and technological expertise could now be implanted without necessarily getting England's political system as well. Some of the explanation of the differences in the various European countries' political development in the 19th and 20th centuries is to be found in the possibilities of developing various strategies to combine old political power structures and modern industrial forms, as Moore pointed out, and which is precisely a main element of Stein Rokkan's model. In theory this latter point may be elaborated by means of Gramsci's concept of "passive revolution."

Gramsci distinguished between two different patterns of bourgeois revolution in Europe. According to Gramsci, the first, classical pattern of bourgeois revolution was the one followed by the Jacobins in France in 1789. The Jacobins transcended the narrow corporate interests of the bourgeoisie and created an equilibrium "in which the interests of the dominant group prevail, but only up to a certain point."[73] The Jacobin methods were not repeated elsewhere. The second pattern occurred when societies, so to speak, had thrust upon them aspects of a new order created abroad, without the old order having disappeared. A passive revolution takes place as a political response when international political and economic forces threaten a country from the outside with dynamic new ideas: "when the impetus of progress is not tightly linked to a vast local economic development which is artificially repressed, but is instead the reflection of international developments which transmit their ideological currents to the periphery"[74]—thus the French Revolution and the Russian Revolution both spurred reform. A passive revolution occurs when no social class is able to present itself as a force capable of presenting its program as a universal programme for the entire nation.

Without a class force to take the lead, the transmission of new ideas is left to the intellectuals, and "the conception of the State offered by them changes aspect; it is conceived of as something in itself, as a rational absolute."[75] The state becomes a means of political transformation itself, rather than a means by which a social class asserts its universal claims. Analyzing the Italian Risorgimento, where what was a revolution from below in France creating conditions for the expansion of capitalism became a revolution from above, Gramsci pointed out that "Piedmont had a function which can, from certain aspects, be compared to that of a party, i.e., of the leading personnel of a social group (and in fact people always spoke of the 'Piedmont party'): with the additional fact that it was in fact a State, with an army, a diplomatic service, etc. This fact is of the greatest importance for the concept of 'passive revolution'—the fact, that is, that what was involved was not a social group which 'led' other groups, but a State which, even if it had limitations as a power, 'led' the group which should have been 'leading' and was able to put at the latter's disposal an army and a politico–diplomatic strength."[76] A major feature of passive revolution was "the *statization* of reorganization or restructuring so that popular initiatives from below are contained or destroyed and the relationship of rulers–ruled is maintained or reimposed."[77] What Gramsci called *transformatio* worked to co-opt potential leaders of subaltern social groups, perpetuating their weakness. Gramsci interpreted the corporatism of the fascist state as an unsuccessful attempt to introduce some of the more advanced industrial practices of U.S. capitalism under the aegis of the old Italian management. One factor of great significance to stability and change at the political level is, then, in the industrial society's "combined, uneven spread."

COMBINED, UNEVEN DEVELOPMENT AND NATIONALISM

One closely related topic is the place of *nationalism* in political development. From the late 18th century a model for a new political organization in Europe emerged: the nation of citizens having equal rights. The nation became the most prominent value from which political loyalty thereafter was to orient itself. To carry through this principle, national movements and organizations emerged. This marks the beginning of modern nationalism. However, it was not only the economic and political aspects of European modernization that appeared in an irregular and complex manner. An important characteristic of the Central and East European modernization was that it was irregular where national homogenization is concerned as well. This poses special problems for the formulation of comparative theories.

Although nationalism, or *patriotism,* is a theme that Rokkan hardly mentioned in his works, nationality conflicts may be given an interpretation compatible with his model, taking the concept of nation building as our starting point. Rokkan's concept of nation building refers to a dynamic process of change along two dimensions: the extension of public authority penetrating new areas of society on the one hand, and the development of political civil rights and citizenship, on the other. Nation building thus becomes a project for territorial integration, based on three main elements: new forms of public authority, the development of an overarching national identity across old subnational affiliations, and the mobilization of new population groups according to universal criteria of participation.

In most of Western Europe, the nation-building process followed the era of absolute monarchies and was the product of the consolidation of these powerful centralized states, which provided the framework for the growth of nations. The absolutist state was transformed into a modern nation-state. This phase, or bundle of problems, of state building consists of an attempt from the center to establish a unified religious and linguistic standard. In the West the church was combined with the state and its supranational ties were cut off. Latin was gradually disappearing as the medium of written communication and was giving way to a standardized vernacular language. As the population as a whole was joined to the state center, and losing their local or international cultural–symbolic loyalty, nation building was taking place. As pointed out by Peter Flora, for Rokkan, "identity-building in the sense of nation building does not merely mean that a new identity comes along to join other age old or relatively recent identities. This process is linked rather with the claim to supremacy for this identity (and the loyalties and solidarities that goes with it) over other collectivities. In this respect it is comparable to the increasing claim of the territorial state to the monopoly on the legitimate use of force."[78] The pattern of development thereby constitutes the conditions of the political system's legitimacy, support for central institutions and rules of the game.

Nation building in the narrower sense of *identity building* thus refers to the processes that generate feelings of identity with the territorial system. How then do nations form? Karl Deutsch's classic work has provided an important point of departure for later studies of nation formation, including those of Stein Rokkan. Deutsch's classical definition of nationality as consisting in a "wide complementarity of social communication" (the same information fed to different subgroups as becoming more important to their members than the subordinate communities' own stores of information) should be borne in mind: "It consists . . . in the ability to communicate more effectively, and over a wide range of subjects, with members of one large group than with outsiders."[79] The rise of particular networks of communication thus constitutes one means of operationalizing the nation concept. But this is not enough; economic intercourse, the mobility of goods and persons, is necessary as well. A nationality involves "an alignment of a large number of individuals from the middle and lower classes linked to regional centers and leading social groups by channels of social communication and economic intercourse, both indirectly from link to link and directly with the center."[80] Deutsch's answer to the question of how nations form, then, is twofold: nations form through the twin process of cultural assimilation and social mobilization. The nation could not emerge without a previous and often long-lasting elaboration of links among its potential members, as well as a political transformation of the old regime, which involved, in the words of Stein Rokkan, a "growing acceptance of the unit citizen of the nation-state acting in abstraction from his particular roles in the organizational and institutional structure of society."[81]

As pointed out by Anthony Smith, the national is anchored in a prehistory of an ethnic, cultural nature. The processing of this "raw material" commonly involved both continuity and rupture, and although it is possible to prove great changes of a qualitative and quantitative nature, and it is quite correct to emphasize innovation in philosophical and theoretical terms, there will be considerable overlap.[82] This raw material also explains the fact that nations become different from each other.

> For, while attention may legitimately be focused on the constant elements of 'nationhood' in the modern world and the universal trends that govern their formation, the variations between nations are equally important, both in themselves and for their political consequences. My belief is that the most important of these variations are determined by specific historical experiences and by the 'deposit' left by these collective experiences. Hence the importance attached here to the various 'myths' and 'memories,' symbols' and 'values,' which so often differentiate nations.[83]

We are here dealing with stereotypes characterizing the mentality of various social groups and populations at different times. At a high social level it is about analyzing a state's national idea: Any idea, including a national idea (concept of state), will be an abstraction bringing together factors in a certain way. Here factors such as country and people, together with other preconditions, are brought in contact with each other, so that subsequently they can be seen as realized in a realm. The term "proto-nationalism" is sometimes used to describe territorial or feudal patriotisms (*Landespatriotismus*) limited to a small ruling class. The underlying stereotypes are resistant to changes of social conditions, but can also be adapted to new circumstances and be assigned a new meaning and be given new functions.[84] Besides, a dynasty was not just the embodiment of a monarchic form of government, but also a personal representation and a carrier of the idea of sovereignty. From the French Revolution the object of identification shifted to the community of equal citizens understood as the *sovereign people*. If the process was successful, the geographical area of the state's authority also defined the boundaries for the population's sense of national identity and its culture. A new loyalty being born, the classes were to a higher degree integrated and the social and cultural segregation of the agrarian society began to disappear through a social communication process, transcending and integrating "high culture" and "low culture" (the educational system was of vital importance here). The periphery-based counterculture was thus wiped out. Accordingly nation building represents, if seen from below, a transfer of loyalty from smaller primary group-oriented social units (family, kinship, locality, household) to aggregate units of a political and administrative nature. This represents a departure from the earlier patterns of social and political organization, with their old local and particularistic mentality.

This form of nation building will have its greatest importance in old, continuous (*historical*) European nations. During this type of nation-formation process "community," in Deutsch's words, is growing faster than "society" as "social mobilization" is taking place (men and women are uprooted from their traditional and agrarian setting). For Deutsch the main index of this cultural assimilation, that is, the absorption of smaller or subordinate communities into the communication networks of the larger and dominant groups, is language adoption. State building has erased or eroded many a viable or potential nation. Nation building goes hand in hand with nation destroying.

However, a state-supporting elitist culture was not the only possible value system by which political loyalty could be reoriented: ethnic minorities with strong integration and loyalty, can survive as nonassimilated pockets and constitute potential threats to the dominating nation state "from below." When, in the age of increasing reform from above, the *scientific state*, in the terminology of Anthony Smith, seeks to homogenize the population in its boundaries for administrative purposes, it produces *sociological minorities.* These are groups with a distinctive culture within a large political unit, who become permanently oppressed. The novelty in their situation is that they are made to become conscious of the fact. The crux of the matter is that the scientific state demands a heavy price for its benefits: it demands the privatization of religion. This shaking of trust in divine authority underlies the crisis of faith among the intelligentsia, who turn to the creating of nations out of the sociological minorities.[85] Rokkan's model seems to fit in very well with this type of situation. Based on Rokkan's model, national conflicts could be understood as expressions of center–periphery conflicts, resulting from the fact that state boundaries and national boundaries do not coincide. Wherever periphery interests are articulated and mobilized political conflicts will arise.

The timing of the different phases in a territory's national consolidation may be decisive. This timing must be understood in a considerably longer historical perspective than the impulse that emanated from the French Revolution. Even older political–institutional arrangements may be of great significance, as frameworks of elite compromises. The accumulation of critical phases that must be dealt with in the nation-building process is an important characteristic of political development outside Western Europe, to Stein Rokkan.

Nationalism was, however, an ambiguous phenomenon and could manifest itself in several forms, when in the wake of the French Revolution the boundaries created by the dynastic autocracies were questioned in a fundamental way. Rokkan lacked an analysis of the differences between the political systems that emerged before the age of nationalism, and those that emerged as part of the patriotic movements—commonly characterized by an overriding political concern with national survival and national equality. He did not ask whether nation building depends on nationalism. This is probably associated with the fact that the East European countries are only summarily involved in his models. Among these one will find numerous examples of nationalism, or rather, patriotism, as the independent variable in the nation-building process. This was especially true of the "peoples without history" (Otto Bauer), or "small nations" (Miroslav Hroch) with no national upper class at the beginning of the 19th century and with no contemporary historical–political framework of their own.

Nation building went along two basic paths: building on the approach of Karl Deutsch, like Rokkan, Miroslav Hroch points out:

> Looking at Europe as a whole, it is clear that it went through two distinct stages, of unequal length. The first of these started during the Middle Ages, and led to two quite different outcomes, which provided contrasting starting-points for the second stage, of a transition to a capitalist economy and civil society. At that point the path to a modern nation in the full sense of the word proceeded from either one or the other of two contrasted socio-political situations (though, of course, there were transitional cases). Over much of Western Europe—England, France, Spain, Portugal, Sweden, the Netherlands—but also farther East in Poland, the early modern state developed under the domination of one ethnic culture, either in absolutist form or in a representative estates system. In the majority of such cases, the late feudal regime was subsequently transformed, by reforms or revolution, into a modern civil society in parallel with the construction of a nation-state as a community of equal citizens. In most of Central and Eastern Europe, on the other hand, an "exogenous" ruling class dominated ethnic groups which occupied a compact territory but lacked "their own" nobility, political unit or continuous literary tradition.[86]

As mentioned above, the first of these paths, "the French or the ruling class model," draws on the previous proto-nationalism as the nation-state gradually merged the concept of citizenship with that of territorial identity. In most of Central and Eastern Europe, on the other hand, the point of departure was different. At the time they were formed into modern nations these peoples

1) did not have a ruling class of their own ethnic group, so that the social structure of the nation was incomplete;
2) did not inhabit an administratively defined political subunit that matched the extent of their ethnic population;
3) lacked a continuous tradition of cultural production in their own literary language.

Because of these weaknesses, the rise of capitalism did not liberate these groups nationally, but placed them under the rule of a new foreign ruling class, the bourgeoisie of another ethnic background.[87]

This provides an opening for a second variety of national identity and nation building. The nation building here took the form of a struggle for equal rights, for national language and culture, for political liberation and autonomy, as well as a share in economic prosperity. Hroch calls this a struggle to provide the missing attributes of full national existence for a *national movement.*

One must therefore distinguish between the national identity in a ruling class and in a small nation. The second path was followed by those nations that lacked a proto-nationalist tradition in the above mentioned sense. Among the illiterate majority of the population, too, the study of *myths, memories, symbols* and *values*, such as are embodied in epic poetry, tales and legends, religion, rituals and forms of collective practice, can give us a more tangible notion of what Benedict Anderson calls "imagined societies"—the varieties of collective affiliation which already existed and which states and nations could mobilize and make work, so to speak, on a macro-scale.[88]

Distinguishing between the two contrasted socio-political situations, Miroslav Hroch sketches three structural phases between the initiation and the successful conclusion of a national movement, "according to the character and role of those active in it, and the degree of national consciousness emergent in the ethnic group at large." During an early scholarly period, phase A, learned researchers "discovered" the ethnic group and laid a basis for the subsequent formation of a national identity. Their energies were first and foremost devoted to scholarly work, but without putting forward specifically national demands. In the second period, or the critical phase B, a new group of activists appeared who sought to win over as many as possible of their compatriots to the idea of creating a future nation by patriotic agitation. Phase C was the stage of the mass national movement during which the major part of the population came to highly value their national identity. The agitation now had its breakthrough into a movement capable of fulfilling the national goals.

In "the century of the third estate," from 1789 to 1914, the struggles for constitutional reforms and for national independence were often joined in one common struggle on two fronts. The thesis of the nation was a source of political legitimacy in the struggle against both the dynastic autocracies and territorial state formations that offended the national cultural community. The logical wish in this period was to transform the nations into nation-states. Unification and self-determination were the basic principles of the nation-state, considered to be the natural and desired unit for the development of a modern society. The movements to establish nation-states must however be analytically distinguished from nationalism. They represented a political program to establish a political structure, which claimed to be founded on the nation. But these programs included other groups of claims as well and separatism was no necessary characteristic of nationalism. The language issue came to be in the foreground of the national programs of nondominant nations, inspired not least by J. G. Herder's fundamental and philosophical reflections on language: it expresses a nation's way of thinking, it is in itself the national thinking. And without a national thinking a national character cannot develop. The ideological mission assigned to language made it the symbol of a nation's cultural independence. Four elements for the inclusion of the language issue in the national programs may, according to Miroslav Hroch, be distinguished: 1) interest in language as a subject of scientific study; 2) formation of a separate identity via a written language, which was standardized and codified, and which was to be used normatively as a literary language; 3) teaching of the new languages in schools, and their upgrading to languages of instruction at all levels of education. This was achieved by, for instance, the Czech national movement. The various national movements, however, obtained very different results in their struggles to reach these goals in the 19th and the early 20th century; 4) At their most advanced level the national programs in this period raised the demand for equality of nondominant nations' written languages with the written language of the dominant nation: to become the administrative language, the legal language and the economic language in areas where a given ethnic group constituted the majority of the people.[89]

Depending on the circumstances, nationalism could, however, be annexed by conservative movements and be separated from the struggle for reforms to which it was originally linked. But it "was only during the final phase C that a full social structure could come into being, and that the movement differentiated out into conservative–clerical, liberal and democratic wings, each with their own programmes."[90] The national movement now turned into a scene of struggle for political and ideological hegemony, or in Hroch's words, a "battlefield for the pursuit of power."[91]

A "development through backwardness perspective" can be linked to the triggering of national mobilization in two ways (or nationalism may be understood as an ideological–cultural response to the unevenness of the modernization process in two ways):

1. In the international arena, the demonstration effect and the challenge from the internationally more advanced countries may give rise to nationalist impulses and an outside model could play a decisive role. The spread of technology, political organizational patterns and ideas now become important issues. Nationalism is the weakest groups' answer to the threat of degradation and dependence in the international community. At the same time as the world tendentially becomes one through the spread of capitalism—something which Marx considered to be a principal aspect of capitalism's civilizing

mission—nationalism contributes to preserving its nation-state fragmentation and segmentation. More than that, as pointed out by Reinhard Bendix, nationalism in the old states,

> though a nearly universal phenomenon in modern history, is not in fact a force that easily unifies countries. Indeed, the old states underwent long periods of intellectual polarization when they had to come to terms with challenges from abroad. The typical response is a polarization of modernizers and nativists" . . . The modernizers and nativists of a country share the desire to preserve and enhance their native land—as they share the hostility to the "advanced country" . . . All the same, such groups are deeply divided over which path to modernization their country should follow . . . the debates between traditionalists and modernizers remain unresolved more often than not, both during the struggle against an old regime and after it has been overthrown and a new regime established.[92]

Reactionary and revolutionary modernizing regimes, both calling for nationalist sacrifice, may be considered to be different answers to the need to relate to the experiences and models of more advanced countries. The dialectics between maintaining the domestic tradition and the models to which foreign countries inspire is precisely one element of the explanation of nationalism's great capacity to synthesize. And it is what classically and universally triggers a political dynamism between Western-oriented and domestically oriented nationalists, of which the zapadniki and the slavophiles in 19th-century Russia are the leading example.

2. In multiethnic societies national tensions will arise if development from a pre-modern to a modern society is regionally uneven and vertically dissimilar. Areas where modernization creates problems it is not yet able to solve, which are at an intermediate level of industrial development, will be especially susceptible to nationalism in this perspective. In the core areas nationalism will most certainly occur either among minority national groups, trying to defend their own privileged positions, or among newly educated strata of hitherto non-privileged nations who are trying to better their own career possibilities parallel with the social advancement of their own nations, as for the first time they are drawn into the modernization process.[93] This understanding of the phenomenon has been developed especially by the English sociologist and anthropologist Ernest Gellner. When the dividing lines and gaps of industrial society coincide with the old society's cultural and ethnic dividing lines, with language as one important distinguishing factor, national tension will of necessity arise, which, in turn, may lead to political mobilization and, in the last instance, require separatist solutions.[94] When national and colonial questions are intertwined, each reinforcing the other, lack of stability may be explained by a combined, uneven development. Under such circum-

stances the class structure tends to be ethnically segregated. This situation has been characterized as *internal colonialism*, a condition in which the uneven development of the economic system causes material and cultural oppression to nations in the making—newcomer ethnic groups tend to constitute internal colonies.[95] When studying social elites, one is not only interested in their objective characteristics, or in the factors that account for their formation. One is also interested in their identity and their capacity for collective action. Ernest Gellner suggested that political nationalism will be more marked when the economy is not able to provide a growth of high-status employment on the same scale as the increase of new applicants.[96]

This kind of nationalism, then, will hardly be articulated without an intelligentsia. This fits in with Hroch's theory, according to which the success of a small nation during phase B was not self-evident. It can only be explained when taking into account a factor that Hroch termed "a national relevant conflict of group interest," meaning a social interest conflict that coincides with linguistic, or sometimes religious, conflicts:

> A common example in the nineteenth century was the conflict between new university graduates coming from a non-dominant ethnic group, and a closed elite from the ruling nation keeping a hereditary grip on leading positions in state and society. But there were also clashes between peasants belonging to the subaltern group and landlords from the dominant one, between craftsmen from the former and large traders and manufacturers from the latter, and so on. It is important to stress that these conflicts of interest which bore on the fate of national movements cannot be reduced to class conflicts—for the national movements always recruited members from several classes and groups, so that their interests were determined by a broad spectrum of social relations (including among them, of course, class relations).[97]

In other words, what is provided here is an alternative analytical approach to important features of the modern political system in Europe, Rokkan's dependent variable. Compared with his "abstract–static" model, the development-through-backwardness model creates a way of regarding *nationalism* as a mediating link between the development of different countries and regions, between relative position in the international system and domestic political development. Here, too, Rokkan's models, where "the interplay between the national and the industrial revolution" is used as a mediating category of variables, will not exclude this type of interaction in concrete research. This second concept of nationalism is thus specified in a different way from the *longue durée* perspective outlined above: nationalism as a political and cultural center–periphery conflict that follows from the attempts at cultural standardization. This concept then is part of a more conjunctural, *moyenne durée* perspective, to use Fernand Braudel's terminology. The two perspectives will be able to supplement each other in a fruitful manner.

CONCLUSION: ROKKANIAN MACRO SOCIOLOGY

Rokkan's research strategy in his late period was highly demanding. The well-known classics in the macro-historical tradition sought to follow somewhat different routes.[98] First, they sought to apply the comparative method in order to determine and explain accurately the dependent variable's value for one single unit like Max Weber and his epigones. Weber defined his overarching problem thus: What chain of circumstances has caused phenomena precisely here—and *only* here—in the West, which nevertheless formed part of a line of development of universal significance and validity? Or they could choose a generalizing strategy, that is, seek to explain the value of one single unit on the dependent variable for all units considered. The well-known J curve of J. C. Davies, used to explain revolutions, which in turn was inspired by the theories of Alexis de Toqueville and Karl Marx, illustrates such a connection between a draft theory and empirical findings. Finally, they could seek to explain the differences in values on the dependent variable for all units considered. This was Barrington Moore Jr.'s approach.

Rokkan's strategy deviated from all of the above. With his model, he wanted to explain all values that the dependent variable (the modern party system) can assume for one single unit (the European, or Western European territorial system). In order to implement such a strategy, one must take the areas' placement in the system as a whole as the starting point for explanations. This thinking is also found in Fernand Braudel and his self-appointed disciple, Immanuel Wallerstein.

Did Rokkan succeed in doing this? The answer is both yes and no. This is the point where he made his most important and original contribution to historical interpretation. While both problems and approach have been thoroughly considered by others before, his procedure for simplifying this enormously heterogeneous historical material—and the underlying idea of how the European system has functioned—is suited to give us completely new insight into the conditions of European politics. His conceptual maps are an enormously elegant heuristic device to solve the demanding task. Variations between today's political systems in Western Europe are explained from the areas' total links with the two most important differentiation processes in European history—summarized by Rokkan in his two-axis system. This outline of the system as a whole and the underlying idea of its functioning was Rokkan's actual and independent contribution to European macro history. Here, as in other fields, he was one of the very greatest innovators of concepts.

However, this reading of Rokkan's later works does not weaken another critical point in my discussion. Despite Rokkan's intellectual openness, which has often been emphasized, his thinking seems to be compatible with a *structural determinism*, which goes hand in hand with a *retrospective determinism:* Alternative projects tend to disappear from history, and thus also their influence on the alternative that wins in the end.

It seems natural to believe that any research strategy that uses the system level and its *logic* as explanation variable will run into such problems. What is common to Rokkan's conceptual maps, in their concrete formulation, and Wallerstein's world system, is a backward projection of contemporary conditions. This is used as a key to grasp the main lines in historical development. In Wallerstein's formulation of the same strategy, the economic system is postulated as an explanation of all other conditions. Economic interaction is postulated as an explanation of the strength and form of a state, whereas the value on the dependent variable is nevertheless deduced, in purely definitional terms, from the connections in his general model.

However, a key of some kind is of course needed if we are to summarize and analyze such highly comprehensive masses of historical material. As long as the scientist is conscious of the shortcomings of his own applied key, there need not, in my opinion, be any significant weakness to the underlying thinking. Where Rokkan is concerned, I believe this weakness is related to an intellectual "lag" connected with his use of a traditional variables-based approach, which, as I have already argued, he was about to put behind him in his later works, although without discarding all of his earlier experiences as a researcher within this tradition. I believe there is in his case no strong necessity of ending up in a structural (or a retrospective) determinism: Rokkan has developed a whole list of the main actors in state- and nation building and pointed out their different alliance options as well as the most likely consequences of these options in terms of future political trajectories. Rokkan's models also allow an introduction of an analysis of sequential interactions. This is quite essential if one does not want to miss an important element of historical creativity and unpredictability. On the background of these two weak points I have suggested two themes of an empirical nature that are suited to place the interaction and communication between different regional development sequences in focus: These are state building and nationalism.

1. *State building.* Perry Anderson's emphasis on the role of *warfare* in state development and changes in a state's form, size and structure, is an illustration of the first theme. It paves the way for alternative or supplementary explanations of the phenomena with which Rokkan is concerned. Above I

have also pointed to features of the *political* processes of change that could help explain specific historical aspects of capitalism as a mode of production. These are dimensions that are neglected in Wallerstein's backward projection of *present-day* capitalism, which is actually an international system. The process of political penetration took place in Western Europe through the formation of nonterritorial-based elites in the absolute monarchies. As a offspring of the Parsonian sociological tradition, the starting point for Rokkan's view of state building, in the more restricted sense, had been a Weberian perspective. State building is then to be understood as constituting a triangular conflict between the supreme ruler, his administrative staff and the population. I will discuss the three following cases: Austria–Hungary until 1918, the All-Russian empire before 1917, and the Soviet Union. Again, my exposition deviates from Rokkan's in that it integrates interaction and communication in the international system as well as between different regional development sequences as independent causal factors.

2. *Nationalism.* Similarly, nationalism is such a theme. Rokkan hardly refers to this in his works. Based on Rokkan's model and fundamental ideas, nationalism must nevertheless be understood as a part of, and an expression of, a historically more long-lasting and fundamental center–periphery conflict. I outlined an alternative approach to the theme. Nationalism is then understood as a mediating link between international and interregional economic interaction and the phenomena constituting Rokkan's analytical focus (modern political systems). Nationalism may be seen as a response to uneven development. In the core areas nationalism will most certainly occur either among minority national groups, trying to defend their own privileged positions, or among newly educated strata of hitherto non-privileged nations who are trying to better their own career possibilities parallel with the social advancement of their own nations, as for the first time they are drawn into the modernization process. When national and colonial questions are intertwined, each reinforcing the other, lack of stability may be explained by a combined, uneven development. Under such circumstances the class structure tends to be ethnically segregated. I will link my analysis of the nationality problems in the All-Russian Empire, the Soviet Union and Austria Hungary to the analysis of state building mentioned above.

In the last chapter I will go into some problems of East European development by using a long-term perspective and following a Rokkanian approach. I will be focusing on regime stability as well as on state building and nationality questions. Here too Rokkan's city-belt theory seems to justify a simple Weberian analysis as. Historically, the typical political form in the region had been either the large multiethnic empire, or the fragmented ethnical groups that had not succeeded in establishing their own, lasting state formations. In the 19th century the position of Eastern Europe resembled that of colonial peoples in Asia and Africa, except that the former were dominated by the land, and the latter by maritime powers. Due to the relative weakness of the East European nations as compared to the outside powers, the politics of the area have been governed by the principle of *Primat der Aussenpolitik* over domestic political developments. The All-Russian empire, the Habsburg monarchy, Prussia (the German Reich) and the Ottoman Turkish empire were not able to penetrate the city belt, but more or less conquered the land between the belt and their respective city centers. The military and fiscal imperatives of the Habsburg and Ottoman empires had not least a retarding effect, demographic as well as socio-economic, on the Balkan borderlands they shared.

My aim is twofold: First I will attempt to answer the questions raised above. Then I will briefly discuss what light my results can shed on the use of a Rokkanian approach outside the region specified by his conceptual maps. This discussion may be interpreted as a small contribution toward pinpointing factors which should be taken into account if one wishes to integrate Europe's Eastern zone into comparative European studies based on Rokkan. I apologize that my exposition is somewhat less systematic than Rokkan's own would have been.

NOTES

1. For a closer analysis of this transition in Rokkan's orientation, reference is made to Jeremy C. Mitchell's contribution, "Velgerskaren og den hemmelige valghandlingen," pp. 207–16, in Bernt Hagtvet (ed.), *Politikk mellom økonomi og kultur. Stein Rokkan som politisk sosiolog og forskningsinspirator.* Oslo: Ad Notam Gyldendal 1992.

2. For a good survey and discussion of the current state of modern macro historical research, see Charles Tilly, *Big Structures, Large Processes, Huge Comparisons.* New York: Sage 1984.

3. Rokkan, Stein, "Eine Familie von Modellen für die Vergleichende Geschichte Europas," *Zeitschrift für Soziologie*, April 1980, pp. 118–28 (pp. 125–26).

4. Ref. Rokkan and Hagtvet's article on the preconditions of the fascist breakthrough in Europe, in S. Ugelvik Larsen, B. Hagtvet and J. P. Myklebust (eds.), *Who Were the Fascists: Social Roots of European Fascism.* Bergen: Universitetsforlaget 1980, pp. 131–53.

5. See Charles Tilly, *Big Structures, Large Processes, Huge Comparisons.* New York: Sage 1984.

6. For an assessment, ref. Charles Tilly, *Big Structures, Large Processes, Huge Comparisons*; and Peter Flora, "Introduction and Interpretation," in Peter Flora, Stein Kuhnle and Derek Urwin (eds.), *State Formation, Nation-Building and Mass Politics*

in *Europe. The Theory of Stein Rokkan*. Oxford & New York: Oxford University Press 1999.

7. Flora, Peter, "Stein Rokkans Makromodell der politische Entwicklung Europas. Ein Rekonstruktionsversuch," *Kölner Zeitschrift für Soziologie und Sozialforschung*, 33:3, 1981, pp. 397–98; Charles Tilly, "Stein Rokkans begrepsmessige kart over Europa," in Bernt Hagtvet (ed.), *Politikk mellom økonomi og kultur. Stein Rokkan som politisk sosiolog og forskningsinspirator*. Oslo: Ad Notam Gyldendal 1992; Erik Allardt & Henry Valen, "Stein Rokkan. An Intellectual Profile," in Per Torsvik (ed.), *Mobilization, Center-Periphery Structures and Nation-Building*. Bergen: Universitetsforlaget, 1981.

8. "Introduction: Center-Formation, Nation-Building and Cultural Diversity: Report on A UNESCO Programme," in S. N. Eisenstadt and Stein Rokkan (eds.), *Building States and Nations*, vol. 1. Beverly Hills: Sage 1973, pp. 20–21.

9. Rokkan, Stein, "Nation-Building, Cleavage Formation and the Structuring of Mass Politics," in Stein Rokkan, with Angus Campbell, Per Torsvik, and Henry Valen, *Citizens, Elections, Parties; Approaches to the Comparative Study of the Processes of Development*. Oslo: Universitetsforlaget/New York: McKay 1970, p. 116.

10. Rokkan, Stein, "The Structuring of Mass Politics in the Smaller European Democracies: A Developmental Typology," *Comparative Studies in Society and History*, 10:2, 1968, pp. 199–202.

11. Rokkan, Stein, with Angus Campbell, Per Torsvik, and Henry Valen, *Citizens, Elections, Parties; Approaches to the Comparative Study of the Processes of Development*. Oslo: Universitetsforlaget/New York: McKay 1970, p. 113.

12. Flora, Peter, "Introduction and Interpretation," in Peter Flora, Stein Kuhnle, and Derek Urwin (eds.), *State Formation, Nation-Building and Mass Politics in Europe. The Theory of Stein Rokkan*. Oxford & New York: Oxford University Press 1999, pp. 13 and 86.

13. Rokkan, Stein, "Eine Familie von Modellen für die Vergleichende Geschichte Europas, " *Zeitschrift für Soziologie*, April 1980, p. 122.

14. Regarding the distinction between formal and empirical theories, associated with development studies, see Raymond Boudon, *Theories of Social Change*. Cambridge, MA: Polity Press 1986, pp. 202–7.

15. Flora, Peter, "Introduction and Interpretation," in Peter Flora, Stein Kuhnle, and Derek Urwin (eds.), *State Formation, Nation-Building and Mass Politics in Europe. The Theory of Stein Rokkan*. Oxford & New York: Oxford University Press 1999, p. 86.

16. Mjøset, Lars, "Er positivismekritikken den eneste kritikk som det er mulig å reise mot norsk sosiologi?" *Sosiologi i dag*, 2:2, 1981, p. 71.

17. Ref. also Einar Berntzen and Per Selle, "Structure and Social Action in Stein Rokkan's Work," *Journal of Theoretical Politics*, 2:2, 1990, pp. 131–49.

18. Rokkan, Stein, *Stat, nasjon, klasse* (ed. Bernt Hagtvet). Oslo: Universitetsforlaget 1987, p. 10.

19. Rokkan, Stein, "Territories, Centers and Peripheries: Toward a Geoethnic–Geoeconomic–Geopolitical Model of Differentiation within Western Europe," in Jean

Gottmann (ed.), *Center and Periphery. Spatial Variation in Politics.* Beverly Hills: Sage 1980, p. 165.

20. Rokkan, Stein, "Eine Familie von Modellen für die Vergleichende Geschichte Europas," *Zeitschrift für Soziologie*, April 1980, p. 180.

21. Tilly, Charles, "Sinews of War," in Per Torsvik (ed.), *Mobilization. Center–Periphery Structures and Nation-Building.* Bergen: Universitetsforlaget 1981, p. 120.

22. In *Exit, Voice and Loyalty.* Cambridge, MA: Harvard University Press 1970, Albert Hirschmann identifies three main types of response that the members (of clients) of a corporative operator can give when the fulfillment of an organization's functions begins to deteriorate. For instance, the citizens of a corrupt state can "elect with their legs," that is, leave it (Exit) (e.g., East Germany 1989). Such a response may involve a price to be paid by the individual (language problems, etc.). The members can also express their discontent more or less aggressively (Voice). This response, too, will come at a price. Or they can endure the bad times, hoping that things will improve, or articulate their wishes themselves (Loyalty). Even this has its price: enduring the suboptimal condition. All three types of response involve a cost, and the analytical problem consists of determining the relationship between them, that is, the conditions determining the occurrence of one strategic choice or the other. Among the factors that made the polarity between Exit and Voice important was the fact that it also reflected a difference of values: Exit was related to the economy, to mobility, *Gesellschaft*, capitalism; Voice was related to politics, to identity, *Gemeinschaft*, socialism.

The relationship between the two main types of response was not an either—or, but a both—and. Stein Rokkan generalized the Hirschmann model in a broader comparative perspective and attempted to determine various mixed types theoretically and historically-empirically. Hirschmann helped him pose the problem of the subdivision of the territories into entities in a new way and to study the dynamism of boundary-drawing. The Exit–Voice polarity raised the question of the significance of forms of boundary control: externally to prevent, permit or enforce Exit (or Entry), internally to channel, tolerate or suppress Voice.

23. Rokkan, Stein, "Entries, Voices, Exits: Towards a Possible Generalization of the Hirschmann Model," *Social Science Information*, 13, 1974, p. 46.

24. Rokkan, Stein, "Cities, States, and Nations: A Dimensional Model for the Study of Contrasts in Development," in S. N. Eisenstadt and Stein Rokkan (eds.), *Building, States and Nations*, vol. 1. Beverley Hills: Sage 1973, p. 79.

25. Ibid.

26. Rokkan, Stein, Derek Urwin, Frank H. Aarebrot, Pamela Malaba, and Terje Sande, *Center–Periphery Structures in Europe. An ISSC Workbook in Comparative Analysis.* Frankfurt: Campus 1987.

27. Rokkan, Stein, "Dimensions of State Formation and Nation Building: A Possible Paradigm for Research on Variations within Europe," in Charles Tilly (ed.), *The Formation of National States in Western Europe.* Princeton, NJ: Princeton University Press 1975, pp. 570–72.

28. Rokkan, Stein, and Bernt Hagtvet, "The Conditions of Fascist Victory," in S. Ugelvik Larsen, B. Hagtvet, and J. P. Myklebust (eds.), *Who Were the Fascists: Social Roots of European Fascism*. Bergen: Universitetsforlaget 1980.

29. On the distinction between formal and scientific theories of social development, see Raymond Boudon, *Theories of Social Change*. Oxford: Polity Press 1986, pp. 202–7.

30. For a discussion of the lines leading from previous Norwegian historians' theories to Rokkan, see Øyvind Østerud, "Nasjonalitetsprinsipp og nasjonsbygging," in: Øyvind Østerud, *Det moderne statssystem og andre politisk–historiske studier*. Oslo: Gyldendal 1987.

31. Rokkan, Stein, "Territories, Centers and Peripheries: Toward a Geoethnic–Geoeconomic–Geopolitical Model of Differentiation within Western Europe," in Jean Gottmann (ed.), *Center and Periphery. Spatial Variation in Politics*. Beverly Hills: Sage 1980, p. 173.

32. Rokkan, Stein, "Territories, Centers and Peripheries: Toward a Geoethnic–Geoeconomic–Geopolitical Model of Differentiation within Western Europe" in Jean Gottmann (ed.), *Center and Periphery. Spatial Variation in Politics*. Beverly Hills: Sage 1980; and Stein Rokkan, "The Survival of Distinctiveness," in Stein Rokkan et al. (eds.), *Economy, Territory, Identity: The Politics of European Peripheries*. Beverly Hills: Sage 1983.

33. Rokkan, Stein, "Territories, Centers and Peripheries: Toward a Geoethnic–Geoeconomic–Geopolitical Model of Differentiation within Western Europe," in Jean Gottmann (ed.), *Center and Periphery. Spatial Variation in Politics*. Beverly Hills: Sage, 1980, pp. 174–78.

34. Rokkan, Stein, "Cities, States, and Nations: A Dimensional Model for the Study of Contrasts in Development," in S. N. Eisenstadt and Stein Rokkan (eds.), *Building States and Nations*, vol. 1. Beverly Hills: Sage 1973, pp. 79–80.

35. Rokkan, Stein, "Nation-Building, Cleavage Formation and the Structuring of Mass Politics," in Stein Rokkan, with Angus Campbell, Per Torsvik, and Henry Valen (eds.), *Citizens, Elections, Parties; Approaches to the Comparative Study of the Processes of Development*. Oslo: Universitetsforlaget/New York: McKay 1970.

36. Flora, Peter, "Introduction and Interpretation," in Peter Flora, Stein Kuhnle, and Derek Urwin (eds), *State Formation, Nation-Building and Mass Politics in Europe. The Theory of Stein Rokkan*. Oxford & New York: Oxford University Press 1999, pp. 82, 85–86.

37. Rokkan, Stein, "Cities, States, and Nations: A Dimensional Model for the Study of Contrasts in Development," in S. N. Eisenstadt and Stein Rokkan (eds.), *Building States and Nations*, vol. 1. Beverly Hills: Sage 1973, pp. 358–59.

38. For the arguments in this section I am indebted to Øyvind Østerud and Lars Mjøset, both of the University of Oslo. For Mjøset's view of historical sociology, see the following articles: Lars Mjøset, "Stein Rokkan's Thick Comparisons," *Acta Sociologica* 43, 2000; Lars Mjøset, "Can Grounded Theory Solve the Problems of Its Critics," *Sosiologisk Tidsskrift*, 13, 2005, p. 379–408; Lars Mjøset, "No Fear of Comparisons or Context: On the Foundations of Historical Sociology," *Comparative*

Education, 42, 2006, pp. 337–62. The term "tick comparisons" to characterize Stein Rokkan's approach is coined by Lars Mjøset in the title of the first of his articles mentioned in this note.

39. Rokkan, Stein, "Territories, Nations, Parties: Toward a Geoconomic–Geopolitical Model for the Explanation of Variations within Western Europe," in Richard L. Merritt and Bruce M. Russett (eds.), *From National Development to Global Community. Essays in Honor of Karl W. Deutsch*. London: George Allen & Unwin 1981, p. 77.

40. Rokkan, Stein, "Territories, Nations, Parties: Toward a Geoconomic–Geopolitical Model for the Explanation of Variations within Western Europe," in Richard L. Merritt and Bruce M. Russett (eds.). *From National Development to Global Community. Essays in Honor of Karl W. Deutsch*. London: George Allen & Unwin 1981, p. 77.

41. Sejersted, Francis, "Norsk historisk forskning ved inngangen til 1990–årene. Et oppgjør med den metodologiske individualisme," *Historisk tidsskrift* 4, 1989, p. 402.

42. For a related, but not identical, critique of Rokkan, see P. Abrams, *Historical Sociology*. Ithaca, NY: Cornell University Press 1982.

43. Mjøset, Lars, "Stein Rokkan's Thick Comparisons," Acta Sociologica 43, 2000, p. 396.

44. Glaser, B. G., & A. L. Strauss. *The Discovery of Grounded Theory*. New York: Aldine de Gruyter 1967, p. 37.

45. Strauss, A. L. "Discovering New Theory from Previous Theory," in T. Shibutani (ed.), *Human Nature and Collective Behavior. Papers in Honor of Herbert Blumer*. Englewood Cliffs, NJ: Prentice Hall 1970, 46–53.

46. Geertz, Clifford, "Thick Description Toward an Interpretive Theory of Culture," in Clifford Geertz (ed.), *The Interpretation of Cultures*. New York: Basic Books 1973, p. 25.

47. Rokkan, Stein, "Territories, Nations, Parties: Toward a Geoconomic–Geopolitical Model for the Explanation of Variations within Western Europe," in Richard L. Merritt and Bruce M. Russett (eds.), *From National Development to Global Community. Essays in Honor of Karl W. Deutsch*. London: George Allen & Unwin 1981, p. 93.

48. Mjøset, Lars, "Can Grounded Theory Solve the Problems of Its Critics," *Sosiologisk Tidsskrift*, 13, 2005, pp. 400, 401, 406.

49. Gramsci, Antonio, *Selections from the Prison Notebooks* (Quintin Hoare and Geoffrey Nowell Smith, eds.). London: Lawrence & Wishart 1971, p. 238.

50. That is, the general dominance of formal rationality. Citation from Max Weber, *The Protestant Ethic and the Spirit of Capitalism*. London & New York: Rutledge 1990, p. 13.

51. For a comparison of Weber and Anderson's conceptual toolboxes, see Lars Mjøset, *Transition to Capitalism: Escalation of Rationalization*, PRIO Working Paper 4/1982, International Peace Institute of Oslo 1982.

52. Andersson, Perry, *Lineages of the Absolutist State*. London: New Left Books 1974, p. 420.

53. Andersson, Perry, *Lineages of the Absolutist State*. London: New Left Books 1974, pp. 395–431.

54. Andersson, Perry, *Lineages of the Absolutist State*. London: New Left Books 1974, p. 421–22.

55. Skocpol, Theda, *States and Social Revolutions*. Cambridge: Cambridge University Press, 1978.

56. Mann, Michael, "State and Society 1130–1815. An Analysis of English State Finances," in Maurice Zeitlin (ed.), *Political Power and Social Theory*, vol. I. Greenwitch, CT: Jai Press 1980, p. 200; and Øyvind Østerud, "Absolutismen som statsbygging," in Øyvind Østerud, *Det moderne statssystem og andre politisk–historiske studier*. Oslo: Gyldendal 1987, pp. 79–80.

57. Anderson, Perry, *Lineages of the Absolutist State*. London: New Left Books 1974, p. 195.

58. Hintze, Otto, *Staat und Verfassung*. Leipzig: Koehler und Amelang 1941; and Otto Hintze, *Historical Essays* (ed. Felix Gilbert). New York: Oxford University Press 1975.

59. Tilly, Charles, "Reflections on the History of European Statemaking," in Charles Tilly (ed.), *The Formation of National States in Western Europe*. Princeton, NJ: Princeton University Press, 1975; Charles Tilly, "Stein Rokkans begrepsmessige kart over Europa," in Bernt Hagtvet (ed.), *Politikk mellom økonomi og kultur. Stein Rokkan som politisk sosiolog og forskningsinspirator*. Oslo: Ad Notam Gyldendal 1992; Theda Skocpol, *States and Social Revolutions*. Cambridge: Cambridge University Press 1978.

60. Skocpol, Theda, and Margareth Somers, "The Uses of History in Macrosocial Inquiry," *Comparative Studies in Society and History*, 22:2, 1980, pp. 87–93.

61. See Jerzy Topolski, "The Manorial Serf-Economy in Central and Eastern Europe in the 16th and 17th Centuries," *Agricultural History*, 48:3, 1974: "The peasant farm within the manorial–serf economy must be considered as a necessary element of the structural system composed of three principal elements: manor—peasant farms—markets . . . In such a structure the nobles' interest in peasant economic activity was limited: the lord's main problem was to ensure the necessary peasant labor for the manorial fields" (pp. 349–50). Witold Kula likewise concludes that the export market was of "very limited importance for overall production," see Kula, *An Economic Theory of the Feudal System*. London: New Left Books 1976, p. 95.

62. Brenner, Robert, "The Origins of Capitalist Development. A Critique of Neo-Smithian Marxism," *New Left Review* 104, 1977.

63. Østerud, Øyvind, "Wallersteins varldssystemanalys. En kommentar," in G. Behre and Birgitta Oden (eds.), *Historievetenskap och Historiedidaktikk*. Lund: Liber/Oslo: Universitetsforlaget 1982.

64. Gourevitch, Peter, "The International System and Regime Formation. A Review of Anderson and Wallenstein." *Comparative Politics* 10:3, 1978.

65. Rokkan, Stein, with Angus Campbell, Per Torsvik, and Henry Valen, *Citizens, Elections, Parties; Approaches to the Comparative Study of the Processes of Development*. Oslo: Universitetsforlaget/New York: McKay 1970, p. 54.

66. Moore Jr., Barrington, *Social Origins of Dictatorship and Democracy. Lord and Peasant in the Making of the Modern World.* Boston: Beacon Press 1966, p. xiv.

67. Rokkan, Stein, "Dimensions of State Formation and Nation-Building: A Possible Paradigm for Research on Variations Within Europe," in Charles Tilly (ed.), *The Formation of National States in Western Europe.* Princeton, NJ: Princeton University Press 1975, 586.

68. Moore Jr., Barrington, *Social Origins of Dictatorship and Democracy. Lord and Peasant in the Making of the Modern World.* Boston: Beacon Press 1966, pp. 413–14.

69. Knei-Paz, Baruch, *The Social and Political Thought of Leon Trotsky.* Cambridge: Cambridge University Press, 1978; Gerschenkron, Alexander, *Economic Backwardness in Historical Perspective.* Cambridge, MA: Belknap Press of Harvard University 1962; Gerschenkron, Alexander, *Continuity in History and Other Essays.* Cambridge, MA: Belknap Press of Harvard University 1968; Trotsky, Leon, *1905.* Harmondworth: Penguin 1972; Trotsky, Leon, *The History of Russian Revolution.* London: Pluto Press 1977; Thorstein Veblen, *Imperial Germany.* New York: Augustus M. Kelley 1964. For a more recent presentation of this theory, see Gunnar Opeide, "Tilbakeliggenhetens problem." Forum Øst 3:3, 1985, pp. 8–30. Øyvind Østerud, "Utvikling gjennom tilbakeliggenhet," in Øyvind Østerud, Det moderne statssystem. Oslo: Gyldendal 1987, pp. 125–44. For a critique see Jon Elster, "The theory of Combined and Uneven Development: A Critique," in John Roemer (ed.), *Analytical Marxism.* Cambridge: Cambridge University Press 1986, pp. 23–54.

70. See Paul Blackledge, "Leon Trotsky's Contribution to the Theory of History." *Studies in East European Thought* 58, 2006, pp. 1–31; Knei-Paz, Baruch, *The Social and Political Thoughts of Leon Trotsky.* Cambridge: Cambridge University Press 1978, p. 93; Trotsky, Leon, *1905.* Harmondworth: Penguin 1972; Trotsky, Leon, "The Peculiarities of Russian Historical Development" in Leon Trotsky, *The Permanent Revolution, and Results and Prospects.* New York: Pioneer Publishers 1965; Trotsky, Leon, *The History of the Russian Revolution.* London: Pluto Press 1977.

71. Knei-Paz, Baruch, *The Social and Political Thoughts of Leon Trotsky.* Cambridge: Cambridge University Press 1978, p. 93.

72. Trotsky, Leon, *The History of the Russian Revolution.* London: Pluto Press 1977, p. 33.

73. Gramsci, Antonio, *Selections from the Prison Notebooks* (eds. Quintin Hoare and Geoffrey Nowell Smith). London: Lawrence & Wishart 1971, p. 182.

74. Ibid., p. 115.

75. Ibid., p. 117.

76. Ibid., p. 104–5.

77. Jessop, Bob, *Putting the Capitalist State in its Place.* Oxford: Polity Press 1990, p. 213.

78. Flora, Peter, "Introduction and Interpretation," in Peter Flora, Stein Kuhnle, and Derek Urwin (eds.), *State Formation, Nation-Building and Mass Politics in*

Europe. The Theory of Stein Rokkan. Oxford & New York: Oxford University Press 1999, p. 67.

79. Deutsch, Karl, *Nationalism and Social Communication.* Cambridge, MA: MIT Press 1966, p. 97.

80. Ibid., p. 101.

81. Rokkan, Stein, "Mass Suffrage, Secret Voting and Political Participation." *Archives Européennes de Sociologie,* 2:1, 1961, p. 133.

82. Smith, Anthony D. *The Ethnic Revival.* Cambridge: Cambridge UP 1981, pp. 1765, 185–212.

83. Smith, Anthony D., *The Ethnic Origins of Nations.* London: Basil Blackwell 1986, Preface.

84. Dann, Otto (ed.), *Nationalizmus in vorindustrieller Zeit.* Munich: R. Oldenbourg 1986.

85. Smith, Anthony. *Theories of Nationalism.* London: Duckworth 1971, chap. 10.

86. Hroch, Miroslav, "From National Movement to the Fully-formed Nation. The Nation-Building Process in Europe." *New Left Review* 198, 1993, p. 3.

87. Hroch, Miroslav, "How Much Does Nation Formation Depend on Nationalism?" *East European Politics and Societies,* 4(1), 1990, p. 109.

88. About popular proto-nationalism, see Eric Hobsbawn, *Nations and Nationalism, Programme, Myth, Reality.* Cambridge: Cambridge University Press 1990, pp. 46–79.

89. Hroch, Miroslav, *Linguistic Conflicts in Eastern Europe and their Historical Parallels.* Prague: Charles University 1990, unpublished.

90. Hroch, Miroslav, "From National Movement to the Fully-formed Nation." *New Left Review* 198, 1993, p. 7.

91. Bendix, Reinhard, "Backwardness and Intellectual Mobilization," in Reinhard Bendix, *Force, Fate, and Freedom. On Historical Sociology.* Berkeley: University of California Press 1984, pp. 120–21.

92. Gellner, Ernest, *Nations and Nationalism.* Oxford: Blackwell1983; and Øyvind Østerud, "Utvikling gjennom tilbakeligenhet," in Øyvind Østerud, *Det moderne statssystem.* Oslo: Gyldendal 1987.

93. Bendix, Reinhard, "Backwardness and Intellectual Mobilization," in Reinhard Bendix, *Force, Fate, and Freedom. On Historical Sociology.* Berkeley: University of California Press 1984; Gellner, Ernst, *Nations and States.* Oxford: Basil Blackwell 1983; Smith, Anthony, *The Ethnic Revival in the Modern World.* Cambridge: Cambridge University Press 1981, chap. 3.

94. Hechter, Michael, *Internal Colonialism. The Celtic Fringe in the British National Development, 1536–1966.* London: Routledge & Kegan Paul 1975.

95. Gellner, Ernest, *Nations and Nationalism.* Oxford: Blackwell 1983, pp. 24, 112.

96. Hroch, Miroslav, "From National Movement to the Fully-formed Nation." *New Left Review* 198, 1993, pp. 11–12.

97. See Charles Tilly, *Big Structures, Large Processes, Huge Comparisons*. London: Sage 1984.

98. See Reinhard Bendix, "Why Nationalism? Relative Backwardness and Intellectual Mobilization," *Zeitschrift für Soziologie*, 8:1; 1981; Gellner, Ernest, *Nations and Nationalism*. Oxford: Blackwell 1983; and Øyvind Østerud, "Utvikling gjennom tilbakeliggenhet," in Øyvind Østerud, *Det moderne statssystem*. Oslo: Gyldendal 1987.

Chapter Two

State-Building, Nationalities, and Conflict Dynamics in the Soviet and Habsburg Empires: A Rokkanian Approach

The Soviet development project after 1922 contained elements of both state- and nation building, as these terms are commonly used in historical and sociological research. The starting point of this comparative analysis can be stated as follows: What light can the experiences of other multinational empires shed on Soviet nationality policy? While Austria and Turkey emerged from the ruins of the Habsburg and Ottoman Empires, no Russian nation-state came into being after 1917. Why was the Russian Empire in the disguise of the Soviet Union (or the Soviet Union in the capacity of successor empire of the former) for a long time obviously successful in neutralizing and to a large extent solving potential conflicts, while other multinational empires facing the same problems collapsed?

I will discuss the three following cases: Austria–Hungary until 1918, the All-Russian empire before 1917, and the Soviet Union.[1] Theoretically I will base my discussion on the assumption that Stein Rokkan's models offer a mode of discussion that may be useful in the comparative analysis of certain important processes of state- and empire building and disintegration also in those cases.

The *Ausgleich* in 1867 altered the state structure of the Habsburg monarchy and thereafter national relations developed along very different lines in the two imperial halves. The *Ausgleich* agreement mirrored an equilibrium between the Habsburg dynasty and the Magyar nobility. The empire was divided into two parts with equal status and rights, the essence of the compromise being the German dominance over Austria and the Magyar over Hungary. A comparison between the two states shows, however, that the shape and structure of nationality conflicts and their available solutions were quite different. Austria, in principle recognized as a multinational state by its own political elite with equal rights for all its nations, was faced with a

Hungary defining itself as a Magyar nation-state—with the concept of a Magyar supreme rule as a common dogma for all parties and with a subsequent suppression of reality. This Magyar supremacy and the following fiction of Hungary as a nation-state could only be maintained by means of an arbitrary and discriminating electoral system and by corresponding administrative practices.[2] For certain comparative purposes Austria–Hungary must therefore be treated as two cases.

To put the distinctive features of the Russian state building into a relief, I will also use the Western European overseas colonial empires as ideal types or examples in the comparative analysis. I feel this is justified because both in terms of methods and institutional solutions, state- and colony building must be seen as variations over related themes or practical problems.

To focus on the social and economic dynamics from which modern nationalism springs, I will present the phases in a somewhat different order from that of Rokkan's model. In the Soviet case the phases were developing simultaneously. This approach should therefore hardly present a problem from a historical–empirical point of view. The fact that the problems associated with the economic redistribution are presented first here should not, of course, be interpreted as an endorsement of an economically deterministic way of thinking.

ECONOMIC REDISTRIBUTION BETWEEN SOCIAL CLASSES AND NATIONS

Nationalism and Combined, Uneven Development

Phase 4 in Rokkan's model—economic redistribution—is associated with the crystallizing of modern class conflicts, and with various types of cleavages between interest groups linked to production and markets. Most distinctive during the industrialization process was the cleavage between the owners of the means of production and the industrial working class. The political breakthrough of social democratic and social liberal values took much of the sting out of this conflict and domesticated, so to speak, both capitalist dynamics and the industrial working class as a potentially revolutionary force. In the case of the USSR, I will emphasize the economic redistribution between regions and nations, not between different social classes, although these two aspects are closely linked in modernizing societies, including the USSR.

Nationalism may be seen as a response to uneven development. I refer to the more detailed discussion of natonalism in chapter 1. Here I will only repeat some key words from the main points as an introduction to subsequent empirical analysis: In the core areas nationalism will most certainly occur either among minority national groups, trying to defend their own privileged positions, or among newly educated strata of hitherto non-privileged nations who are trying to better their own career possibilities parallel with the social advancement of their own nations, as for the first time they are drawn into the modernization process.[3]

When national and colonial questions are intertwined, each reinforcing the other, the class structure tends to be ethnically segregated. This situation can be characterized as *internal colonialism*, a condition in which the uneven development of the economic system causes material and cultural oppression to nations in the making—newcomer ethnic groups tend to constitute internal colonies.[4] Under such circumstances lack of stability too may be explained by a combined, uneven development.

Patriotic, or national, mobilization under these circumstances will hardly come about without an intelligentsia. When studying social elites, one is therefore not only interested in the factors that account for their formation. One is also interested in their identity and their capacity for collective action. Miroslav Hroch and Ernest Gellner suggested that political nationalism will be more marked when the economy is not able to provide a growth of high-status employment on the same scale as the increase of new applicants.[5]

The scenario of national opposition and separatism due to economic factors may, however, be defeated. Federalism may be seen as an instrument to handle the economic aspects of ethnic conflicts, by leaving room for the central authorities to redistribute a larger or smaller part of the society's resources. However, even if the state is seeking to act in the interest of the community as a whole, it must be prepared to face serious problems, as the involved parties may always interpret its policies as unjust in its effects. The idea that some nations profit at the expense of others may form the basis for political mobilization of the community as a whole, it must be prepared to face serious problems. As a way to approach such questions I will also discuss if, or to which degree, the dominant nation's culture and nationalism influenced the policy toward minorities. The answer to these questions places nationality policy on a continuum that varies from strict cultural standardization and discrimination against some distinctive subgroups toward cultural tolerance, even including an active stimulation of cultural differences.

Considering the greater degree of stability in the USSR, as compared to the conditions in Austria, some comparative questions need to be further elaborated:

1. Were the geographical discrepancies following from budgetary allocations, that is, between the origin and the spending of the national income, greater in the case of the USSR than in the Habsburg monarchy?

2. Did the leveling in the standard of living and life chances which was brought about by the Soviet policy of regional redistribution essentially contribute to political stabilization?
3. To what extent were the occupational structure and the labor market segregated along ethnic lines in such a way that the national minority intellectuals ended up as career losers?

Modernization and Nation building

The industrial development of the Habsburg monarchy began only slowly. Historical research on the economic development in the 19th century shows this general trend: In the first half of the century, the monarchy became more backward from a European perspective, because of the absence of economic growth in its eastern parts. This picture, however, conceals the growth taking place in its German core areas due to the capitalist development already starting at the beginning of the century. There was no gap between those areas and the leading Western European countries, neither in 1800 nor in 1850.[6]

After the mid-century, the gap between the monarchy as a whole and the Western countries stabilized. Toward the end of the century the monarchy began to catch up, a fact accounted for by Hungary's rapid economic growth, especially from the 1880s. Right up to the end of the monarchy the economic and social structures in the eastern parts were dominated by great landowners, a fact which, however, retarded neither capitalist development nor the country's industrialization.[7]

All things considered, a model of "development through reaping the benefits of backwardness," à la Gerschenkron, based on the backward countries borrowing and learning from more advanced ones seems to fit the Habsburg case, or at least some of its most important areas, better than a theory of underdevelopment, which postulates that the beneficial effects of industrialization cannot be spread, great regions being doomed to remain dependent suppliers of raw materials and labor.[8] This is the case both with regard to the monarchy's relative position in Europe and to the relationship between its own two halves.

As concerns the All-Russian Empire, one of its main features had been the disparity in development levels between different regions, both in terms of economy and culture. A conspicuous feature was the fact that the Russian nation was not the dominant one in the All-Russian Empire economically speaking, when compared to some of the national minorities. Great discrepancies were also to be found in the regions and among their various ethnic groups.[9] Although the foundations of the later Soviet drive for modernization were laid during the last decades of Tsarist Russia, the disruptive economic factors that took such strong effect in the Habsburg case were therefore far less noticeable in All-Russia.

In Austria–Hungary industrialization transformed the sociological basis of the national opposition and changed the composition of nationalities in important regions through migration. As more and more workers of various nationalities migrated into the principal cities of the monarchy to get work, the towns became the main areas of conflict. Therefore there is reason to believe in the relevance of an approach stressing the causal importance of uneven development, and to assume that nationalism is at its strongest where social cleavages and discrimination follow ethnic lines, as in the tradition based on Otto Bauer.[10] Miroslav Hroch's comparative–historical approach to the study of the *patriotic movements* of small nations, with his emphasis on an *X-factor* to explain the movements' breakthrough into mass movements, is located, in analytical terms, in this Marxist tradition from Otto Bauer.

National feelings and assertiveness, according to Bauer, became more strongly developed among minorities, both ruling and oppressed, living in districts overwhelmingly populated by a different people belonging to another culture and speaking another language and where national differences were coupled with social conflicts. The strongest nationalism would occur among a nationally conscious minority in a situation where it did not occupy positions of privilege and the right to exploit, but lived as a servile and exploited social class.[11] In such cases, nationalism developed among the exploited class out of hate for the exploiters: "National hate was transformed class conflict."[12]

As urbanization proceeded, the newcomers to the city proletariat were generally excluded from the benefits of prosperity by their more privileged German fellow workers. A fierce urban class competition also reduced to a mockery the supposed unity of the working class. In the midst of this competition culture and language became particularly important. One distinctive feature of the Austrian nationality conflict was that the national movements for the first time embraced the working classes of the populations, both among historic and non-historic nations, and that the working classes were split along national lines. In Austria people's social and economic situation was determined by the national group to which they belonged, so that collectively German workers were better protected, better educated, and had an easier access to skilled and supervisory positions than others. They also had stronger trade unions at their disposal.

A nationality dynamics highly similar to that in the Austrian half of the Habsburg monarchy was to be found in the USSR during the implementation of the nationality policy introduced by Lenin: the policy of indigenization, or *korenizatsiya.* Processes comparable to those described in Austria–Hungary did not occur in the All-Russian Empire, and in the case of the USSR, they were, so to speak, *embedded* in the overall processes characterizing the Soviet road to modernity: *nation-building processes (natsional'noe stroitel'stvo)* initiated from above through massive literacy campaigns that encouraged the use of minority languages as mediums of instruction in local schools, and "upgrading" by the Soviet authorities of a number of preliterate minority languages by giving them alphabets. In addition, national infrastructures of mass communication were built and higher education strengthened. The social structures of the various nations were transformed through social and geographical mobility, that is, through urbanization and formation of working classes and new intellectual elites among non-Russian nations.[13] Terry Martin in his survey of interwar nationality policy, therefore, offered the metaphor of an "affirmative action Empire" referring to "a set of fundamental rules that structure the political life" of the USSR, "a strategy designed to avoid the perception of empire" and which "decisively rejected the model of the nation-state."[14]

The unintended effects of Soviet modernization began to be noticeable to the country's rulers in the period immediately after Stalin's death. Important nation-building processes had taken place especially through the formation of new non-Russian educated elites.[15] Political control of higher education therefore became an everlasting concern of Soviet nationality policy. For decades access to higher education was controlled through a system of national quotas that gave preferential treatment to representatives of the titular nations in their home republics.[16] In contrast to the older social elites from Tsarist times, which were wiped out by Stalin in the 1930s, the new intelligentsias had the Soviet system itself as their basis.

In the Habsburg monarchy the centrifugal influences stemming from the spread of capitalism in the economic sphere was above all coupled with the "Great Depression" from 1873 to 1896. The national movements of Austria then had their political breakthrough. In the wake of an economic crisis, the political climate changed and the political hegemony of Austrian–German liberalism was broken for the benefit of conservative, socialist and nationalist movements. The broad masses were now for the first time drawn into the political struggle, altering both its form and content.[17]

As the united German political front disintegrated, and with it the influence and prestige of the Austrian Germanness (*die deutsche Kulturgemeinschaft*), Slavic peoples displayed increasing political energy and their positions were strengthened. The social and regional impact of the crisis thus was to make national opposition fiercer. This also seems to make plausible the thesis that the most important social carrier of national hatred was the *petite bourgeoisie, in the classical Marxist sense*, in the Austrian part of the monarchy. While the traditional small bourgeoisie was hardest hit in Cisleithania (i.e., Austria), the group that felt the impact of the Great Depression in Hungary strongest was the gentry. The gentry also was to become the foremost exponent of anticapitalist and nationalist feelings.[18]

Some economic factors that influenced Habsburg nationality conflicts ought to be mentioned: Even if German capital was necessary in the beginning for Czech and Hungarian industrialization, the dependence and lack of proportion between *national* and *foreign* capital and personnel that followed offended the Czechs and the Hungarians, whose self-esteem had been considerably enhanced as a consequence of their unequivocal industrial progress.[19] Tendencies toward autarky among non-Germans were also reinforced due to pressure from competition with the initially more advanced German industry. The Czechs are the most conspicuous example here. Strengthening national credit institutions became a matter of greatest importance, and patriotic slogans such as "Do not make your purchases from Germans!" were followed by a boycott of German goods.[20] In Hungary, where a modernizing elite had at its disposal a state apparatus, a persistent policy was pursued to further the building of a national industry. Hungarian opposition toward Austria was kept alive as a means to reach such a goal. This policy was largely very successful.

Economic Transfers—A Means to Counteract National Opposition?

As regards the Soviet case, it is well worth emphasizing the following aspect of the Soviet nationality policy in a comparative perspective: Even if the existing regional hierarchy of consumption per capita remained unchanged, one basic aim of Soviet regional policy was to promote economic development even in the regions with the highest birth rates, Central Asia, so that this region would not lag further behind in the future. To achieve this, income produced in one republic was transferred and used for consumption and investment in others. A strong financial redistribution took place during the whole period of Soviet rule in the framework of the budgetary process and was closely tied to social economic planning.[21] An important means in the income transfers was the turnover tax, a differentiated tax on consumption introduced in 1930 as a purely all union tax leaving room for Moscow central planners to allow different republics to retain unequal shares for local use.[22] Also investment allocations had as one of its aims to redistribute resources so as to promote complex and parallel economic growth among the various republics.[23]

Soviet modernization resulted in perceptible improvements from one year to the next for Soviet citizens, as long as economic growth increased steadily. From 1950 to 1980, real consumption per capita increased by 3.4 percent in the average each year and the standard of living was tripled.[24] As regards social expenditures payments from social consumption funds, a conspicuous leveling was taking place in medical care and pensions, through subsidization of house rents, and through support and subsidization of education and general enlightenment of the people.[25] This included, as an aspect of paramount importance, the equalization of educational opportunities for members of all Soviet nations, a factor that brought about a dramatic rise in the level of education among the non-Russian nations.

Also in Austria a transfer of income through taxation took place. The higher tax revenues received from the Germans were above all used in the regions of Cisleithania as an addition to the capital injection from the Vienna banks, and made possible both Czech and Hungarian industrialization.[26] Even if both the pronounced aim of the transfers, and their most important effect,[27] was to spread economic growth and even out developmental differences among the regions, their political impact was the sharpening of national opposition in the Habsburg monarchy. The principal explanation for this was the character of the political system of Vienna and the permanent tug of war between the nationalities in economic issues that made the national struggles fiercer.

The conflict between Hungary and Austria over the distribution of common public spending was recurrently sharpened every tenth year when the renewal of the *Ausgleich* was to be negotiated. In Cisleithania the conflict over each Crownland's share of public spending and the distribution of public transfers kept the national conflicts warm.

Considerable importance must be attached to social and economic factors in explaining the high degree of stability in Soviet Central Asia (the former colonies of Tsarist Russia) until the Gorbachev era. Despite Central Asia's peripheral position and high birth rate, it was relatively protected against exploitation, and the region's republics profited as consistent recipients of resources transferred from other parts of the USSR, probably during the whole Soviet era.[28] Its labor-intensive agriculture, its relative degree of self-sufficiency in farm products, and its industry, deviating from the Soviet pattern based on heavy industry, mainly geared to the needs of agriculture, and dominated by small-scale production, raised popular consumption levels. In addition mass education coupled with social mobility neutralized the local intelligentsia. These are factors contributing to an explanation of why the Central Asians on the whole remained locked in a pre-nationalist stage.[29]

Central Asia was in fact the most conspicuous example of developmental disproportions on the republic level, disproportions that made it possible to employ an intellectual elite to manage a large cultural infrastructure that was out of all reasonable proportion to the local economy. This policy was dependent on a strong central power relying on extensive economic growth and gave the state the opportunity to protect the interests of the groups that were most receptive to nationalist attitudes, according to Western theories on the subject. Its result was that a uniform institutional pattern of science, art and culture was imposed on all union republics regardless of their different histories, cultures and levels of industrial development. The disproportions following from this were accentuated by ongoing demographic and ethnic processes.[30] At the same time, Soviet policy was not effective in weakening the influence of sub-national identities connected with universal organizations (clan, kinship, family, neighborhood) at the grassroots level.

The Ukraine found itself in a position completely opposite to that of Central Asia. To be sure, here too the republic leadership was prepared to create new job opportunities and open up careers to the new intellectual strata. But here more than 10 percent of the republic's gross national income (or perhaps as much as 14 percent in the most recent period) was transferred to other republics; that is, national income produced in the Ukraine exceeded the income used there by that amount, without any compensation.[31] At the same time members of the Ukrainian intelligentsia experienced a crisis with regard to their social mobility in the home republic.[32]

The stability in national relations in the Ukrainian republic cannot be accounted for by factors of economic redistribution in Rokkan's macro model. The stabilizing influence exerted by economic factors in the USSR as a whole probably came to an end in the second half of the 1970s. In the same way that the European "Great Depression" sharpened national opposition in the Habsburg monarchy, the stagnation of economic growth in the late 1970s now contributed to hardening the political atmosphere between the Soviet nations. This conflict was particularly related to the professional interests and careers of "native" elites of non-Russian origin.

As a conclusion it is quite reasonable to maintain that an approach like that of Otto Bauer, focusing on *the uneven development of capitalism* as one way of concretizing the economic problems with which state builders have to cope, is an apt theoretical starting point to explain the dynamics of national conflict in Austria–Hungary.

I have maintained that in the case of the Soviet Union the economic transfers partly explain political stability after the Second World War. But naturally the Soviet developmental policy alone is not capable of explaining the, at any rate apparent, absence of signs of national opposition. Similar transfers also took place between regions in Austria without the same effect. On the contrary, the unconcealed tug of war concerning economic burdens and benefits rather sharpened the national opposition here. Seen from a comparative point of view, economic factors are therefore not an adequate explanation for Soviet stability. In the Habsburg monarchy the same economic factors exerted their influence on the relationship between the nations, but they did so in one particular political arrangement that acted as more than a mere *superstructure* possessing a limited *relative autonomy*, and thus contributed to defining a quite unique ethnic–topographical structure. Granted other political conditions, the influences of the economic factors might have been quite different also in the case of the USSR. This leads us to the next set of problems, as defined by Stein Rokkan's model.

CULTURAL STANDARDIZATION AND NATIONALISM

Stein Rokkan and the Theory of *Sociological Minorities*

This phase, or bundle of problems, of state building consists of an attempt from the center to establish a unified religious and linguistic standard. In the West the church was combined with the state and its supranational ties were cut off. Latin was gradually disappearing as the medium of written communication and was giving way to a standardized vernacular language. As the population as a whole was joined to the state center, and losing their local or international cultural–symbolic loyalty, nation building was taking place.

If the process was successful, the geographical area of the state's authority also defined the boundaries for the population's sense of national identity and its culture. A new loyalty being born, the classes were to a higher degree integrated and the social and cultural segregation of the agrarian society began to disappear through a social communication process, transcending and integrating "high culture" and "low culture" (the educational system was of vital importance here). The periphery-based counterculture was thus wiped out.

Nation building represents, if seen from below, a transfer of loyalty from smaller primary group-oriented social units (family, kinship, locality, household) to aggregate units of a political and administrative nature. This represents a departure from the earlier patterns of social and political organization that follows from a definite tendency to level down all intermediate structures between the state and the individual and tie influential elites to the state's bureaucratic structure. However, a state-supporting elitist culture was not the only possible value system by which political loyalty could be reoriented.

Ethnic minorities with strong integration and loyalty can survive as non-assimilated pockets (or *sociological minorities*) and constitute potential threats to the dominating nation state "from below." The novelty in their situation is that they are made to become conscious of the fact.

Based on Rokkan's model, political conflicts will arise wherever periphery interests are articulated and mobilized. In the following I will again ask whether, or in what ways, the dominant nation's culture and nationalism influenced the policy toward minorities. Did the institutional policies of the centers allow, or to what degree did they allow, particularist loyalties and defense of separate identities of distinct subgroups?

Austria and Hungary Representing Two Distinctive Nationality Policies

The development of the Habsburg monarchy from 1848 to 1918 was, before the disintegration phase of the Soviet Union, the most important sequence in European history for the study of the political consequences of the ethnicity principle. The fragmentary dynamics vis-à-vis the state organization and the tension between state organization and nationalist mobilization were, in other words, more strongly expressed here than in the Soviet Union for the larger part of its history.

The Habsburg state remained to the end a *Hausmacht,* a collection of dynastic possessions without a common ethnic or territorial denomination and without a coherent state structure. As for the pre-*Ausgleich* Habsburg monarchy, from one point of view, the Josephine experiments of the 18th century (Joseph's envisaged *Gesamtstaat*), their failures and successes prefigure the nationality conflicts of a later date.[33] Nationalism in this period emerged as a response to policies pursued during Rokkan's phase 1 (state consolidation) and hindered the standardization of phase 2.

Social, economic, ecclesiastical, and military reforms were implemented as parts of the project of Maria Theresa and Joseph (her son) to try to restructure the disparate lands as an organized whole. The practical concern of the *Aufklärung* for welfare and improvement created two particular areas where statecraft and national interest might stimulate each other: first was an attention to vernacular languages at a lower level in education and instruction. The second common ground was the concept of citizenship, the idea of a community of *Staatsbürger*, contributing to ambiguity as to the extension of any particular community, stimulating alternative patriotic loyalties. "Joseph II, we might say, climbed aboard the train of *Aufklärung,* only to stop at the station marked '*Staatsbürgertum.*' National communities in his monarchy simultaneously climbed aboard a Josephinist tram, only to alight at the station marked 'nationhood' (those having farthest to travel being most moulded by the impetus)."[34]

In Hungary all the Josephine reforms were enforced despite vehement Magyar protests. The nobility was partly panicked by the possibility of losing their exemptions from taxes and compulsory military service, as well as their control over serfs. The *Natio Hungarica* did not mean a community of those speaking Hungarian, but a ruling class; for many members Hungarian was not their mother tongue. When the enlightened absolutist Joseph II decided in the 1780s to switch the language of the state from Latin to German (the point was administrative efficiency, and not the creation of German cultural hegemony), he was met with enraged opposition from the Latin-speaking nobility in Hungary.

"The existence of the Hungarian Diet as political forum for the nobility, the existence of Hungary as a separate entity within the Empire, enabled national claims not only to transcend the purely cultural domain and the relationship to the central power, but also to include questions of social and even economic development."[35] During the early 19th century reform of the language was prioritized. Slowly increasing literacy, the spread of Magyar in printed texts, also stimulated a nationalism different from that of the nobility. This nationalism had its hour in the Revolution of 1848.

However, the process was strongly influenced by the fact that less than half of the population was Hungarian. "As a 'state bourgeoisie' in the making, the liberals could not be expected to preside over the diminution or truncation of the territorial unit whose management would provide them with social status, purpose, and security."[36]

For certain comparative purposes post-*Ausgleich* Austria–Hungary must, as mentioned above, be treated as two cases. In total agreement with the differences between the official ideologies dominating Austria and Hungary respectively, the political democratization, seen from a nationality perspective, proceeded along very different tracks in the two imperial realms. While the Austrian nations were able to develop their national culture year after year, the opposite tendency was the case in Hungary. The strongest Hungarian non-Magyarian national group was weaker in the political and public arena than the weakest non-German one in Austria. While there did not exist any *cultural standardization strategy* in Austria, either from the political elite or from the German–Austrian side, Hungary was the clearest example of such a cultural standardization strategy outside the All-Russian Empire.[37]

Crownland federalism played an important role in the political conflicts in the Austrian half of the monarchy. Cisleithania consisted of 17 autonomous Crownlands, all of them with their own local parliaments and separate administrations. In addition there was a central national assembly and administration in Vienna. Every territorial assembly elected a governor as head of the autonomous administration. There was also a governor appointed by the emperor, to be responsible for matters common to all lands. There were important minorities in most Crownlands, and every nation spared no effort to ensure administrative, cultural and economic privilege for itself. They therefore became important hotbeds for national conflicts. The majority nation, such as the Czechs or Poles, stubbornly asserted the Crownland's autonomy, as did the Germans when they were the majority. One of the most important problems that would have had to be resolved to reconcile the nations was the principle on which administrative reforms were to be founded (or the language of the local administration) in mixed-population areas. The majority nations defended a *territorial principle*, whereby individual rights were derived from the autonomous position of the actual area. The minorities, on the other hand, demanded either further territorial partitioning according to national settlements or autonomy based on a *personal principle*.

> The Crownlands are the internal enemy of the Hapsburg monarchy. They, and no one else, are the breeding ground for irredentists, they create the desperate minorities and the ruthless majorities. . . . But precisely because the Crownlands give their national majorities a hope of national dominance, the majorities in all Crownlands and also the majority of the *Reichsrat* cling to them, even the Germans! North Bohemia is suffocating under the pressure of the Bohemian royal throne and cries for help, the German Alpine lands, however, will continue to be Steiers, Carinthians, Tyroleans. . . . As long as this ghost from bygone days, the idol of the homogenous territory, has not been laid to rest, there will be no national peace.[38]

In Austria the new national movements could develop spontaneously from small intellectual circles into large, socially all-embracing mass movements. "The nations without a history" (i.e., without their own national upper class and without a historically developed political institutional framework by the beginning of the 19th century) had the German nation's cultural dominance working against them, a fact which came to expression in the secondary schools and at the university level, and in the widespread opinion that such nations were incapable of creating their own higher culture. On the cultural level, the construction of national infrastructures for the emerging nations was of prime importance. It is therefore not a mere coincidence that the foundations of Slavic philology, archeology, and ethnography were laid by Austrian Slavs during this period. General compulsory education and the rise in the average standard of this education contributed to hasten the nation-building process, as did the spreading of newspapers and publishing houses, pedagogic literature, specialist literature and terminology. In Hungary the transition from embryonic national movements to embracing mass movements was retarded by the use of political instruments.[39]

When the Habsburg monarchy collapsed, before Entente troops had been stationed in its territory, all national movements in Cisleithania (Austria) proved strong enough to take power in their own ethnic areas. Only in some particularly disputed areas did bloodshed actually take place. In the Hungarian half of the realm, in contrast, the government attempted to save historical Hungary (with the exception of Croatia and Vojvodina). The tradition of

Magyar dominance and political pressure proved sufficiently strong to secure the initial recognition of the authority of the new government. Only the military invasion by the *successor states* and the decisions and treaty of the peace conference put an end to Magyar power. The elections after the First World War, moreover, showed a deviation between the "objective" ethnical composition as reflected in the census of these territories and the national political orientation (as reflected in the results of elections on the subject of the new post-war state).[40]

From a comparative perspective, there are periods in the history of Tsarist Russia characterized by a *nationality policy* similar to that of Hungary. In these periods there is an intensification of an elite-based cultural standardization of the kind referred to in Rokkan's four-phase model: In the wake of 18th-century Westernization, a stimulus toward an aggressive policy of integration, including a violent missionary activity, made itself felt. The reason for this was a desire to unify, systematize and modernize the empire according to Western standards, including the standard set by Western intolerance toward non-Westerners. Still no particular national considerations existed with regard to implementing a cultural Russification of non-Russians in this period; functionally what took place was the same process of standardization that was occurring during the enlightened autocracy in the West as a prerequisite for the emergence of culturally homogeneous nation states.

Late 19th-Century Russification and Magyarization

The Russification of the last decades of the 19th century can, as a point of departure, be understood as a parallel to the Magyarization process in Hungary. Both cases were an anticipatory strategy from groups, traditionally alien to national ideas but now threatened by marginalization through social modernization and its accompanying political mobilization. Neither the Russification nor the Magyarization were influenced by the patterns given by the French and the American Revolutions. In both Russia and Hungary a superficial and illusionary image of national unity was created by suppressing the national self-assertion of the minorities.[41]

In one basic aspect the Russian and the Magyar policies of unification were, however, fundamentally different. In the All-Russian case orthodox Christianity was the main instrument in the drive toward a unitary state, not the nationalism of the dominant nation, as was the case in Hungary. This must be explained by the fact that in Hungary the impulse toward unification emanated more clearly from the interests of the upper social groups—or ruling classes in an economic sense—while in Russia its sources were to be found among the dynastic circles of the imperial or patrimonial state bureaucracy.

In societies in which the majority of the population lacks both political experience and education, one of the main preoccupations when political minority programs are being formulated, will be the language issue. The national movements in Austria–Hungary achieved very different results in their struggle to carry out their language programs, the use of their own mother tongues. In Hungary national movements were prevented from reaching phase C (the phase of mass mobilization in Miroslav Hroch's terminology) by political means. The strategy of "forced Magyarization" of the Hungarian education system was in fact aimed at impeding non-Hungarian nationalities from developing their own educated elites. This was openly acknowledged by the Magyar leaders. It is important to emphasize the political linkage between the language question and the social-class conflicts (i.e., social conflicts lying outside the sphere of a nation's existence). Equally important was the linkage between nationality policy and class policy. Thus the Magyars were on the defensive in a twofold sense: their defense of their national dominance was also an anticipatory strategy against a development that in the long run threatened to undermine the old latifundia system of class dominance (i.e., the political and social ramifications of capitalist industrialization).[42]

With the spreading of education and the increase of industrialization, the Hungarian middle classes expanded by absorbing newcomers. The new groups were of artisan and peasant origins and bourgeois elements assimilated from other nationalities, the majority of which consisted of Jews and Germans, but were also Slavs and Romanians. Representatives of the suppressed nations considered, on their part, their own *Magyarons* to be renegades. Magyar nationalism therefore became the ingredient cementing the heterogeneous Hungarian middle and upper classes.[43]

The crisis of Dualism in 1903–1906 tied the deeply discriminating election system to the preservation of the old Habsburg army regulations in Hungary. Traditionally, the language of command (*Kommandosprache*) in the common army (*k.u.k. Arme*) had been German. However, the Hungarian Parliament now put forward a bill declaring Magyarian to be the language of command in the Hungarian part of the empire. After a long-lasting conflict the king-emperor threatened through the minority government led by Fejevary, to introduce universal suffrage in Hungary if the bill was not revoked. As a consequence the opposition surrendered its vehement nationalism. This made clear that the perpetuation of the monarchy depended on the continued dominance of the Magyar agrarian upper class.[44] On the other hand, the hegemonic position, or dominating influence of the state structure over other societal domains, or spheres of social action, in All-Russia, as later in the USSR, raises the following question: Did the cultural norms implemented in the Russian case represent only the ideological–cultural interests of the state regime as such, without clear reference to any particular social class in the population, in contrast to the situation in Hungary? In my opinion this must be answered in the affirmative—the driving force behind the development of Russian official nationalism was the patrimonial bureaucracy itself—and the political positions of these two presumptively *state-supporting nations* in state structure were therefore quite different in the two empires during their last decades. Paradoxically, during the last decades of the 19th century the relative position of the Russians in the hierarchy of All-Russia's nations was becoming, according to my perception, more and more similar to that of the Germans of contemporary Austria. A development in the opposite direction of the one the Russians went through was occurring from a different starting point for the German part, in such a way that a convergence was taking place.

THE CONTRADICTORY NATURE OF RUSSIAN AND GERMAN IDENTITIES

The relative position of the Russians in the All-Russian Empire had, up to the middle of the 19th century, been the opposite of that of the Austrian-Germans in the Habsburg monarchy. The use of non-Russians in offices of confidence in the patrimonial administration obstructed the Russian nobility from constituting itself as an independent political force against the emperor-tsar. While the Russians made up a considerably larger part of the total population than the Germans, the more purely patrimonial state in All-Russia rendered possible the limitation of their social and political influence.[45]

Russia under Alexander III increasingly became a sheer police state and an exceptional regime giving vast powers to the police and civil service in most areas. The objective was to limit the reforms of the 1860s and 1870s, and in general the effects of modernization. The regime relied solely on the aristocracy for support and sought to strengthen its position. The dawning national awareness in some of the non-Russian population groups was seen as a threat to the unity of the state, as when traditional methods of handling the Polish elites failed during the 1860s. This caused an intensification of administrative Russification that was directed toward the preservation of the government through "greater administrative unity and coordination."[46]

In the All-Russian, as opposed to the Hungarian case, the efforts to build a unitary state can be described as a national leveling, the result of which was the strengthening of a group previously discriminated against, namely the Russians. This was done in a way that affirmed the patrimonial system of government and the political principle of autocracy, and implied that no formal rights were granted to any nationality, including the Russians. In addition to them, a number of minority groups in the category *inorodtsy* (non-natives) in Central Asia also benefited from their annexation by the All-Russian Empire during the Russification campaign of the late 19th century.[47] Tsarism was thus "able simultaneously to repress and Russify in its Western borderlands while promoting indigenous languages in the east and south."[48] But all in all the Russian influence on non-Russians in Central Asia was slight. For the Estonian and Latvian "nations without a history," which lacked an upper class of their own ethnicity; the mounting pressure on the German Baltic nobility for the first time opened up the possibility to constitute themselves as separate nations, particularly in education and culture, but also in the economic domain.[49]

The Russian national identity consisted of various components in the form of characteristic myths: the realm (*russkaya zemlya)*, orthodox Christianity and the autocracy/tsar. These components can be seen as "chemical substances" which can be mixed together in different ratios and give rise to different political trends.[50] Russian nationalism remained closely tied to the social and political contradictions of Russian society throughout the entire tsar period. Toward the end of the 18th century there had been three variants of Russian proto-national feelings. These came to expression through three different social strata or classes: the predominantly politically oriented state patriotism of the upper ecclesiastical and aristocratic strata which were closely linked to the state; the religious and xenophobic, potentially anti-state feelings of the broader masses; and a culturally, linguistically and historically motivated national consciousness of segments of the secularized, Western-oriented, educated elite.[51] Although the existence of an ethnie (i.e., of a pre-national ethnocultural group) in Russia to which political elites could have appealed is indisputable, "no actual or potential political leaders chose to appeal to it." "Because the Russian-educated elite followed the tsar in identifying the Russian people with a universal religion, they also were never able to produce the sort of particularistic and secular nationalist ideology that arose in Western Europe."[52]

In the 19th century, therefore, these three forms of Russian national identity remained separate from one another, and a fusion into one single political and social nationalism never took place. Russia remained divided in its national identity. The state could not make use of slavophile nationalism for its own ends and at the same time did not succeed in transforming traditional state patriotism to be a source capable of binding all strata and groups together, nor was the national consciousness of the Russian elite capable of creating a lasting bond either to the state or to masses of the Russian people.

As the empire entered its last decades Russian nationalism became the expression of the most conservative groups in the country, who identified loyalty with an ethnic Russianness, the definition of which included religion, however putting the interests of the empire—"Russia one and indivisible"—over those of the nation. It was not totally without impact on the regime, whose nationality policy remained contradictory to the end. Nationalism in prerevolutionary Russia being more a state of mind than a political force, never succeeded in fulfilling the socially integrating functions it had in the old historical nations of Western Europe. Its relationship to the state was one of fateful ambivalence, which caused it "for the most part to remain a cultural and psychological rather than a political phenomenon."[53] Since the parties on the left put the interest of class over the interests of nation, non-Russian parties looked for alliances with supranational left-wing parties.[54]

From a Rokkanian point of view Peter Flora stressed that "identity-building in the sense of nation-building does not merely mean that a new identity comes along to join other age old or relatively recent identities. This process is linked rather with the claim to supremacy for this identity and the loyalties and solidarities that goes with it over other collectivities. In this respect it is comparable to the increasing claim of the territorial state to the monopoly on the legitimate use of force."[55] Therefore, Russia in 1917 fell apart by the presence of faultlines that "were precisely the divisions that would have been resolved by the development of a national unity." But even then there "was no political party—or even a single individual—calling for the Russian heartland to let go of its empire and to create a government of, by, and for Russians."[56]

During the 19th century the development of the Austrian state of affairs was, as seen from the German–Austrian point of view, the other way around. Two factors were of importance: The disintegration of the German cultural and political hegemony in the Habsburg monarchy, and the role of Great German nationalism, first in the German Confederation, afterwards in *das Reich*. Before 1815 "the Old Austrians" were feeling both a part of the German nation and as good Austrian patriots. However, a constantly increasing gulf was gradually developing between Austrian state patriotism and Great German patriotism in the course of the 19th century. Unlike all other groups in the Habsburg monarchy the German–Austrians could not, moreover, on their part, clearly differentiate between their own nationality, with its particular interests, and their Habsburg identity. Instead they found themselves permanently torn between a universal state ideology and their particularly German identity. The unification of Germany by Prussia thus caused a crisis of loyalty to the dynasty among the Germans.[57]

Aside from the failed Josephine policies of the 1780s and the 1850s (the system of Bach), there was however little concerted effort to impose the German language on diverse regions of the realm. The Habsburgs took pains to stand above the modern German nationalism that emerged in the 19th a pre-national ethnocultural century.

Probably the most important unifying ideological putty in the Habsburg state edifice had been provided by the Roman Catholic Church. The universal spirit of Catholicism did not promote an attitude emphasizing special national characteristics and differences. Ever since the Counterreformation it had placed its entire religious and political power unreservedly at the disposal of the emperor in his efforts to prevent the Empire from disintegrating. The Church was far removed from any German nationalistic leanings. Its clear opinion was that a unified Habsburg monarchy, with the Church itself as its prominent moral component, was incompatible with a rejection of the cultural efforts of the Slavic majority.[58]

As for the USSR, Stalin's attack on non-Russian nationalism as well as his use of Russian nationalism can be given a plausible interpretation in the context of Soviet modernization. While turning to the principle of discipline in every realm from the family to the factory, he embraced Russian nationalism as well. A rehabilitation of the position of the Russian population element was now taking place as a part of the post-revolutionary, state-building project, after a period in which the *decolonizing aspect* of the Bolshevik revolution had entailed a condemnation of Great Russian nationalism as "the worst form of deviation from the correct Leninist course."[59] The change was brought about more as a response from the center to the anti-Russian feelings among the political leaders and party members in the non-Russian republics due to the violent measures used by Stalin to enforce his revolution from above, than it was an abandonment of old objectives on grounds of principle. Stalin accused the national elites in the non-Russian republics of "bourgeois nationalism" and liquidated them completely, killing more communists than the world's fascist dictators together. The purge extended throughout the party from the highest to the lowest level. It also extended to those outside the apparatus, particularly members of the intelligentsia who might serve as alternate sources of leadership. They were replaced by new elites, socialized in complete agreement with Stalin's new non-egalitarian, centralized and Russian-inspired ideology. With local leadership decimated, control over the non-Russian nations was secured through "foreign cadres," mainly Russians who were placed in positions of responsibility.[60]

With Stalin's death in 1953 it seemed as though the authority of "the Russian elder brother" was complete and the question of nationality consequently solved. The national tensions that had been revealed by the war were, by all appearances, eliminated. Not even at that point of time, however, was the official policy formalized on the basis of the Russian nation, but on Soviet patriotism and socialism. This form of state nationalism, consequently, was building more on the old state patriotism of the patrimonial, All-Russian autocracy, than on nationalism in the modern sense. Also in the case of the USSR, the achieved unity was illusory and short lived, despite Stalin's use of methods that none of the rulers of the old authoritarian states, such as Tsarist Russia, had at their disposal. Moreover, it soon was to be clear that Stalin's successors were more sensitive about national differences than what the apparent national peacefulness immediately after World War II suggested.

Soviet State Building and Russian Nationalism

As for the Russians, the internal contradictions and tensions afflicting their national identity was probably perpetuated into the post-war period, despite the mobilization of Russian nationalism under *the Great Patriotic War*. Lenin himself was a Russian, the Revolution had been Russian, consequently the Russians were supposed to be typical representatives of the Soviet citizen, and the Russian culture was treated accordingly. While the flag waving from the governmental quarters of every non-Russian Soviet republic was a cross between the titular nation's original national symbol and the Soviet banner, only the red Soviet banner itself was waving from Moscow's Kremlin. Russian national pride could, moreover, be attached to the international strength of the USSR and its presumed prestige as a superpower. While non-Russians could easily describe their problems within the Soviet system in terms of national oppression by attributing their difficulties to a "stupid Russian speaking bureaucracy," such an escape route was more difficult for Russians to embark upon.

My answer to the question concerning the role of Russian nationalism in the state-building projects of All-Russia and the USSR is that none of the Russian social groups, nor the state and its elites, gave voice to a nationalism directed against non-Russian ethnic groups before 1917. The suppression of national minorities under Alexander III must therefore be seen as an expression of contemporary general reaction, characterized by "defensive modernization," which sought to preserve the autocratic state structures and considered all signs of opposition a threat to the unity of the state. This process is summarized by Andreas Kappeler:

> Although the government also remained skeptical about the Russian national movement, it was an obvious idea to instrumentalize the integral power of Russian nationalism and anti-Semitism in order to neutralize the growing problems with which it was confronted as a result of modernization and industrialization, and the growing social tensions and opposition movements. . . . However, neither the church nor the extreme nationalists triumphed completely, and in principle the state adhered to the dynastically legitimated autocratic system.[61]

Both before and after 1917 the state was at times pursuing a policy of standardization, aimed at reducing all subjects to a common denominator in accordance with a non-ethnic model. Before 1917 orthodox Christianity was the distinguishing element of this policy and after 1917 the Marxist–Leninist ideology. After 1881 the Jews became the main scapegoats for the problems following the policy of modernization. Even if the medium of this supranational Soviet culture, as it was developing in the USSR during the last two generations, was the Russian language, it is still possible to argue that it was not so much a Russian as a meta-culture above ethnic distinctions. It therefore seems unreasonable to interpret the Soviet nationality policy during the post-Stalinist period as consistently offensive and assimilating toward non-Russian ethnic groups. Rather it expressed a strategy that sought to balance non-Russian ethnic groups and the Russian majority. Although limited by elevation of the Russians, *affirmative action* programs would continue; the "Friendship of the Peoples not the dominant nationality was the Soviet Union's imagined community."[62]

This answer must also be seen against the background of the Russians still not having reached a stage of reconciliation and integration between the different components constituting their collective identity. This state of dissension was sharpened, evolving into something like an identity crisis during the Gorbachev era.

CONTINUITY AND BREAK IN THE SOVIET CASE

The dual structure of the Austrian–Hungarian political system was of course present neither in the All-Russian nor the Soviet polity. The question then is which of the two Habsburg nationality policies was closer to the Soviet case. The answer is, as suggested above, that both parallels are to be found to be contradictory, mutually undermining components of Soviet policy, the first one being more influential at some points of time, the second one at others.

A periodization of Soviet policy based on the dynamics between the two components is possible. Ethnic–linguistic policy was thus marked by three phases: The first phase, the policy of indigenization (*korenizatsiya*), was characterized by a large degree of linguistic pluralism and upgrading and alphabetizing of several minority languages.[63] The Latin alphabet—"the alphabet of the world revolution"—was chosen.[64] In this work no resources were spared and the efforts can hardly be described as anything but an attempt at a highly genuine linguistic pluralism with a basis in reality, as the recognition of various separate languages—even when they were closely related, as in the case of Tatar and Bashkir, or Kazakh and Kirgiz.[65] In the second phase, the study of Russian language became obligatory for non-Russians, a change to the Cyrillic alphabet took place, and linguistic pluralism was succeeded by bilingualism.[66] The third phase was marked by a pronounced desire to construct a meta-culture in the country as a whole, with a partial de-ethnicized Russian language as the medium. The use of Russian language was increased in the higher echelons of the educational system and in official domains related to the all-union level.[67]

In the first of the periods mentioned above, "the Austrian element" was dominant; in the second one it was weakened; in the third it is tempting to jump to the conclusion of a parallel with Hungary, but the mixture is more diffuse and contradictory as is also the tension between the components, and various interpretations can therefore be applied to different geographical regions and functional groups. On the individual level, the perspective will vary according to each Soviet citizen's national background, due to the fact that the tension between the "Austrian" and the "Hungarian" component in a very direct way was being built into and reflected in the Soviet state structure. A departure from the Austrian pattern was the way in which the recently formed or newly transformed nations not only were recognized and stimulated, but even institutionalized as the only officially acknowledged criterion of differential treatment of Soviet citizens. The internal passport system, which listed the owner's nationality, had a negative impact on integration. It made nationality instrumental when dealing with educational authorities and essential for the distribution of labor. By actively consolidating the nations and using them as the strategic mediating institutions between the citizens and the state, the Soviet state made nationality into perhaps the best possible basis for collective political action in a period of social crisis and collapse. To what degree did these fluctuations and ambiguities reflect a deviation or a continuity compared to the All-Russian Empire?

Seen in a *longue durée* nationality perspective, the Soviet Union and Tsarist Russia in many respects seem to have been moving along parallel tracks. These tracks also led to similar terminal points. The Soviet nationality policy thus had several features that quite obviously match pre-revolutionary patterns, such as the vacillation between flexibility and stimulation of non-Russian groups on the one hand, and a policy of cultural regimentation and Russification in order to remove impediments to modernization on the other, not to mention a comprehensive cooperation with loyal non-Russian elites, which, just as in All-Russia, contributed to the creation of a supranational social stratum consisting of groups whose loyalty was to the leadership in St. Petersburg before 1917.

The 1930s, with its Stalinist revolution from above, the forcible industrialization and reconstruction of the Soviet economic order, involved, however, a radical departure from the pattern set by Tsarist Russia by a dramatic reconstruction of the entities— the populations and elites that the nationality policy of the USSR was to handle. One of the officially pronounced long-term aims of the Soviet development policy from now on was the creation of a uniform social structure throughout the country.

As part of an effort to prevent socioeconomic dynamics generated by Soviet modernization from resulting in a political fragmentation of the autocratic Stalinist political structure, there was increasing pressure on non-Russian social elites to adapt to a supranational standard dominated by the Russian language and culture. Even if the Russification of the language was successful to a considerable degree, it is much more essential to ask what kind of connection existed between this linguistic mobilization and political support of the system.

The cultural sector gradually became cause for anxiety, seen from the point of view of non-Russians. The emphasis on bilingualism was a fact already in the 1930s but was intensified during Brezhnev's "mature socialism" with its compulsory use of the Russian language. Attempts were made at establishing Russian as the medium of inter-ethnic communication in as many sectors and functions as possible and as the main language of science, technology and culture. Seen from one perspective, this use of a *lingua franca* was of course a sheer necessity in a multinational state. But even if there was a considerable increase in the use of the Russian language, to many members of the minority peoples the dominant position of Russian symbolized their own subordinate status and was perceived as a threat to their mother tongues. Consequently there were signs of resentment and disdain toward the Russian language. By 1978 there had already been massive demonstrations in Tbilisi demanding that the titular language should be designated in the constitution of the Georgian republic as the state tongue, a demand which Moscow had to satisfy.[68]

Saying that the chances for a genuine Russification to succeed were small would thus be a clear understatement. The use of the Russian language as the cement of the Union impeded rather than promoted the emergence of a transnational political community; in fact it demonstrated the precarious foundation of the whole Soviet state-building process. The first open manifestation of the shifting of balance between center and periphery was to be the passing of local language laws in 1988–1989 under Gorbachev, when six other republics adopted legislation establishing a state language. Indigenous cultural, educational, and scientific elites were particularly eager to maintain their own languages as the languages of discourse in their professions.

Efforts at Cultural Integration Interpreted through Rokkan's Model

How does this relate to the Rokkan model? As already mentioned, nationalism according to Rokkan's model may be interpreted as a political and cultural conflict between center and periphery. At first sight, the Soviet experience seems to confirm the relevance of this model. This assumption, however, needs to be further questioned. According to Stein Rokkan, it was of decisive importance for the development and historical fate of a language to emerge as a relatively stable norm for a territory before the development of technologies for mass reproduction. This was the case with the Russian language. The prospects for survival for the peripheral languages were far weaker, unless they had reached the establishment of an institutionally anchored set of norms in education and printing before the industrial revolution.[69] Only very few non-Russian languages had in fact reached such a stage so early. According to Rokkan's schemata, the new geographical mobility in the wake of industrialization would expose large parts of the rural vernacular-speaking populations to the dominating languages of the industrialized areas. But in the Soviet case, the policy of the center itself strengthening these vernaculars broke the expected pattern, rendering an unusual outcome possible. This explains the continued existence on a massive scale of ethnic pockets that resisted integration in the Soviet system.

The prospects of success for a political integration process depend, however, according to Stein Rokkan's model, on the relative duration of time between the different phases of territorial consolidation. The efforts of Soviet authorities to forge a unifying and integrating "Russian" meta-culture during the 1960s and 1970s ("the Soviet People as a new historical community") came too late. The national consolidation of the cultural sub-entities as a consequence of "the interaction between the industrial and national revolutions" (i.e., the intermediary variables when Stein Rokkan constructed his conceptual maps that traced political variations in Western Europe) was already a fact—a fact which to a large extent was a result of the favorable conditions offered by the Soviet nationality policy.

As a conclusion it can be stated that stability in the Soviet case cannot be explained by referring to phase 2, the phase of cultural standardization, in the Rokkan model. Moreover it can be argued that linguistic mobilization may be inversely correlated to political stability—that if, in an attempt to integrate ethnic minorities, language assimilation is pursued too assiduously without a parallel political, social and economic equalization, the development of political loyalty may actually be impeded.[70] In addition, Soviet stability also points, in my opinion, to another problem connected to the application of Rokkan's model to societies outside Western Europe: the cumulation-of-challenges thesis. This thesis sees the success of state building as dependent on the passing of an adequate amount of time before one phase in the process is followed by the next. This passage of time is a necessary condition for the emerging state to be able to cope separately with each set of challenges in different societal domains.

The question is whether one must not also allow for interaction and penetration from one of those domains to the other, that is, for the hegemonic and encompassing influence of one domain, such as politics, law or cultural practices or economy, on social stability and intergration? For example, the overwhelming dominance of Islam, Hinduism, Christianity and Juadism in their respective classical eras implies not only a thorough immersion of religious teachings into the fields of law, rulership, family life, and so forth, but also their deep penetration into the economy. Max Weber also pointed to cases where certain types of rulership became so deeply entrenched in the social fabric that they also dominated patterns of action in economic and religious domains, for example the manorial–feudal rulership in the medieval Occident.[71]

In the Soviet case the superior influence of the political structure, the primacy of political design over other domains, and especially over inter-ethnic relations, seems to be a phenomenon that needs to be investigated more precisely.

MILITARY–ADMINISTRATIVE PENETRATION

Some Differences between East and West, and between Russia and Central Europe

In the context of the three cases under consideration here, this phase can be analyzed in greater detail from a Weberian perspective. State building in the more restricted sense is then to be understood as constituting a triangular conflict between the supreme ruler, his administrative staff and the population. Max Weber emphasized explicitly that he was mainly interested in dominance only so far as it is manifested through administration, that is, in its instrumental aspects.[72]

The main focus in an analysis of territorial integration, successful or not, is on the use of various strategies and power resources associated with the means and positions of administration. The process of political penetration took place in Western Europe through the formation of nonterritorial-based elites in the absolute monarchies. In the words of Otto Hintze: "Absolutism . . . can be regarded as concomitant of that process of political organization in which a conglomerate of separate territories becomes fused into a unitary political structure . . . The efforts of monarchical authority to fuse these parts into a whole which was administratively, financially and militarily unified, produced modern absolutism."[73] A major part of Max Weber's analysis is dedicated to the way in which armies can be set up and held together. It describes the administrative problems military conquerors will have to face when trying to integrate a conquered territory, and the factors that determine the size of an army, that is, why *the military skeleton* of a state tends to be large or small, centralized or decentralized, collegial or hierarchical. With territorial expansion, a dynamics toward progressive fragmentation takes effect. Transferring more authority to subordinate links makes it increasingly difficult for the prince or the commanding leader of the state to maintain his personal control of the administration and his subordinates. At the same time, these subordinates start to receive material rewards on a larger scale and on a more permanent basis than before. This increases their social status and consequently their independence from the prince as their supreme overlord.

When comparing the Central European and Russian zones, a purely instrumental view of state integration is clearly inadequate to answer questions relating to long-term historical development. Introducing Antonio Gramsci's concept *cultural hegemony* as a supplementary analytic device however, makes possible a more thorough analysis of the relation between the phases of political penetration and cultural integration in Rokkan's model. To Gramsci, the pre-modern state was

> in a certain sense a mechanical bloc of social groups, often of different race: within the circle political–military compression, which was only exercised harshly at certain moments, the subaltern groups had a life of their own, institutions of their own, etc., and sometimes these institutions had State functions which made of the State a federation of social groups with disparate functions not subordinated in any way . . .The modern State substitutes for the mechanical bloc of social groups their subordination to the active hegemony of the directive and dominant group, hence abolishes certain autonomies, which nevertheless are reborn in other forms, as parties, trade unions, cultural associations.[74]

To Antonio Gramsci, his concept of cultural hegemony underlaid the relations between social classes. Each class seeks to secure a governing position, not only in public institutions, but also in opinions, values and standards acknowledged by the majority. Oppressed classes must, before they can gain political power for themselves, conquer their own cultural hegemony by establishing their own values in the public opinion. Gramsci's cultural hegemony refers to a structural differentiation in European state development between the Eastern and the Western front (first and foremost Russia versus the West), that is between societies basing political power on force, and those basing it on consensus, in which domination therefore must be understood in a wider context. As pointed out by Christine Buci-Glucksmann, "The more authentically hegemonic a class really is, the more it leaves opposing classes the possibility of organizing and forming themselves into an autonomous political Force."[75] The civil society in the West is a highly complex subsystem, which allows its intellectual life to be controlled by purely cultural means, a control that is one variety of the process of cultural integration described by Rokkan.

As for the peripheral zone of the European system, without a class force to lead the way, the state, captured by a small fraction, emerges as the dominant force in national politics. The state, then, becomes a means of political transformation itself, rather than a means by which a social class asserts its universal claims, "it is conceived of as something in itself, as a rational absolute."[76] When the state replaces class as a motor of socioeconomic development, the inevitable result is what Gramsci called a *dictatorship without a hegemony,* resulting in a *passive revolution,* "which by cutting off the leaderships of the allied and opposing classes, deprives them of their own political instrument and creates an obstacle to their constitution as autonomous classes."[77] A passive revolution—the introduction of changes that did not involve any arousal of popular forces—occurs when no class is able to present itself as a potential hegemonic force, a force capable of presenting its program as a universal program for the entire nation.

Gramsci's thesis was that the Russian Revolution was aimed at a type of historical state different from the one prevalent in the West. In Russia special circumstances associated with the formation of the state had as their consequence an autocratic state controlling the country's resources and population in a way that was unknown in the West. "In Russia the State was everything."[78] As Russian historians long have been aware, the absence of a true bourgeoisie made the state bureaucracy a mouthpiece for bourgeois interests. The Russian absolutism's government in the 19th century was bourgeois, but unofficially, in the intrigues and the cliques of the landowning aristocracy, the regime was "feudal." Russian capitalism was used by the absolute state that could not claim any great credit for its establishment, according to Pavel Volubuev, to strengthen its feudal character, and therefore it remained absolute up until the 1917 revolution.[79]

Society's integration took place exclusively by means of the state, which, together with the Church, was the only organized institution. The regime did not understand that the Russian state could be strengthened only by being seemingly weakened, and was thus an obstacle to political and social *Europeanization* (to borrow a term frequently used by Georgii Plekhanov).[80]

Also in the case of the relations between the different nations of the Habsburg Empire, Antonio Gramsci's ideas about hegemonic struggles are highly pertinent. Here "two and sometimes even three possibilities of national identification faced the inhabitants . . . of 'small nations.'"[81] Gramsci's class perspective on hegemonic struggles are also related to Otto Bauer's classical distinction between two different social structures, "nations with history" ("socially complete," all social classes present) and the "the nations without history" ("socially incomplete," without an agrarian upper class of its own). This distinction constitutes a historical basis for the development of the nationality question, tying it explicitly to a social class analysis and a class perspective.

The German–Magyarian hegemony in the Dual Monarchy emerged from a long historical development influenced and determined by the German dynasty, bureaucracy, army and capitalism on the one side, and Magyar feudalism on the other. Despite the fact that the Habsburg administration and political system influenced the basis of this hegemony, it is unreasonable to maintain that is was based on pure political coercion toward the other nationalities only.

The German–Magyar political hegemony in the Dual Monarchy was not based on any numerical superiority of these two nations either. The Austrian half of the empire was the product of German colonization, and the culture integrating its economy, administration and army was German. The situation in the Hungarian half of the empire was similar. The feudal structure, by which the large landowning interests were able to determine the content of the country's political and social life, was based on the Magyar nobility, the non-Magyar nobility that was completely assimilated into the traditions and ideology of the Magyar upper classes, and on the middle class. For all intents and purposes, all nations without history in the Habsburg Empire were retarded in their national development up to the middle of the 19th century by German–Austrian and Magyar cultural hegemony and economic dominance.

For centuries the Habsburg policy emphasized flexibility and a "calculated indifference" toward the subjects of the monarchy. The centralizing and standardizing modernization policies between 1849 and 1860 was the one and only exception, not the rule. "Instead of trying to invade and swallow up the society, or more correctly, the societies, the state tried as much as possible to avoid any kind of contact with them in the extent to which this was possible."[82]

Outside and beside this administrative apparatus, Habsburg allowed the many societies and cultures (linguistic communities) of the empire to lead their own lives. This opened up to the nations without history a cultural space that made possible a cultural and political consolidation prior to their attaining national independence and states of their own, a space from which new national movements were to emerge, acting as *independent variables* in the nation-building processes.[83]

Analyzing these movements, Miroslav Hroch, famously distinguishes between three structural phases between the starting point and the successful conclusion of a national movement, "according to the character and role of those active in it, and the degree of national consciousness emergent in the ethnic group at large."[84] During an initial period, phase A, learned researchers "discovered" the ethnic group and laid a basis for the subsequent formation of a *national identity*. The energies of the activists were above all devoted to scholarly inquiry, but without pressing specifically national demands. In the second period, or the critical phase B, a new range of activists emerged who sought to win over as many as possible to the project of creating a future nation by patriotic agitation. Phase C was the final stage during which the major part of the population came to put great store in their national identity and the agitation passed over into a mass movement capable of completing the national program. "It was only during the final phase C that a full social structure could come into being, and that the movement differentiated out into conservative–clerical, liberal and democratic wings, each with their own programmes."[85]

How should one assess the national issue's significance to the various nations in the Hapsburg monarchy? Robert Kann launched two dichotomies relating to the "awakening" of nations, which are useful in this connection: First, he distinguished between nations where the social conflicts in this period took place primarily within the specific population group, and nations where they did not; second, between nations where the national issue dominated party formation and the political life, and nations where it did not. [86]

On the basis of the first of these distinctions he gave the following classifications of the monarchy's population groups: Among the German–Austrians, Italians, Croats, Poles, Czechs and Magyars the social conflicts take place chiefly within the specific population group, while among Romanians, Ukrainians, Serbs, Slovaks and Slovenes the social struggle in the period is chiefly directed against superior classes of another nationality. Kann himself believed that the national awareness is all the more fully developed where the nation gives room for the whole political spectrum, and where social conflicts can take place within specific ethnic communities. The social and the political spectrums therefore supplement each other, in his opinion.

On the basis of the second dichotomy he talks about nations where the problems of politics were partly or largely, but not chiefly, dominated by *the national issue*. These were the German–Austrians, Italians, Poles, Slovenes and Czechs. The other group he refers to includes the nations where nationalistic aims, ethnically and in terms of international law, were in the foreground and dominated political thinking and actions. These were the Croats, Magyars, Romanians, Ukrainians, Serbs and Slovaks. This, of course, does not mean that social conflicts were ignored in the latter group. Although the nationality conflicts that took place in the first category were of considerable significance to the monarchy as a whole, for instance among Czechs and Germans and Italians and Slovenes, they did not, in Kann's opinion, dominate the problems of politics in these population groups.

The opposition of non-dominating nations was mainly directed against the two leading nations' economic and cultural monopoly. Twenty years after *Ausgleich*, however, the German relative position in Cicleithania was weakened to the advantage of the other national groups; the German culture no longer had supranational pretensions. The German–Austrian position as a national group until 1918 was one of the first among equals, not of superiority. In Hungary the decisive "non-event" was the collapse of the Magyar cultural hegemony that failed to come. This hegemony lasted until 1918 because it was bolstered by political means until 1918.

In the USSR Stalin's post-revolutionary dictatorship was based on a strong state confiscating the civil sphere, extremist forms of political mobilization and the use of terror. Stalin himself in his political report to the 16th Congress of the Communist Party in 1930, for the first time explicitly modified the doctrine of the withering away of the state: "We stand for the withering away of the state. At the same time we stand for the strengthening of the dictatorship of the proletariat, which is the mightiest and strongest state power that has ever existed. The highest development of state power with the object of preparing the conditions *for* the withering away of state-power—such is the Marxist formula. Is this 'contradictory'? Yes, it is 'contradictory.' But this contradiction is bound up with life, and it fully reflects Marx's dialectics."[87] Referring to the political organs of the USSR, and diverging completely from classical Marxism, Stalin finally in 1950 simply stated in his last theoretical pronouncement: "Furthermore, the superstructure is a product of the base, but this by no means implies that it merely reflects the base, that it is passive, neutral, indifferent to the fate of its base, to the fate of the classes, to the character of the system. On the contrary, having come into being, it becomes an exceedingly active force, actively assisting its base to take shape and consolidate itself."[88] Stalin's turning Marx on his head was just, of course, mirroring actual political developments which "paradoxically had generated a passive revolution within 'Socialism in one country.'"[89] In the case of the USSR I therefore will follow Terry Martin's suggestion of a fourth phase in addition to Miroslav Hroch's three, when nation building is conducted from above by the state itself: "The Soviet state . . . literally seized leadership over all three phases: the articulation of a national culture, the formation of national elites, and the propagation of national consciousness. It went still further and initiated even 'Phase D' . . . measures typical of newly formed nation-states: established a new language of state and a new governing elite."[90]

However, the relationship between the new educated national elites and the Soviet nations was not that of "a social group which 'led' other groups, but a State which . . .'led' the group which should have been "leading."[91] Using the Gramsci-inspired distinction between the *ruling class* and the *dominant class*, the new meritocratic national elites—the intelligentsia as broadly conceived in Soviet parlance—became the dominant class ("that sector of society whose function, interests and outlook contribute most to the general character of the system"). But the ruling class ("the sector where power actually resides even though its effective exercise must respect the interests of the dominating class") was recruited in the 1930s and restaffed among young apparatchiki risen from the proletariat during the purges and mentally adapted to Stalinist values.[92] It created all kinds of obstacles to the emancipation of the dominating class. Thus the main contradiction in the Soviet elite during its early days between state class and internationalists in the CPSU "was shifted to the nomenclatura itself."[93] Thus the hegemony was "exercised by a part of the social group over the entire group, and not by the latter over other forces in order to give power to the movement, radicalize it, etc."[94] On the one hand, what Gramsci called *transformatio* worked to co-opt potential leaders of non-Russian national groups. By extension *transformatio* served as a strategy of assimilating and domesticating potentially dangerous ideas by adjusting them to the policies of the ruling class and thereby obstructing the formation of an organized opposition. On the other hand, before Gorbachev the state suppressed nationality conflict in ways of which the Habsburg could not dream (as a *dictatorship without hegemony,* in Gramsci's terms). The slightest hint of nationalist mobilization was met with repression. In both ways, through co-optation and repression, the "statization" of social relations meant that popular initiatives from below were contained or destroyed and the relationship of rulers–ruled was maintained.

Russian State and Empire Building in a Comparative European Perspective

In All-Russia, the state carried out a decisive role in the integration of the empire. As the chief agent of Russian imperialism, the army embodied the presence of the Russian state in the different corners of the empire, thereby giving the administration as a whole a distinct military cast.[95] This dominant position of the army in All-Russia must be seen in the context of the country's relative social and economic backwardness as compared to Western and Central Europe of the time. Part and parcel of this backwardness was the weakness of the civilian parts of the Russian state; in Weberian terms, the absence of a strong bureaucracy, or an institutionally anchored set of formalized regulations, which were capable of effectively integrating and pacifying its enormous territory.[96] Antonio Gramsci's distinction between West and East therefore seems to pinpoint the essence of the difference in territorial integration between the Habsburg monarchy and All-Russia.

One perspective first represented by Otto Hintze, and later further developed among others by neo-Marxist authors Perry Anderson and Theda Skocpol, may throw additional light on our subject at this point. This tradition emphasizes that an element of interaction operates, where the international state system modifies the building of individual states. This happens when innovations in the art of warfare and in exercise of authority are transferred from one country to others through warfare. Taxes and consequently a unified national administration are necessitated by pressures that the external state system places on rulers in the form of military competition or threats of conquests. The political elites, therefore, make their maneuvers in the intersection between pressures of international conditions and the domestic class-structured economies, from which they must extract resources and build their administrations. States in underdeveloped and backward societies, such as Tsarist Russia, attempted to keep up with more economically advanced societies in the field of military technology. The Russians could not in the long run rely on buying the arms they needed from abroad; accordingly they had to build these industries themselves to secure a constant supply. This factor strengthened the position of the military in All-Russia further as compared with their colleagues in Western Europe.[97]

It is difficult to imagine how Russia, lying outside the European system as summarized by Rokkan's center–culture axis and his West–East center–economy axis, can be integrated into perspective building on Rokkan's European model without taking into account the element of international interaction mentioned above. If it is taken into account, however, Russia's political development as a backward country can be explained in the context of broader European development. The military part of the state apparatus has been *lying ahead of* (*operezhenie*) the stagnating society, as a compensation for its weaknesses, and has perhaps itself in turn decisively contributed to its stagnation by confiscating a disproportionately large part of its resources and economic surplus.

Consequently, the relationship between state and backwardness is not the most easily determined in a comparative perspective. If one excludes the political-institutional arrangement in the shape of the tsarist state, there is nothing to prevent one from characterizing Russia up until the abolition of serfdom in 1861 as feudal, as long as one gives a static description of social structures. Soviet historians, however, encountered a problem relating to the social dynamism. Going back to Karl Kautsky and the Second International, the classical interpretation of Marx' theory of history rests on Marx' famous 1859 "Preface to *Contribution to a Critique of Political Economy.*" The "Preface" describes the gradual growth of productive forces as the fundamental determinant of historical change, where the technological aspects of production determine the pattern of economic relations, which in turn form the basis of the superstructure. The dynamics of history therefore arises from the productive forces' development. When the relations of production fall behind this development, an "epoch of social revolution" must begin in order to bring the relations of production and the political and economic superstructures back into correspondence.[98] In the study of Russian development it became difficult, in a comparative perspective and based on such a Marxist development schema, to explain why no capitalism arose in the womb of Russian feudalism. Marxist studies of West European history have often seen the absolute monarchy as an important link between feudalism and capitalism and an important precondition of the breakthrough of capitalism. Aron Avrekh thus defined absolutism as "a feudal monarchy, which by virtue of its internal nature is especially capable of development and transformation into a bourgeois monarchy."[99] In the study of Russian development this "transitional problem" (that is the transition from feudalism to capitalism) may therefore generally be expressed by asking whether the absolutist Russian state was an appropriate and useful instrument in overcoming the country's backwardness and economic stagnation, as in Western Europe, or whether the Russian state was a cause of that backwardness.

In a very interesting discussion among Soviet historians in the late 1960s and early 1970s it was recognized that the state cannot be dismissed as a mere element of the superstructure, and the prevailing general formulas were brought into question. The debate was inspired among other things by a revival of the category of the Asian mode of production that had been suppressed in the 1930s. As generally known Marx did consider the Asian mode of production to be a static order that could not generate capitalism without a violent shock from the outside. As early as 1966 Iurii Garushyants referred to the temptation of reexamining the whole of Russian history on the basis of the concept of the Asian mode of production.[100] It was thus maintained from some of the participants that the Russian absolute state was a reactionary force and did not clear the way for the transition from feudalism to capitalism, as in France. The state used capitalism without having any part in it and must be understood as "an intermediary type between Asian despotism and European absolutism."[101] The term *mnogoukladnost* (*multistructuredness*, i.e., the very complex interaction of socioeconomic formations in Russian society) was coined, referring to Russian backwardness, the entrenchment of feudalism, which for a long time blocked, hindered and distorted the development of capitalism and the powerful compensatory role of the state.[102]

If applying as one's point of view the constraints on implanting a capitalist dynamism (with productive investment of profits and rentability as the main rationality criterion) one may, in Weberian terms, argue that the authoritarian external ethics of obedience of the absolute state cannot replace an internalized ethics of conviction favouring the development of personal qualities, or an *ethos* (as in the ethics implanted by the Protestant sects in North America).[103] Alexander Gerschenkron, in his discussion of backwardness and economic development, distinguishes between a "traditional" and an "all-European pattern" of industrial growth. The former is based on the military needs and the exigencies of power politics and does not lead to self-increasing growth. It has the character of being intense, of short duration and periodical. This model is intended as an explanation of earlier Russian attempts at industrialization (i.e., prior to the industrialization of the 1890s). When, nevertheless, Gerschenkron sees a strong state as favourable to a backward country, this is due to the role he ascribes to the state in his "all-European pattern" where he offers purely economic, as opposed to political, explanations. The tension between the real and the possible in the form of economic reality in more advanced countries triggers the development. He sees the state's strength and the degree of "mercantilistic elements" in the economy as a function of the degree of backwardness and as a substitute for the absence of economic conditions. A specific state policy yielding material results in the form of facilitating subsequent industrialization is seen as part of a "backward pattern of development." However, he does not consider a strong state as an element of backwardness. Backwardness to him is a purely economic category. Alexander Gerschenkron interprets Russia's strong ecnomic growth from 1890 to 1914 as the classic example of a decisive period of growth, of more than 8 percent per year. It was a model case to other countries that were so backward that they needed state funding to overcome the worst difficulties. The decisive threshold was crossed in the 1907–1914 period.

In my opinion, however, it is not very fruitful to put these two explanatory models up against each other as alternative patterns. The tension in economic terms between the real and the possible equally affects both private and state actors. Where private economic actors have great political influence, the state should be seen more as a passive economic instrument. Where they have little influence, the state is more of an independent actor. The star example is of course the German Empire where both private capitalist actors and the state felt the tension, and both were active to realize the promise it represented. The private actors did so to reap economic profit, the state in order to obtain political gains.[104] In the case of Russia the strength of the state cannot, in my opinion, be considered in the way that Gerschenkron does in his all-European model. The degree of strength and weakness of the state is determined by factors that chronologically precede the period in which "development through backwardness" can be assumed to occur. The tension between the real and the possible, which Gerschenkron emphasizes, could not be released until the state itself could reap the profits of it. In Russia a serious economic breakthrough, therefore, could not come until the time at which considerable industrialization required the state to act as a practical instrument and when this was in the interest of the state itself. The view of a strong state as a functional imperative derivable from a relative position within a graduated system of economic development can also be problematized. Could the opposite just as well be the case, that is, that the state does not act unambiguously as a positive factor but could equally well be seen as a cause of the backwardness?[105]

Where the Soviet period is concerned, the pattern seems to repeat itself. The most important decision in the Soviet Union in the 1920s was perhaps Stalin's decision to modernize Soviet economy by forced industrialization and collectivization. Stalin was, as the tsars before him, in large part motivated by security concerns. Speaking in 1931, he said: "We have lagged behind the advanced countries by fifty to hundred years. We must cover that distance in ten years. Either we'll do it or they will crush us."[106] A series of five-year plans that transformed the Soviet Union was initiated in October 1928. The conventional view has been that Stalin's revolution from above was based on genuine economic planning, and although harsh and cruel, was forward-looking and effective, forcing the Soviet Union to modernize and construct the economic base for victory in the Second World War and for superpower status thereafter. With time, this view has had to give way to the view that an economic foundation was created, seemingly dynamic, but ultimately operating, as Soviet theorists of the Perestroyka period charcterized it, as the new "braking mechanism" as shock workers and enthusiasm substituted rationality and planning. To cite a leading senior expert in the field:

> Again and again stirred up against the managers and the technical intelligentsia . . . Attempts at scientific management gave way to work styles seemingly grounded in the peasant experience: furious effort at times and on certain projects, as in the Stakhanovite movement and the "shturmovshcina" at the end of every plan period, but otherwise a totally uneconomic approach to time, productivity, and efficiency at the macro level and over the long haul, and no effectiveness of capital investments . . . Under Stalin, true economic planning gave way to propaganda campaigns to increase efforts and enthusiasm . . . When shortfalls inevitably appeared, Stalin would intervene with frantic decrees, all enhancing the priority of heavy industry. In effect, he was altering an unrealizeable plan in mid-stream, while blaming shortfalls in any sector of the economy on wreckers and sabouteurs . . . the key economic decisions were shaped much more by the personalities and politics at the moment.[107]

All-Russia as a *colonization project,* was wearing the stamp of backwardness as well. Just as the administration of All-Russia had a more military form than the societies characterized by more elaborate bureaucracies, the situation inside Russia was that the degree of militarization was proportional to the distance from the center.[108] The militarization of the administration was a fact not only in Russia proper but also in the empire. Lacking the organizational bonds tying the overseas colonies to their motherlands—that is, the powerful trading companies and concessionaries—the Russian *colonial administration* was dominated by the army and the army by powerful and strong individual leaders as *namestniki, voevody,* vice regents, governors or military governors-general.[109] The army was made up by Slavs and the officer corps endorsed the official state patriotism. This kept in check possible opposition and guaranteed the loyalty of the local pillars, the co-opted elites of the non-Russian peripheries.[110]

In the European expansion throughout the 19th century, it was certainly a common trait that the generals led the way more than ever: Kaufmann in Turkestan was matched by Custer in Dakota and Kitchener in the Sudan. The often ideologically motivated expansion, that is, "the White man's burden" to carry the torches of civilization to all corners of the world, at this stage often boiled down to the conquest of territories that the companies of earlier times had deliberately left untouched, since no profits were expected there.

In this perspective, however, a main difference between the Russian and the Western European expansion seems to be the high degree of uniformity characterizing the administrative arrangements of both the colonial center and its peripheries in the All-Russian case. This, rather than the deviations from the Western colonial pattern, distinguished Russia in a comparative perspective. This interpretation is strengthened by the fact that instituting supreme state ownership of all land in the colonial areas was an important aspect of the standardization and uniformization of the empire. Such state ownership of land was, according to the Weberian tradition, a definitory characteristic of patrimonialism, the most marked feature of the Russian state.[111] The comparative perspective thus seems to give new meaning to the great historian Kliuchevskii's word that "Russian history is the history of a country colonizing itself."[112]

Political Integration in Tsarist Russia and the USSR

The uniformity of the organizational patterns of the state before 1917 continued into the Soviet period, and was further elaborated so as to fit the new state building processes. Right from the start it was the policy of the Soviet regime to give the citizens of each titular nation preferential treatment in admittance to higher education and recruitment to leadership and administrative positions inside its own territory. To pursue a policy of equal opportunities for titular nations in every single republic, each of them was, as earlier mentioned, equipped with the same set of institutions. Leadership and administrative positions in almost all of the republics were in the hands of the titular nations from the 1950s and their share of leadership positions were greater than their share of the population as a whole.[113] Although Soviet federal republics had very little power compared to all-union institutions, the multinational nature of the Soviet state had real significance for social mobility and for the existence of national hierarchies.

One difference between the Soviet states and the old regime, from a state-building perspective, was the following: After 1917, an increasingly planned economy required a much higher degree of formal bureaucratization than both *l'ancien regime* and the contemporary market-oriented economic systems of the West. The Soviet Union consequently shared with giant organizations everywhere an urge to organize all human activity rationally. It also shared with them a thoroughly authoritarian political structure, in which the elite is above control from the lower-ranking members of the organization.[114] To Max Weber, bureaucracy, seen from a territorial point of view, was an exceptionally efficient organizational device in the realization of political aims because of its capacity to integrate and keep organizations together. The bureaucratic state became predominant because of its functional superiority in pacifying large territories. Externally it is efficient in its capacity to support large armies with equipment, and internally it shows great resilience in the face of the threat of disintegration from civil war or revolution.

Of course, the political struggle for control of the administrative apparatus in Western Europe did not cease with the breakthrough of bureaucracy; it has only been transferred to new arenas, in which bureaucrats or expert officials tend to make their political superiors into mere figureheads. Knowledge of official forms, procedures, appeal channels, and precedents can easily degenerate into special "techniques" of bureaucratic abuse. The internal dynamics of bureaucracy tend to transform its individual departments into interest groups representing only their own restricted field. Instead of serving the common good, each begins to fight for its own specialized interests against the interests of other departments. This results in a systematic displacement of goals where partial concerns will win over the interest of the whole. More generally, the necessity of delegating powers from the center to the periphery, from the top to the lower-ranking levels, contains an objective dynamics toward a progressive fragmentation of authority, that is to say, toward absence of stability in the relations between the center and the peripheries of the state.

As a consequence of Soviet policy, each union republic gained "all of the characteristics of former independent states having lost their independence."[115] In spite of this, in the same way that the All-Russian state had succeeded in preserving the loyalty of both the military governors and the co-opted local non-Russian elites, in the Soviet case the non-Russian members of the all union elite accommodated themselves to the multinational state, and became its most strategic pillars after the purges of the 1930s.

Which kinds of constraints were brought about by the Soviet reliance on elite politics, and how can these constraints explain the remarkable stability of the peripheries? Which were the mechanisms counteracting the dynamics toward fragmentation? Did the Soviet elite itself have characteristics that prevented independent political action by its individual members? How can the remarkable internal loyalty and external concord of the Soviet elite be accounted for?

Uni-hierarchical and Multi-hierarchical Societies

In a comparative perspective, the Soviet uni-hierarchical system of social stratification and social control was a unique way of organizing an industrial society. All the institutions were parts of a single hierarchy where the state gave both the criterion for the ranking of social groups and for the transfer of individuals from one group to another. The common link was the system of the *nomenklatura*, in which the party's personnel department assigned people to jobs in all sub-hierarchies. The Habsburg monarchy lacked such tools for social engineering: it was unable to manipulate the social structures of its nations and to integrate its elites in a way comparable to that of the USSR.[116]

An important point of view on the historical development in Russia deserves mention here, the fact that the state preceded the classes, both temporally and causally: The state creates the social estates before they can create themselves. The state was society's demiurge, wrote Pavel Miliukov, historian and leader of the Liberal Party in 1917.[117] This is attributed to the country's "delay," which caused strong opposition between its external and internal resources. The imposition of new taxes made it necessary to create new classes of taxpayers for whom these taxes were appropriate. George Plekhanov, the father of Russian Marxism, on his part highlighted as a main difference between Russia after the Kiev state and the classic Asian despotisms, the fact that in Russia it was not the need to establish the economic conditions for production which created a despotic state. It was the need to provide defense against attacks and raids by nomads.[118] Owing to their special method of production, the nomadic tribes were militarily stronger than the sedentary farming peoples inhabiting the Russian plains. The development of farming involved division of labor between the producer and the warrior. Only a small group undertook the military tasks, thereby preserving their own mobility. This meant that the sedentary peoples on the East European plains were at a disadvantage in their encounters with equestrian peoples. They therefore had to join forces in a strong political union, pooling all their military resources. "The erection of a Leviathan state on such a primitive economic basis could be achieved only if the statebuilders were able to squeeze from the tillers of the soil an extraordinary share of their meagre output. This was possible only if the state assumed control of landed property and, therewith, the power of life and death over its subjects."[119] At the same time the tsar took into his hands—to the detriment of private trade—so large a share of the nation's commerce that he was thought of as the country's "first merchant." This increased as well as extended the power of the prince, at the same time as the internal life of the state came to resemble the big, agrarian-based despotisms of the Orient.[120]

The vastness, and the absence of diversity, of the East European plain thus gave rise to Russia's distinctiveness, which consisted of fluctuating between two main trends or currents, the European and the Asian.[121] Before the 16th century this was an obstacle to the emergence of feudal relations between aristocracy and peasants, as in Western Europe, and more generally the creation of feudal relations at a higher social level. The Russian *druzhinniki* became much weaker than the military-service class in the West. Plekhanov also emphasized the remarkable stability of Russia's Oriental society. "He had in mind not merely the relative absence of ferment and upheaval but, more generally, a pace of social development so slow as to be almost imperceptible. . . . The patterns of social life become so fixed that no other socio-political order is even conceivable. That was why popular rebellions in Russia generally were directed not against the system as such, and why the peasants irrationally persisted in regarding the tsar as a paternalistic protector."[122]

As state-building projects, there are some conspicuous historical parallels between the All-Russian Empire and the later USSR. Both Peter the Great and Joseph Stalin were highly active as builders and warriors; in the reign of Peter the Great the nobility was mobilized to carry out the emperor's comprehensive military and civilian projects. Joseph Stalin, on his side, played a major role in creating the Soviet privileged estate, or ruling class, the *nomenklatura*. The Soviet system eliminated almost every income from property, and the state decided on the scales of wages and salaries and on the distribution of privileges in general. The state also reconciled all the more or less conflicting demands from numerous interest groups, including nationalities, inside one single hierarchy. Stalin's *nomenklatura* can consequently be seen as a parallel to, or an elaboration of, Peter's famous table of ranks. This table of ranks formalized the gentry's obligation and became an effective device in forging a single state-supporting estate (*soslovie*), the *dvoryanstvo*, through the cooptation of the non-Russian social elites. Thus there was created, in the Soviet case, a multinational elite, within which there were national ladders to climb.

In Tsarist Russia the state was continually confirming already existing privileges for social groups and local elites, granting new ones when expanding into new territories. Even if the recruitment of non-Russian elites was indispensable for the Russian state to retain its newly conquered territories, this strategy must also be understood as part of the patrimonial techniques of domination. Openings for non-Russians in the All-Russian elite, were to be found not only in the periphery, but also in the center, a fact which created a heterogeneous supranational elite. No other European aristocracy had as weak indigenous roots as the Russian one.

Peter the Great and his successors, while introducing technological changes, continued with the well-established pattern of bypassing the members of the old administrative staff and the old nobility in favor of foreign-born and low-born groups when they renewed their administrative staff. The most important posts in St. Petersburg were filled by members of different non-Russian groups, such as Tatars, Germans from the Baltics and Swedes from Finland. The court language was French in the 17th and 18th centuries, not Russian. This gave rise to a Russian culture open to members of all educated classes, regardless of national background.

In the same way in the Brezhnev era, non-Russians could be found strategically placed among all the most important pillars of the empire such as the army, the police, the state and the party, and among members of other all-union structures and institutions, that is to say in the central bureaucracy with its subdivisions and territorial ramifications. Seen from this point of view, it is an open question whether the essential features of the social class structure had been fundamentally changed at all by 70 years of ideological domination emphasizing *socialist development*.

The All-Russian-Soviet parallel was also reflected in thoughts concerning polity. From Peter the Great the state concept rested on an idea of All-Russia as one vast monarchy, although consisting of a large number of nationalities and territories. This was expressed through the differentiation in the official title of the imperial majesty. In Tsarist Russia the rulers and state officials preferred to look on the *ethnical conglomerate* of the population as an undifferentiated mass of subjects. The adjective *rossiiskaya* had a special meaning in the formation of the Russian state and in the development of the Russian identity. The All-Russian Empire was known as *Rossiiskaya imperiya,* which implied the idea of a unitarian, although multinational state under a Russian monarch, and of a particular kind of loyalty to this state on the part of its subjects, independent of their ethnic and cultural background. The concept had a territorial, as opposed to ethnic, connotation and referred to the geographical extent of the state's authority and possessions. *Rossiiskaya* was distinguished from the plain and ordinary adjective *russkaya,* which indicated the particular Russian component of the population.[123]

The dominating culture of All-Russia was, according to the view of Slavophiles, not genuinely Russian, but a thin Western European varnish, introduced and upheld from the outside, in much the same way as its main seat, St. Petersburg, was characterized by a slavish imitation of Western Europe. Consequently this ethnic–cultural Russian nationalism was hardly a suitable ideological basis for the state; it came instead to be regarded as a permanent threat against the ruling elite, persistently suppressed and in general devoid of independent political significance.[124]

The Russian state was, as formerly mentioned, expanding continuously beyond the original Russian core areas. Russia's central position on the Eurasian continent by turns naturally invited confrontations and withdrawals in relation to both Europe and Asia. Finns and Turks were under Russian political authority, already at a very early stage of the state building process, and later the number of non-Russian groups was permanently increasing. Only in the original Russian core areas, in the northwestern part of the later USSR, was ethnic unification taking place through natural assimilation processes; elsewhere continual migrations were only increasing the local ethnic and religious heterogeneity. The geographical expansion, therefore, was perceived more as a spontaneous and natural process than a result of a conscious policy, and in the early stages of empire building there was very little awareness of the fact that Russia was about to become a multinational polity.[125]

State Concepts Before and After 1917

All-Russia developed politically as one single and continuously overarching process that encompassed both state formation and *colony building* as two closely interrelated and simultaneous aspects, not as two distinct processes separate in time and space as in Western Europe. This characteristic of the Russian state did not remain without influence on the concepts and methods of the Russian administrators. The political elites of St. Petersburg hardly distinguished between domestic and colonial policies. From an administrative, or rather a political perspective, the empire was regarded as a unified whole. It encompassed an enormous area, especially against the background of the means of transportation and communication available at the time. This vast extension generated an urgent need for regional decentralization, delegating certain functions to local institutions in the peripheries. Again it is conspicuous that compared to countries like France and Prussia, and above all to the

Habsburg monarchy, the administrative build-up of the Russian empire was dominated by a basic uniformity in all its regions.

The *Rossiiskaya* concept allowed for a considerable non-Russian cultural influence in the All-Russian system. The political structure depended, however, on a powerful ideology for continuous mass support. The only ideology sanctified by the church was not based on orthodox religion, as such, but centered around the person of the tsar as the father of All-Russia. There was also a powerful folklore mythology worshipping the tsar's fatherhood of the nation. The two views were, nevertheless, deeply divided concerning the interpretation of the tsar as a political symbol of autocracy: as the absolute monarch of divine right, *Gosudar Imperator*, proudly and independently ruling over his empire, or as the humble monk in union with Holy Russia. This tension on the mythological level was confirmed and strengthened during the reign of Peter the Great, as the exercise of state authority was freed from the limitations set by orthodox religion and thereby no longer restricted by the specific Russian element of the population. Liberation from tradition gave rise to an approximately pure patrimonial system. Although it was inconceivable to contradict tsarism within the context of Russian culture, the division concerning the tsar as a political symbol was to become the basis of church schisms, as well as of social opposition to the state in the name of orthodox religion as the hallmark of the Russian nation.

The struggle for cultural hegemony between different social strata or classes among the Russian population also partly overlapped a conflict between a "native" Russian agrarian population and a "foreign" ruling class, as was the case in the Habsburg Empire. However, All-Russian state patriotism, as the dominant ideology of social integration, was not to be challenged in any serious manner before 1917. A main reason for this was the absence of a social class, or estate, sufficiently independent of the state to act on behalf of the Russian nation. Here the general conditions under the patrimonial regime must be borne in mind: the state's dominant position vis-à-vis the society; the nobility's lack of independence from the state and its permanent inner intrigues; the embryonic character of the emergent *civil society*—the intermediary organizations between the state and the citizens. The absence of a political culture and social sub-structures to support it was to prove a fateful flaw of the Russian state edifice, which in reality was held together only by the outward power and glory of the autocracy. When the central power collapsed, a situation of social disintegration arose.

From the middle of the 1920s a change was taking place in the new regime's official ideological self-representation. In less than a decade the role of the USSR was transformed from champion of world revolution to guarantor of socialism in one country, a reversal that has been described as one "from utopia to realism."[126] Stalin committed Russia to a vast program of industrialization and modernization, a program that made little sense in the context of classical Marxism. At that point, there was little to distinguish the aspirations of Russian nationalists from those of Russian Marxists. A fusion of developmental and nationalist aspirations took place.[127] Russia was to become a great nation, never again to be defeated in the field, capable of defending itself against a conspiracy of capitalist powers. As long as the "capitalist encirclement" remained, the state was to remain as the focal institution of the Soviet system.[128] In the summer of 1934 the doctrine of Soviet patriotism was introduced to fill the ideological vacuum in the post-revolutionary society.[129]

An ideological current that could serve as a pattern for the new doctrine was the so-called national Bolshevism. After the revolution this national Bolshevism had contributed to the legitimacy of the new regime among its former opponents by depicting it as the true heir to the Russian historical tradition.[130] All later variations of the "national Bolshevist theme" pinpointed the fundamental importance of the continued territorial integrity of the Russian-dominated Soviet state. This attitude must be seen as the fundamental ideology of the ruling all-union elites. In my interpretation it represents a continuation of pre-revolutionary state patriotism.

The Nomenklatura and Center–periphery Relations

The parallel between the All-Russian and the Soviet efforts at state building does not stop at the creation of new state-supporting service classes, which were highly dependent on the sovereign ruler. Soon after the death of Peter the Great the members of the nobility were able to free themselves from compulsory state service—it was abolished in all its forms by Peter III in 1762—to become a privileged estate. However the change was without any real consequence for their lifestyle. The Russian gentry always lacked the de facto independence and authority of the West European feudal lords, and the members of the *dvoryanstvo* still had to serve the crown to maintain their social prestige even after they were freed from state service.

Also Stalin, on his side, made the lives of individuals extremely insecure, depending on his arbitrary and personal whims. After Stalin's death, the system created by him, as the one by Peter the Great, proved itself durable, and became more firmly established. However, in the post-Stalinist era a number of guarantees were built in to secure the *nomenklatura*, the backbone of the state, from being torn up by terror and to guarantee the lives of individuals. Efforts were also made to protect to a somewhat higher degree the functions of the bureaucratic machinery from interference and disruption by a despotic ruler.[131] But these guarantees were far from absolute.

Under Brezhnev the general secretary of the all-union Communist Party still had the authority to replace regional party secretaries. However from now on cadre stability and noninterference in local personnel questions was to become the rule. This opened up for a positive preferential treatment of the titular nationalities in their republics, making the local elites dependent on the local party leadership for their positions. Ethnicity was institutionalized both on the individual and on the group level, ruled over by indigenous political elites and organized through a single but complex administrative hierarchy. The importance attached to having strong but loyal individuals to maintain political stability in the non-Russian areas was again in accordance with the pre-revolutionary pattern. Even though Stalin arrested the development toward a genuine federalization in the form of an "absolute equalization" between the nations during the *korenizatsiya* period, a framework for cooperation with loyal non-Russians was still available through the Soviet federal-state structure. Instead of the *korenizatsiya* policy, which emphasized the goal of giving the titular nations almost full control over the institutions in their territories, the era of "high-Stalinism" brought with it the pursuit of a long-term strategy to grant all the nations a proportional representation in the most important sectors of social life in their home republics. After Stalin's death, the tempo toward proportionality was accelerated, and Russian overrepresentation slowly declined.[132] During the Brezhnev era, Soviet scholars explicitly defined the objective of equalization between the Soviet nations in higher education as aiming for representation of a titular nation corresponding to a that nation's proportion of the titular territory's population.[133] Where recruitment to the Communist Party was concerned, a similar objective of proportionality in the admission of members was expressed: the composition of Communist Party membership in any given administrative-territorial area should reflect the national composition of that territory's population.[134]

In the USSR, the center's strong support of local political elites, was, however, combined with a system of political appointments of republic leaders from Moscow. Their dependence on the center for their power, plus a tight control system, maximized the costs of supporting national aspirations for these local leaders. Another important control mechanism against regional tendencies was the mobility of high-ranking administrative personnel between the all-union center and the republics. Moscow authorities placed a small number of political cadres from the all-union center in key positions in the republics, and circumscribed the experiences of the rest of the nomenklatura officials to one local republic.[135] Altogether this system made it possible to join the federal structure to a strong central state power. The Soviet system could thus be described as a hybrid between a consociated system and an empire. The reason why the centrifugal, disintegrating dynamics of the Soviet state organization did not become more manifest lies in the how and why the inner solidarity of this hierarchy, as well as the loyalty of its individual parts to the center, was not broken. The absence of a "space" for alternative forces was based on a variety of techniques, which joined control to self-interest, autonomy to centralism, cooperation to the threat of expulsion.

Austria as a Contrasting Example

The difficulties of the Habsburg monarchy to reach a kind of *proportional equalization* including the non-German and non-Magyarian nations in the Habsburg monarchy must, in a comparative perspective, be seen in the light of the more complex multi-hierarchical, rather than the All-Russian uni-hierarchical, social substratum on which the Austrian state system was based. By this is meant both the separation of the economic, political and religious ideological hierarchies and their elites and the more complex social formation in which a multiplicity of communities not only existed simultaneously, but also overlapped in space, forming a multilayered network.

In their efforts to centralize and unify the empire, the Habsburg dynastic state too had placed great emphasis on building an absolutely reliable and loyal bureaucracy. Under German administrative personnel, the unity of the empire had been gradually strengthened. This administration aimed at leveling national particularism and eliminating all serious signs of local autonomy. The state administration had an evident caste character: originally the Habsburgs readily had preferred foreigners and adventurers without any social and territorial connections in the boundaries of the monarchy, similar to the Russian tsars. The ideal Austrian official of the Crown had a perfect knowledge of the German language and was for the rest completely devoid of any national consciousness, even if he himself was originally a German.[136]

In Austria German supremacy was gradually modified. This meant allowing people with a multilingual competence a career in the Crownlands (*Konländer*) and in the capital, and it meant the admittance of more non-German students to qualify for positions in the state. Despite the poor salaries, a position in the imperial administration was a sign of social prestige, and the awakening Austrian nations were determined to secure their own sons their rightful shares of governmental positions. The struggle to replace monolingual Germans was the basis of countless intrigues in the national assembly and the cabinet. These efforts were at least partly successful. A survey from 1914 based on most of the *Zentralstellen* in Vienna revealed that 24 percent of the civil servants were non-Germans.[137] The policies of encouraging ethnic minorities to express their identities through bureaucratic channels were similar in both Austria and the USSR.

The relation between state and society in Austria was, however, different from the Soviet case, in spite of the parallels between the Soviet project and the dynastic monarchies of the European *ancien regime.* Instead of embodying a uni-hierarchical social structure like that of the USSR, the Austrian state administered a motley social patchwork of old and new, agrarian and industrial, feudal and capitalistic. This complexity was also reflected in the sphere of each national group, in the conflict between historic tradition and ethnic claims. Often these claims were wider, though sometimes even narrower, than the historic state concepts of specific Habsburg domains, of which Bohemia, Hungary and Croatia serve as outstanding examples.[138] One must also distinguish between the federalism of the Habsburg Crownlands (*Kronländer*) and the traditions of the *historicopolitical entities* out of which the Habsburg Power was developed. "The true significance of this concept of the historicopolitical entities within the Austrian national problem is based on the specific nature of the conservative social forces behind it."[139] The emergent party system was therefore extraordinarily heterogeneous. In the party formation, clubs dominated by the estates stood side by side with modern mass parties in an unusually heterogeneous party pattern, which, along with the mixing of a Western subjective principle of nationality with the Eastern objective principle, made a resolution of the nationality problem difficult.[140]

The Habsburg dynastic idea had, as formerly mentioned, rested on the assumption of the precedence of the German culture. The weakening of the German cultural hegemony in Austria in the era of the nationality principle had left the state without any supreme principle of legitimacy. The failure of all plans to federalize the state along ethnical lines also meant that the possibility to create a *supranational* or an *international* state concept had failed. During the last decades before the First World War the Habsburg administration therefore was debilitated both morally and intellectually at the same time as nationalist ideals were gaining in strength.

From one point of view it could be said that it was the struggle over language that tore the empire apart. Although uncompromising extremists were fewer than moderates among the German-speaking population, they were dominant in mixed-language areas and in institutions of higher education. Here they prevented a compromise solution. The German government's support, and that of the German nationalists from *das Reich,* gave German–Austrian nationalism a significance it would otherwise have lacked. The democratic process was slowed down, and the emperor's possibilities for reaching a compromise with the Slavs were hindered. The government therefore had to suspend the *Reichsrat* and govern by decrees.[141]

The main contentious issues in the struggle between Germans and Czechs were about and were associated with the interpretation of article XIX in the

1867 constitution, which recognized and guaranteed equal rights to all of Austria's nationalities. It promised equality for all spoken languages in the educational system and in public life, and required all Crown lands inhabited by more than one nationality to give all inhabitants instruction in their own language.[142]

However, the constitution did not define *nationality* and omitted to clarify whether this equality was to be applied to all individuals, to the members of a nationality as an organized group, or to the territories largely inhabited by one specific nationality. The constitution also failed to provide a more detailed interpretation of what *spoken languages* meant; the term could refer to all spoken languages in a Crownland or just those spoken in a more restricted area. Finally, the constitution did not specify a body having the authority to interpret it: The government through decrees, the *Reichsrat* through interpretive acts, or an executive body through administrative interpretations.

The *furor teutonicus,* which the language ordinances caused in 1897, brought Austria closer to revolution than she had been since 1848. With the equal status of the Czech and German languages the German–Austrians saw a threat to their own control of the state. They were particularly upset by the ordinance's reference to "the Bohemian Kingdom," which implicitly involved recognition of historical Bohemian state rights, and would mean a step toward federalism.

In the 1890s, when the nationality conflicts between the Czechs and the Germans entered an acute phase, the German government thus resolutely and continuously supported the German–Austrians, a support that supplemented the considerable political, financial and propagandistic support from German nationalists in *das Reich.* This process let loose inner bureaucratic dynamics toward fragmentation and resulted in the formation of local "principalities." There was an increasing need for bureaucrats who spoke the local languages, without any corresponding wish in Vienna to relax the administrative centralization. Although there was an overwhelming grassroots loyalty among the Habsburg subjects right down to 1918, nationalist bureaucrats were looking forward to the dismantling of the Habsburg monarchy and the building of independent local administrations for their own compatriots. This again contributed to the administrative deadlock. Also certain features of the Habsburg ethnic–topographic structure restricted the range of possible political solutions to the nationality problem:

1) The distribution of ethnic groups between the two imperial states, which must be seen in light of the very different ideologies dominating the public and social lives of Austria and Hungary and their dissimilar political systems. The distribution of ethnic groups between the two parts of the monarchy implied that five out of eleven groups were living in the territories of both the

two constituent states. These groups, accounting for about 45 percent of the total population, were the Germans, the Croats, the Serbs, the Romanians and the Ukrainians. The main obstacle to the federalization plans was the impossibility of unifying these nationalities without the constitutional reorganization of the Dual Monarchy as a whole. A step-by-step solution, reorganizing the state along ethnic–federal lines, would be blocked also in Austria, as long as the Magyarians were unwilling to recognize that Hungary was also a multinational unit, and not a nation-state.[143]

The USSR, as opposed to Austria–Hungary, was, of course, in the first place one single state system, not two states. Second, through the use of Soviet patriotism and through the formulation of the concept of "the Soviet-people as a new historical community" the state leadership was attempting to procure a common ideology, balancing the elements of a state that was both unitary and multinational at the same time. This balancing was gradually becoming more and more precarious (during the Brezhnev era).

2) Seen in the light of *phase 3 of Stein Rokkan's model*—the political mobilization and incorporation of the population—in light of this phase another feature of the ethnic–topographic structure of the Habsburg monarchy must be emphasized: it did not primarily consist of complete nations, but of fragments of nations. The majority of the population in six of its eleven nationalities were to be found living outside its borders: the Germans, the Italians, the Romanians, the Ukrainians, the Serbs and the Poles. This was a period of considerable irredentist mobilization. At the same time nationalism was evolving into a mass phenomenon, and democratic currents were undermining the political supremacy of the old social elites. All these factors put together meant that the unity of the monarchy was irretrievably lost. Absolute demands, no longer relative ones, characterized the type of nationalism now flourishing in Cisleithania. These demands were too particular to be weighted against the claims raised by other nations.[144]

In the case of the USSR, the potential irredentist problem was not connected with modern nations, but with pan-Turkish and pan-Muslim currents. The formation of modern nations, as a process engineered from the center, could therefore paradoxically be used to neutralize this danger, through the use of two fundamental strategies available to Moscow: First by splitting up the larger groups and then through gerrymandering. This meant drawing the borders so as to circumvent their ostensible raison d'être by incorporating alien persons or purposefully leaving segments of the titular groups outside. Second there was the possibility of population redistributions so as to perpetuate the ethnic heterogeneity in the non-Russian units. The boundaries between the units of the Soviet federation were in fact often based precisely on a "divide and rule principle," without considerations for historical traditions or contemporary ethnic realities. This limited the scope for potential alliances between the periphery nations against the center, particularly in Central Asia.[145]

The official registration of ethnicity on the individual level contributed to segregating the Soviet nations from one another and established a rigid ethnic affiliation for every citizen. Although this was not intended, it frustrated the process of assimilation and the creation of a new supranational community. The challenges of independent political mass participation, that is, unmanipulated participation through organizations constituting a civil society, mediating between state and individual, was, however, postponed in the Soviet case until the Gorbachev period. The system was thus capable of maintaining internal stability, despite the fact that the Soviet nations had acquired the preconditions for independent existence through the nationality policy.

3) Another feature of the ethnic–topographical structure is thrown into relief by the comparative perspective: The existence of a mixture of ethnic groups in a population can be interpreted, after Stein Rokkan, as an additional cost complicating the state-building process, since the integration of these heterogeneous groups and periphery societies in the territory-controlling system also implies a potential for periphery protests and politization. Forestalling the release of this potential makes the tasks of center penetration (taxes, army, administration) and cultural standardization more difficult to handle.

As we have just seen, the costs for the Habsburg empire of its ethnical heterogeneity were high. As modernization was disturbing the old balance between its nations, it was almost logical that the ethno-topographical structure became a negative constraint on the possibilities to compromise. This made the search for a new balance between the nations extremely complicated, once the original equilibrium from 1867 (the *Ausgleich*) had given way.

Such problems existed neither in the All Russian Empire, nor in the Soviet Union: The Habsburg monarchy was the only European power (if we do not take into consideration the mainly Asian Ottoman empire) that consisted of a number of national groups, none of which constituted a majority of the population. The strongest group, the Germans, accounted for a fourth of the total population. The next strongest group, the Magyarians accounted for about one-fifth of the total population. In the empire as a whole, no ethnic–national group could assume the role of uncontested leader in relation to the others; no nation could act as the cement keeping the whole conglomerate of nations together.

By comparison, the *ethnic-topographic* basis of the All-Russian Empire and of the Soviet Union was more favorable. The relative size of the Russian nation simplified the task of neutralizing the potential of national conflict in the rest of the population. The Russian relative proportion varied from 70.7 percent in 1719 to 44.6 percent in 1897, and the Russians were thereafter the only ethnic group with a continually increasing share of the population up to 1959, when it settled around 50 percent.

Under otherwise equal conditions this composition of the population made the Russian population element and the Russian language into a better catalyst in the political integration process than any of the nations of the Dual Monarchy. The Russians in fact became the cement holding the multinational state together. It should of course be noted that parts of the Soviet Union, especially Estonia and Latvia, experienced rapid and fundamental changes in their ethnic structure. The implications of these changes may still prove to be dramatic.[146]

POLITICAL PARTICIPATION AND THE DISINTEGRATION OF THE USSR

Last, I will briefly discuss the dissolution of the USSR. I will start with the changes in variables that explain the long-term political stabilization after the Second World War.

The basic contradiction of Soviet society on the eve of Gorbachev's assumption of power was between the so-called command administrative system and the new social dynamics. Underlying these dynamics were societal modernization, the scientific–technological revolution and particularly the spectacular growth of the newly educated social elites.[147] The problems relating to the stagnation of political structures were reinforced by a sustained economic crisis starting in the late 1970s. The recession meant that the stabilizing influence of a long-lasting period of economic growth came to an end. Gorbachev's policy can be interpreted as an attempt to trigger a societal learning process, whereby the state structures were to be adjusted to a civil society in the making. However, in this process a goal conflict arose between the demands of economic and political reforms. In Rokkanian terms, the unintended effect of Gorbachev's political liberalization was to precipitate an accumulation of crises on several fronts that occurred simultaneously.

As the existing political power was dismantled, without a corresponding recentralizing into new democratic institutions, the dynamics toward progressive political fragmentation immanent in the Soviet state was let loose. Power did rapidly diffuse, but very little of it went to the elected Congress of Peoples' deputies, the Supreme Soviet, or the political parties represented there. Power drifted inexorably to the republics while political decay in the party, the military, and the economic organs was rapidly advancing.[148] At the union republic level, the process of disintegration of the USSR can be described as follows, by using Miroslav Hroch's well-known model:

> The patriotic movements of both the Habsburg monarchy's and the USSR's non-ruling nations, propagated their national programs to mass audiences. The important difference between the Soviet and the Austrian cases, however, was the remarkable speed characterizing the transition of the non-Russian national movements to phase 3, the stage of mass participation. At this stage the intellectual leaders of the national movements succeed in penetrating the population majorities with their patriotic messages. Another conspicuous feature in the Soviet case is how swiftly the demands listed in the national programs were to be fulfilled.[149]

An explanation must allow for a pivotal conjunctural component, crisis accumulation in Rokkanian terms, in the disintegration of the USSR. This component can be defined and evaluated as a causal element only by reference to the critical level at which it occurs: the contextual level. This means that the same causal factor varies in its effect depending on its context. Indeed, at times kaleidoscopic alterations take place that lead to a dynamic fusing of heretofore separately unfolding patterns of action orientations. Often fully unforeseen developments are called forth by the conjunctural dynamics set into motion.[150]

In the USSR at least three sets of causal factors interacted with economic stagnation in conjunctural dynamics, as favorable conditions to the growth of national movements.

1) The social and political dynamics generated by the weakening of the ruling all-union *nomenklatura* class.
2) The possibility, offered by the federal state structure, of combining different types of demands in more comprehensive national programs. The same federal structure also made it possible for the national movements to move beyond their purely linguistic–political phase in a short period of time.
3) As *glasnost* liberalized the Soviet media policy by removing the heavy hand of censorship, modern mass-media technology made possible the fast spreading of new models for political mobilization outside the centrally controlled institutions and organizations.

During the Gorbachev era the nationality question passed from a stage with a strong Hungarian element to a stage more reminiscent of Cisleithanian Austria after 1867. Also the conflict dynamics of the two empires seem to have been moving along paralleled tracks: Gorbachev's tactics of granting limited concessions to the non-Russian nations did not contribute to rendering the nationality conflicts less fierce. During the Brezhnev era, when the slightest hint of nationalist mobilization were met with repression as all other forms of political mobilization not organized by the Soviet state, an outside observer who based his views on appearances might have believed that the Soviet Union, like Hungary after 1867, was a country without a nationality problem. On the other hand, it was clear for all to see that Austria, like the Soviet Union during Gorbachev, was passing from one crisis to another because of nationalist unrest. Why did the USSR fall apart precisely when it was in the process of becoming the sort of *Rechtsstaat* that Austria was from the 1860s?

Paradoxically, the more the demands of the nations were satisfied, the more oppressed the non-ruling nations felt. The Czechs, just like the Balts, were more vociferous, the more their old demands were met, and the more the Germans, respectively the Russians, were on the defensive. The Austrian nationality conflicts gradually achieved their own dynamic momentum (*dynamisches Entwicklungsmoment*) in the Weberian sense, and finally paralyzed the normal functions of the political system, thereby forcing the government to rule by decrees. In the case of the USSR, the paralysis of the political system was manifested in a somewhat different manner: members of the all-union elite were polarized between two different positions. One group wanted to maintain the "inner empire" and resist further democratic reform, whereas another advocated a persistent pursuit of democratic reform and were ready, if necessary, to let the empire go. In the face of this polarization Gorbachev's policy was doomed.[151] Originally no such coupling existed between attitudes favoring the dissolution of the empire and democratization on the one side, and continued authoritarian rule and maintaining the empire on the other.[152]

In contrast to the situation in the Habsburg monarchy, and also in the Western overseas colonies, the conflict between center and periphery in the USSR was not just a question of the *form* of the state—unitary versus federalized, or federation versus separatism—but, equally important, it was a question of its *content*—a single party system versus a multiparty system. The two conflicts reinforced each other, thereby accelerating political development.[153] Nor was the latter conflict one of opposition between the Russians as a group and the non-Russians. It was rather a struggle between the supporters of the old centralized power structure, with the Communist Party as its only legitimate political force and those wanting a society based on political pluralism, the rule of law, constitutional government and the dismantling of the old command–administrative system. Rather than strengthening the thesis of an necessary causal link between socioeconomic modernization and nationality conflicts, the dissolution of the USSR is explained by specific political dynamics during the Gorbachev era. Here "empire savers"[154] came out strongly against political democratization, creating a situation where democratization necessarily would lead to a separation between center and periphery.

The struggles for political independence escalated because it was possible to detach, by a few simple movements, the already existing state units, that is, union and autonomous republics.[155] The Baltic strategy was to issue their own local laws on one societal domain after another. This meant the overruling of Soviet laws and thereby causing *legal chaos* in which they were perceived as sovereign states by the international community. The basis of this policy were the Declarations of Independence by some of the democratically elected national assemblies in May 1990.

In societies where the citizens had been deprived of political participation for several decades, the language question soon became a mobilizing factor of paramount importance, and, as the old bonds were weakened, linguistic identity took on socially integrating functions. An important part of the new national self-assertion was the passing of laws making the local tongues the official languages of the republics. An important means in Moscow's control of the republics, the deployment of Russian-speaking cadres from the all-union center to local power positions was thereby blocked. The use of local ethnic Russian residents as guarantists for the republics falling into line was likewise made more difficult. With regard to the importance of the linguistic demands of the non-Russians, there are obvious parallels between the USSR and other multiethnic empires in their periods of decline. Seen from one point of view, also the Habsburg Monarchy was torn apart by a protracted language conflict, in that case between the Czechs and the Germans.[156]

The weakening of the central and supranational power structures, and of the groups relying on it, opened up a new political space to ethnic and national movements "from below." The founding of the "Popular Fronts" was partly a spontaneous process, partly a process initiated from above, in an attempt to channel the various grassroots initiatives into an acceptable direction, that of *perestroyka*. Political mass participation first appeared in the Baltic republics. In Gorbachev's opinion such mass participation was necessary for the success of *perestroyka*. The first popular fronts had hardly been founded, however, before they perceived of the nation as the basic and privileged unit for the development of democracy and social progress. After it had become possible to champion democratic rights openly, all issues—language, culture, ecology, democracy, social rehabilitation of the victims of Stalinism—were connected and combined in one single, all-embracing national program. In this way it was soon possible to create genuine mass movements that enjoyed the active support of hundreds of thousands of people.[157]

However, it seems justified here to question to what extent the ostensibly same phenomenon was just that in the various areas. The Polish historian Marek Waldenberg said this in his book on nationality issues in Eastern Central Europe:

> Only where certain national groups are concerned, above all the Lithuanians, the Estonians and the Latvians . . . could it be said that the will to create an independent state was widespread and, to a varying degree, rooted. But it is difficult to know how matters stood in Moscow after the August coup (1991) and whether any will might exist in other population groups. One may doubt whether the results of the organised referendums fully reflect well thought-through and reasoned attitudes. One may wonder at the extent to which they were an expression of moods that had suddenly emerged, of promises and pressures from the political elites and from certain groups within the intelligentsia.[158]

The Soviet nationality policy had created a double set of loyalties toward one's own nation and region and toward the Soviet state, at least among the members of the all union *nomenklatura*. As the political center and therefore the supranational political elites were stripped of their main functions relating to the administration of the economy and supervision of the mass media, the political system was doomed to collapse. This in turn triggered national conflicts as the old elites now had to find a power base in their local populations. National conflicts in the post-Soviet political space, then, from one point of view, should rather be considered as the result of the process of disintegration rather than its cause. The elites were forced to play the nationalist card to survive, as the all-union political context of the USSR was in a constant flux, a state on which these elites were completely unable to influence.

The continual and rapid change of the elites' preferences as a consequence of these experiences can, from one point of view, be seen as parallel to the dissolution of the Habsburg monarchy due to the First World War. Before the First World War the national leaders of Central Europe, thus, only sought autonomy in the old dynastic, multinational states and the Habsburg subjects were overwhelmingly loyal to the monarchy. The First World War was, however, fought as a war between several states and the principle of national sovereignty was interpreted as synonymous with state sovereignty by the Peace Settlement of 1919–1920. Self-appointed leaders spoke on behalf of the peoples of the region and their future states. Only in retrospective did they seek democratic legitimacy at home. Finally there was the question of the new state borders to be solved.

Although independence came to the Soviet republics as a result of the collapse of central authority, not as a result of direct struggle, the collapse nonetheless was preceded by three years of mass mobilization, interethnic conflict and center–republic tensions, which conditioned the circumstances under which that collapse took place. At the same time the Soviet and post-Soviet ethnic and national tensions cannot be properly understood without making allowance for the economic crisis and disruptions, prior to and accompanying the process of imperial disintegration. A reasonable contrafactual question is therefore whether the consequences would have been the same had these policies been introduced under Khrushchev?

Even if this question cannot be answered in the strictest sense, a closer analysis of the effects of the Brezhnev period in a regional perspective may shed some light on it:

1) The stabilization of nationality relations during Brezhnev was based on the functioning of the political system. It assigned to the nations the role as the main mediating units between authorities and Soviet citizens. Although it existed already before the Brezhnev period, this system was strengthened by the policies pursued during his reign.

2) This system made all Soviet citizens conscious of their nationality as the only officially recognized distinction between the citizens, registered in each person's internal passport, and taken into account at every important event in the individuals' lives. The classification created practically impenetrable barriers between the different nations, and the nations became the most potent units for political mobilization; and nationalism became the medium through which discontent could be expressed, during a period of crisis. Here too already existing traits were strengthened.

3) Could stability in multinational states be maintained under other conditions than those of the Soviet Union during the Brezhnev period? My answer is that other forms of federalization, not territorially based (the phrase national cultural autonomy has been used) are at least conceivable.[159] For my part, I will therefore refuse a determinist comprehension of the disintegration of the USSR: given the reform policy "lightening the pressure," things had to turn out as they did, "the whole boiler exploding." This of course, is not a repudiation of Alexis de Toqueville's thesis of the liberalization of despotic regimes, but an emphasizing of the primacy of politics also in the context of the decline and fall of the USSR.

NOTES

1. The use of the Habsburg monarchy for comparative purposes has been considerably facilitated by the publication of the multivolume *Die Habsburgermonarchie 1848–1918* by the Austrian Academy of Sciences starting from 1973 onward, edited by Adam Wandruszka and Peter Urbanitsch. I have in this chapter made extensive use of volume 1, *Die wirtschaftliche Entwicklung*, Vienna: Verlag der Österreichischen Akademie der Wissenschaften 1973; volume 2, *Verwaltung und Rechtwesen*, Vienna: Verlag der Österreichischen Akademie der Wissenschaften 1975; and volumes 3/1 and 3/2, *Die Völker des Reiches*, Vienna: Verlag der Österreichischen Akademie der Wissenschaften 1980. For an interesting collection of papers relating to some of the questions treated in this paper, see also Richard L. Rudolph and David Good (eds.),

Nationalism and Empire. The Habsburg Empire and the Soviet Union, New York: St. Martin's Press 1992.

2. Jaszi, Oscar, *The Dissolution of the Habsburg Monarchy*. Chicago: University of Chicago Press 1929; Kann, Robert, *The Multinational Empire: Nationalism and National Reform in the Habsburg Monarchy 1848–1918*, vols. 1 & 2. New York: Columbia University Press 1950.

3. See Reinhard Bendix, "Why Nationalism? Relative Backwardness and Intellectual Mobilization," *Zeitschrift für Soziologie*, 8:1; 1981; Gellner, Ernest, *Nations and Nationalism*. Oxford: Blackwell 1983; and Øyvind Østerud, "Utvikling gjennom tilbakeliggenhet," in Øyvind Østerud, *Det moderne statssystem*. Oslo: Gyldendal 1987.

4. Hechter, Michael, *Internal Colonialism. The Celtic Fringe in the British National Development, 1536–1966*. London: Routledge & Kegan Paul 1975.

5. Gellner, Ernest, *Nations and Nationalism*. Oxford: Blackwell 1983, pp. 24, 112.

6. Berend, Ivan T., "Besondere Characterzüge der Industrierevolution in österreichisch-ungarischer Monarchie," *Zeitgeschichte*, 1:11–12, 1974, pp. 222–38; Berend, Ivan T., and Georgy Ranki, *Hungary: A Century of Development*. New York: Newton Abbot, David & Charles 1974; Good, David, "Modern Economic Growth in the Habsburg Monarchy," *East Central Europe*, 7:2 1980, pp. 248–68.

7. Berend, Ivan, and Georgy Ranki, "Ungarns wirtschaftliche Entwicklung 1848–1918," in Adam Wandruszka and Peter Urbanitsch (eds.), *Die Habsburgermonarchie 1848–1918*, vol. 1, *Die Wirtschaftliche Entwicklung*. Vienna: Verlag der Österreichischen Akademie der Wissenschaften 1973.

8. For an introduction to this perspective, see Alexander Gerschenkron, *Economic Backwardness in Historical Perspective: A Book of Essays*. Cambridge, MA: Belknap Press of Harvard University Press 1962; Alexander Gerschenkron, *Continuity in History and Other Essays*. Cambridge, MA: Belknap Press of Harvard University Press 1968; and also Thorstein Veblen, *Imperial Germany and the Industrial Revolution*. New York: Augustus M. Kelley 1964.

9. Kappeler, Andreas, *The Russian Empire. A Multiethnic History*. New York: Pearson 2001, chap. 8.

10. Bauer, Otto, *Die Nationalitätenfrage und die Sozialdemokratie*. Vienna: Wiener Volksbuchhandlung 1924 (1907); Fran Zwitter, *Les Problemes nationaux dans la Monarchie des Habsbourg*. Belgrade: Comité national yougoslave des sciences historiques 1960, pp. 17–18.

11. See Otto Bauer, "Schlusswort zur Minoritätenfrage," *Der Kampf. Sozialdemokratische Monatschrift*. Vienna 1911, 4, pp. 201–9.

12. Bauer, Otto, *Die Nationalitätenfrage und die Sozialdemokratie*. Vienna: Wiener Volksbuchhandlung 1924 (1907), pp. 262–63.

13. Simon, Gerhard, *Nationalismus und Nationalitätenpolitik in der Sowjetunion. Von der totalitären Diktatur zur nachstalinschen Gesellschaft*. Baden-Baden: Nomos Verlagsgesellschaft 1986, pp. 34–83; Isaev, M., *Iazykovoe stroitelstvo v SSSR*. Moscow: Nauka 1979; Clem, Ralph S., "The Changing Geography of Soviet Nationalities Socioeconomic and Demographic Correlates," in Peter J. Potichnyj and Jane Shapiro Zacek (eds.), *Politics and Participation Under Communist Rule. Selected Papers From the Second World Congress for Soviet and East European Studies*. New York:

Praeger 1983; Arutiunian, Iurii, "Izmenenie sotsialnoi struktury sovetskikh natsii," *Istoriia SSSR*, 4, 1972, pp. 3–20.

14. Martin, Terry, *The Affirmative Action Empire. Nations and Nationalism in the Soviet Union, 1923–1939*. Ithaca & London: Cornell University Press 2001, pp. 18, 19, 15.

15. Simon, Gerhard, *Nationalismus und Nationalitätenpolitik in der Sowjetunion. Von der totalitären Diktatur zur nachstalinschen Gesellschaft*. Baden-Baden: Nomos Verlagsgesellschaft 1986, pp. 299–316; Ostapenko, L. V., and A. Susokolov, "Etnosotsialnye osobennosti vosproisvodstva intelligentsii," *Sotsiologicheskie issledovaniia*, 1, 1983, pp. 10–16.

16. Karklins, Rasma, "Ethnic Politics and Access to Higher Education: the Soviet Case," *Comparative Politics* 16:3, 1983–84, pp. 277–94.

17. For a general survey of the crisis in various countries, see Peter Gourevitch, *The Political Response to an International Trade Crisis: Comparative Responses to the Great Depression of 1873–1896*. Paper delivered to the Canadian Political Science Association, Edmonton Alberta, June 1–5, 1975. As concerns Central Europe, see Hans Rosenberg, *Grosse Depression und Bismarckzeit. Wirtschaftablauf, Gesellschaft und Politik in Mittel-Europa*, Veröffentlichungen der historischen Kommision zu Berlin beim Friedrich-Meinecke-Institut der freien Universität, vol. 24, Berlin: 1967, chap. 3, pp. 58–118; and also "Wirtschaftskonjunktur, Gesellschaft und Politik in Mitteleuropa" and "Political Consequences of the Great Depression" in Hans Rosenberg, *Machteliten und Wirtschaftkonjunkturen: Studien zur neueren deutschen Sozial- und Wirtschaftsgeschichte*. Kritische Studien zur Geschichtswissenschaft 31, Göttingen 1978.

18. About the impact of the Depression in Hungary, see Ivan T. Berend and Georgy Ranki, "Economic Factors in Nationalism. The Example of Hungary at the Beginning of the Twentieth Century," *Austria History Yearbook* 3/3 1967, p. 168; about Hungarian agriculture during this period, see Andrew C. Janos, *The Politics of Backwardness in Hungary: 1815–1945*, Princeton, NJ: Princeton University Press 1982, pp. 118–21. About the impact in Austria, see Hans Rosenberg, *Grosse Depression und Bismarckzeit. Wirtschaftablauf, Gesellschaft und Politik in Mittel-Europa*, Veröffentlichungen der historischen Kommision zu Berlin beim Friedrich-Meinecke-Institut der freien Universität, vol. 24, Berlin: 1967, pp. 54–57, 96–97, 102, 236, 239–41, 246ff, 249–52; Bernhold Sutter, "Politische und rechtliche Stellung der deutschen in Österreich 1848–1918, in Adam Wandruszka and Peter Urbanitsch (eds), *Die Habsburgermonarchie 1848–1918* vol. 3/1: Die Völker des Reiches. Vienna: 1980, pp. 212–13.

19. Offergeld, Wilhelm, *Grundlagen und Ursachen der industrielle Entwicklung Ungarns*. Jena: G. Fischer 1914.

20. März, Eduard, and Karl Socher, "Währung und Banken in Cisleithanien," in Adam Wandruschka and Peter Urbanitsch (eds.), *Die Habsburgermonarchie 1848–1918*, vol. 1, pp. 334, 342–43, 358–62, 364; Kramer, Hans, *Die Italiener unter der österreichisch-ungarischen Monarchie*. Wiener historischer Studien Band 2, Vienna: Herold 1954, p. 83.

21. Granberg, Aleksander G., *Optimzatsiia territorialnykh proportsii narodnogo khoziaistva*. Moscow: Ekonomika 1973.

22. Lavrov, V. V., and K. N. Plotnikov (eds.), *Gosudarstvennyj biudzhet SSSR*. Moscow: Finansy 1975; Penkaitis, Norbert, *Der Finanzausgleich in der Sowjetunion und seine Bedeutung fur die Wirtschaftsentwicklung der Unionsrepublikken*. Giessener Abhandlungen zur Agrar- und Wirtschaftsforschung des europäischen Ostens, 89. Berlin: Dunker und Humblot 1977.

23. Granberg, Aleksander G., *Optimzatsiia territorialnykh proportsii narodnogo khoziaistva*. Moscow: Ekonomika 1973, p. 180.

24. See Gertrude Schroeder, "Soviet Living Standards: Achievements and Prospects," in 97th Cong., 2nd sess., joint committee print. "December 31, 1982," vol. 2, *Selected Papers Submitted to the Joint Economic Committee, Congress of the U.S.: Soviet Economy in the 1980's: Problems and Prospects*. Washington: GPO 1983, p. 367ff.

25. Schroeder, Gertrude, "Regional Differences in Incomes and Levels of Living in the USSR," in V. N. Bandera and Z. L. Melnyk (eds.), *The Soviet Economy in Regional Perspective*. New York: Praeger 1973, p. 173.

26. Herz, Friedrich, *The Economic Problems of the Danubian States. A Study in Economic Nationalism*. London: Gollancz 1947, p. 42; Wesseley, Kurt, "Österreich-Ungarns Wirtschft vor dem ersten Weltkrieg," *Donauraum*, 12, 1967, p. 26.

27. Wysocki, Josef, *Infrastruktur und wachsende Staatsausgaben. Das Fallbeispiel österreich 1868–1913*. Forschungen zur Sozial und Wirtschaftsgeschichte, 20, Stuttgart: G. Fischer 1975, p. 190.

28. McAuley, Alastair, "Economic Development and Political Nationalism in Uzbekistan," *Central Asian Survey*, 5:3/4, pp. 61–182; Davies, R. W., *The Development of the Soviet Budgetary System*. Cambridge: Cambridge University Press 1958, pp. 310, 305, table 47; Wilber, C. K., *The Soviet Model and Underdeveloped Countries*. Chapel Hill: University of North Carolina Press 1969.

29. Iskanderov, I., *Tekstilnaia promyshlennost Uzbekistana*. Tashkent 1974, p. 36; Plotnikov, N., "Transformation of the Uzbek republic," in E. Robinson, (ed.), *Backward Areas in Advanced Countries: Proceedings of a Conference Held by the International Economic Association*. London: Macmillan 1969, pp. 319–26; Wilber, C. K., *The Soviet Model and Underdeveloped Countries*. Chapel Hill: University of North Carolina Press 1969, p 194.

30. See Philip Goldman, Gail Lapidus, and Victor Zaslavsky, "Introduction: Soviet Federalism—Its Origins, Evolution, and Demise," and Victor Zaslavsky, "The Evolution of Separatism in Soviet Society Under Gorbachev," both in Gail W. Lapidus, Victor Zaslavsky, with Phillips Goldman (eds.), *From Union to Commonwealth. Nationalism and Separatism in the Soviet Republics*. Cambridge: Cambridge University Press 1992.

31. For a discussion of the extent of resource transfers from the Ukraine, see I. S. Koropeckyj, "A Century of Moscow-Ukraine Relations: An Interpretation," *Harvard Ukrainian Studies*, 5:4, 1981, pp. 467–96.

32. The native Ukrainian share of the salaried employees in the Ukrainian USSR was reduced between 1939 and 1970 according to Soviet statistics; compare Iurii Arutiunian, "Izmenie sotsialnoi struktury sovetskikh natsii," *Istoria SSSR*, 4, 1972,

p. 6; and Iu. Bromlei, *Sovremennye etnicheskie protsessy v SSSR*. Moscow: Nauka 1977, p. 131.

33. Evans, R. J. W., "Joseph II and Nationality in the Habsburg Lands," in H. M. Scott (ed.), *Enlightened Absolutism: Reform and Reformers in Later Eighteenth-Century Europe*. Houndmills: Macmillan, 1990; Beales, Derek, *Enlightenment and Reform in Eighteenth-Century Europe*. London & New York: I. B. Tauris 2005, chaps. 11 & 12.

34. Evans, R. J. W., "Joseph II and Nationality in the Habsburg Lands," in *Enlightened Absolutism. Reform and Reformers in Later Eighteenth-Century Europe*. London: Macmillan 1991, p. 219.

35. Niederhauser, Emile. *The Rise of Nationalism in Eastern Europe*. Budapest: Corvina Kiado 1982, p. 202.

36. Janos, Andrew C. *The Politics of Backwardness in Hungary: 1815–1945*. Princeton, NJ: Princeton University Press 1982, p. 69.

37. Accounts of Hungarian political development are found in R. Kann, *The Multinational Empire: Nationalism and National Reform in the Habsburg Monarchy 1848–1918*, vols. 1 & 2. New York: Columbia University Press 1950, I; Katus, Laszlo, "Über die wirtschaftlichen Grundlagen der Nationalitätenfrage in Ungarn vor dem ersten Weltkrieg," in Peter Hanak (ed.), *Die Nationalitätenfrage in der Österreichisch-ungarischen Monarchie 1900–1918*. Budapest: Akadémiai Kado/Verlag der Ungarischen Akademie der Wissaenschaften 1966, pp. 149–217; and Katus, Laszlo, "Die Madiaren," in Adam Wandruszka and Peter Urbanitsch (eds.), *Die Habsburgermonarchie 1848–1918*, vol 3/1. Vienna: Verlag der Österreichischen Akademie der Wissenschaften 1980.

38. Springer, Rudolf (Karl Renner), *Der Kampf der österreichischen Nationen um den Staat*. Leipzig: Deuticke 1902, pp. 42–43.

39. An account of the structure of the Austrian part of the monarchy is found in Gerald Stourzh, "Die Gleichberechtigung der Volksstämme als Vervassungsprinzip 1848–1918," in Adam Wandruszka and Peter Urbanitsch (eds.), *Die Habsburgermonarchie 1848–1918*, vol. 3/1; see also Miroslav Hroch, *Linguistic Conflicts in Eastern Europe and their Historical Parallels*, Paper, Charles University, Prague 1990.

40. Zwitter, Fran, "Nationale Probleme und gesellschaftliche Struktur in der Habsburgermonarchie," *Österreichische Osthefte*, 13:3, 1977, pp. 147–60.

41. Jaszi, Oscar, *The Dissolution of the Habsburg Monarchy*. Chicago: University of Chicago Press 1929, pp. 338, 286; Anderson, Benedict, *Imagined Communities. Reflections on the Origin and Spread of Nationalism*. London: Verso 1986, chap. 6.

42. Barany, George, "Hungary: the Uncompromising Compromise," *Austria History Yearbook*, 3:1, 1967, pp. 234–59, 255; Jaszi, Oscar, *The Dissolution of the Habsburg Monarchy*. Chicago: University of Chicago Press 1929, p. 347.

43. Hanak, Peter, "Verbürgerlichung und Assimilation," and "Ungarns Gesellschaft am Anfang des 20. Jahrhundert," in his *Ungarn in der Donaumonarchie. Probleme der bürgerlichen Umgestaltung eines Vielvölkerstaates*. Schriftenreihe des Osterreichischen Ost- und Sudosteuropa-Instituts 10. Vienna: Verlag fur Geschichte un Politik 1984.

44. About the Hungarian election system, see Laszlo Katus in Adam Wandruszka and Peter Urbanitsch (eds.), *Die Habsburgermonarchie 1848–1918*, vol. 3, pp. 469–76. About the crisis of Dualism, see Norman Stone, "Constitutional Crisis in Hungary 1903–1906," *Slavonic Review*, 45, 1967.

45. Dolgorukov, Peter Vladimirovich, *Rossiiskaia rodoslovnaia kniga, izdavaemaia kniazem Petrom Dolgorukovym*. St. Petersburg: V tipografii Karla Vingebera 1855, 2: 111ff; Francis Dvornik, *The Slavs in European History and Civilization*. New Brunswick, NJ: Rutgers University Press 1962; Amburger, Erik, *Geschichte der Behördenorganisation von Peter Grossen bis 1917*. Studien zur Geschichte Osteuropas 10. Leiden: E. J. Brill 1966, 517.

46. Hosking, Geoffrey, *Russia: People and Empire*. Cambridge, MA: Harvard University Press 1997, p. 397.

47. Kappeler, Andreas, "Czarist Policy toward the Muslims of the Russian Empire," in Andreas Kappeler, Gerhard Simon, and George Brunner (eds.), *Muslim Communities Reemerge. Historical perspectives on Nationality, Politics, and Opposition in the Former Soviet Union and Yugoslavia*. Durham & London: Duke University Press 1994; Slocum, John W., "Who, and When, Were the Inorodtsy? The Evolution of the Category of 'Aliens' in Imperial Russia," *Russian Review* 57, 1998, pp. 173–90; Pearson, Raymond, "Privileges, Rights and Russification," in Olga Crisp and Linda Edmondson (eds.), *Civil Rights in Imperial Russia*. Oxford: Clarendon 1983, pp. 83–102; compare I. E. Andreevskii (ed.), *Entsiklopedicheskii Slovar*. Sankt-Peterburg: Izd. F. A. Brokgauz & Efron 13, 1894, pp. 224ff.

48. Suny, Ronald Grigor, "Nationalities in the Russian Empire," *Russian Review* 59, 2000, p. 490.

49. Loit, Alexander, *Socio-Ethnic Structures and National Movements in the Late Russian Empire: The Baltic Countries,"* University of Stockholm, 1990/Paper World Congress of Soviet and Eastern European Studies, Harrogate, 1990, pp. 22–23; Hellmann, Manfred, *Grundzüge der Geschichte Litauens und des litauischen Volkes*. Darmstadt: Wissenschaftliche Buchgesellschaft 1966; Wittraum, Reinhart, *Baltische Geschichte. Die Ostseelände Livland, Estland, Kurland 1180–1918*. Munich: R. Oldenbourg 1954.

50. See Michael Cherniavsky, *Tsar and People. Studies in Russian Myths*. New Haven, CT: Yale University Press 1961.

51. About the development of the Russian national identity, see Michael Cherniavsky, "Russia," in Orest Ranum, *National Consciousness, History, and Political Culture in Early-Modern Europe*. Baltimore: Johns Hopkins University Press 1975, pp. 118–43; and Michael Cherniavsky, *Tsar and People. Studies in Russian Myths*. New Haven, Ct: Yale University Press 1961; and two works by Dmitrii S. Likhachov, *Natsionalnoe samosoznanie Drevnei Rusi. Ocherki iz oblasti russkoi literatury XI–XVII vv*, Moscow & Leningrad: Izdatelstvo Akademiia Nauk SSSR 1945, and Likhachov, *Velikoe Nasledie. Klassicheskie proizvedeniia literatury Drevnei Rusi*. Moscow: Sovremennik 1979.

52. Rowley, David G., "Imperial versus National Discourse: the Case of Russia," *Nations and Nationalism* 6:1, 2000, pp. 33, 32.

53. Rogger, Hans, "Nationalism and the State: A Russian Dilemma," *Comparative Studies in History and Society*, .4:3, 1961.

54. See Andreas Kappeler, "The Ambiguities of Russification," *Kritika: Explorations in Russian and Eurasian History*, 5:2, 2004, pp. 291–97; Ronald Grigor Suny, "Nationalities in the Russian Empire," *Russian Review* 59, 2000, pp. 487–92.

55. Flora, Peter, "Introduction and Interpretation," in Peter Flora, Stein Kuhnle, and Derek Urwin (eds.), *State Formation, Nation-Building, and Mass Politics in Europe. Theory of Stein Rokkan.* Oxford: Oxford University Press 1999, p. 67.

56. Rowley, David G., "Imperial versus National Discourse: The Case of Russia," *Nations and Nationalism*, 6:1, 2000, pp. 29, 28.

57. Bugge, Peter, "Habsburgmonarkiets tysk-østerrikere," *Den Jyske Historiker*, 57, 1991, pp. 64–65; Urbanitsch, Peter, "Die deutschen in Österreich," in Wandruschka and Urbanitsch (eds.), *Die Habsburgermonarchie 1848–1918*, vol. 3/1.

58. For the Counter-Reformation and the Catholic Church see Oscar Jaszi, "Part II. The Historical Atmosphere," in *The Dissolution of the Habsburg Monarchy*. Chicago: University of Chicago Press 1929; Perry Anderson, *Lineages of the Absolutist State*. London: New Left Books 1974, pp. 300, 305, 307, 310.

59. Kossior, S. V., and P. P. Postyshev, *Der bolschewistisiche Sieg in der Ukraine. Reden auf dem Vereinigten Plenum des Zk und ZKK der Kommunistischen Partei der Ukraine (Bolschewiki) in November 1933*. Moscow/Leningrad: Verlagsgenossenschaft ausländischer Arbeiter in der UdSSR 1934, p. 165; Stalin, Joseph, "Extract from the Report on the Work of the Central Committee of the CPSU Delivered at the Seventeenth Party Congress, January 26, 1934," in Joseph Stalin, *Marxism and the National and Colonial Questions*. New York: International Publishers 1935, pp. 267–68.

60. See Robert Conquest, *The Great Terror: Stalin's Purge of the Thirties*. London: Macmillan 1968. See particularly the section titled "The Nationalities," pp. 77–82. See also Roy Medvedev, *Let History Judge: The Origins and Consequences of Stalinism*. New York: Vintage 1973; Nikita S. Khrushchev, *Khrushchev Remembers*. Boston: Little, Brown & Co 1970, pp. 106, 108; and T. H. Rigby, *Communist Party Membership in the USSR 1917–1967*. Princeton, NJ: Princeton University Press 1968, pp. 204, 370.

61. Kappeler, Andreas, *The Russian Empire. A Multiethnic History*. New York: Pearson 2001, p. 277.

62. Martin, Terry, *The Affirmative Action Empire. Nations and Nationalism in the Soviet Union, 1923–1939*. Ithaca & London: Cornell University Press 2001, p. 461.

63. Isaev, Magomet I., *Iazykovoe stroitelstvo v SSSR*. Moscow: Nauka 1979.

64. Sak, L. M. and M. I. Isaev, "Problemy pismennosti narodov SSSR v kulturnoi revoliutsii," *Voprosy istorii* 2, 1966, p. 11; Khansuvarov, I., *Latinizatsiia—orudie Leninskoi natsionalnoi politiki*. Moscow: 1932.

65. Guboglo, M. N., "Razvitie mnogonatsionalnoi sovetskoi pechati v 1917–1940 gg," *Istoriia SSSR* 6, 1972, p. 124; Simon, Gerhard, *Nationalismus und Nationalitätenpolitik in der Sowjetunion. Von der totalitären Diktatur zur nachstalinschen Gesellschaft.* Baden-Baden: Nomos Verlagsgesellschaft 1986, pp. 59–60, 64–65; Bennigsen, Aleksandre and Chantal Lemercier-Quelquejay, *Islam in the Soviet Union*. London: Pall Mall Press 1967, p. 127.

66. Baranova, T. J., "Iz istorii prepodavaniia russkovo iazyka v nerusskikh shkolakh SSSR," *Sovetskaia pedagogiga*, *12*, 1977, pp. 115–23 (116ff).

67. Isaev, M. I., "Natsiia i iazyk," *Voprosii istorii*, 2, 1968, pp. 99ff; Bilinsky, Yaroslav, "Expanding the Use of Russian or Russification? Some Critical Thoughts on Russian as a Lingua Franca and the 'Language of Friendship and Cooperation of the Peoples of the USSR,'" *Russian Review*, 40:3, 1981, pp. 317–32; Desheriev, Iu. D., "Bytovaia kultura i ee otrashenie v iazyke," in Iu. D. Desheriev, *Natsionalnyi iazyk i kultura*. Moscow: Nauka 1978.

68. Suny, Ronald Grogor, "Georgia and Soviet nationality Policy," in Stephen F. Cohen, Alexander Rabinowitz, and Robert Sharlets (eds.), *The Soviet Union since Stalin*. Bloomington: Indiana University Press 1980, pp. 213–19. See also *Izvestia*, February 25 1989; Charles E. Ziegler, "Nationalism, Religion and Equality among Ethnic Minorities: Some Observations on the Soviet Case," *Journal of Ethnic Studies*, 13, 1985, pp. 9–32 (p. 27).

69. Rokkan, Stein, "Territories, Centers and Peripheries: Toward a Geoethnic–Geoeconomic–Geopolitical Model of Differentiation within Western Europe," in Jean Gottmann (ed.), *Center and Periphery. Spatial Variation in Politics*. Beverly Hills: Sage 1980; and Rokkan, Stein, "The Survival of Distinctiveness," in Stein Rokkan et al. (eds.), *Economy, Territory, Identity: The Politics of European Peripheries*. Beverly Hills: Sage 1983.

70. For an interesting comparative discussion of the implications of language choices for political community, see William Safran, "Language, Ideology, and State-Building: A Comparison of Policies in France, Israel, and the Soviet Union," *International Political Science Review*, 13:4, 1992, pp. 397–414.

71. Weber, Max, *Economy and Society* (eds. Guenther Roth and Claus Wittich). Berkeley: University of California Press 1968, pp. 577, 1181.

72. Ibid., p. 948.

73. Hintze, Otto, *Historical Essays* (ed. Felix Gilbert). New York: Oxford University Press 1975, pp. 173–74.

74. Gramsci, Antonio, *Selections from the Prison Notebooks* (eds. Q. Hoare and G. N. Smith). London: Lawrence & Wishart 1971, p. 54, n. 4.

75. Buci-Glucksmann, Christine, *Gramsci and the State*. London: Lawrence & Wishart 1980, p. 57.

76. Gramsci, Antonio, *Selections from the Prison Notebooks* (eds. Q. Hoare and G. N. Smith). London: Lawrence & Wishart 1971, p. 117.

77. Buci-Glucksmann, Christine, *Gramsci and the State*. London: Lawrence & Wishart 1980, p. 57.

78. Gramsci, Antonio, *Selections from the Prison Notebooks* (eds. Q. Hoare and G. N. Smith). London: Lawrence & Wishart 1971, p. 238.

79. Volobuev, P.V. in S. D. Skazkin (ed.), *Dokumenty sovetsko-italiansko konferentssii istorikov 8–10 aprelja 1968 goda: absoliutizm v Zapadno Evrope i Rossii: russko-italianskie sviazi vo vtoro polovine XIX veka*. Akademiia nauk SSSR, Institut vseobshcheĭ istorii, Institut istorii SSSR. Moscow: Nauka 1970, p. 192.

80. See Samuel H. Baron, "Plekhanov, Trotsky, and the Development of Soviet Historiography," *Soviet Studies*, 26:3, pp. 380–83.

81. Hroch, Miroslav, "How Much Does Nation Formation Depend on Nationalism?" *East European Politics and Societies*, 4:1, 1990, p. 109.

82. Magris, Claudio, *Donau*. Oslo: Cappelen 1991, p. 270, translated from Norwegian by this author.

83. For an interesting discussion of these questions among Miroslav Hroch, Ernest Gellner, and Roman Szporluk, see *East European Politics and Society*, 4:1, 1990, pp. 101–50.

84. Hroch, Miroslav, "From National Movement to the Fully-formed Nation. The Nation-Building Process in Europe," *New Left Review*, 198, 1993, p. 6.

85. Ibid., p. 7.

86. Kann, Robert, "Zur Problematik der Nationalitätenfrage in der Habsburgermonarchie 1848–1918," in Adam Wandruszka and Peter Urbanitsch (eds.), *Die Habsburgermonarchie 1848–1918*, 3/2. Vienna: Verlag der Österreichischen Akademie der Wissenschaften 1980, pp. 1321–330.

87. Stalin, Joseph, "Political Report of the Central Committee to the Sixteenth Congress of the CPSU b June 27, 1930," *Pravda*, 177, June 1930; Stalin Reference Archive, marxists.org 2000: http: //www2.cddc.vt.edu/marxists/reference/archive/stalin/works/1930/aug/27.htm.

88. Stalin, Joseph, "*Marxism and Problems of Linguistics,*" published in the June 20, July 4, and August 2, 1950 issues of *Pravda*. Stalin Reference Archive, marxists.org 2000: http: //www2.cddc.vt.edu/marxists/reference/archive/stalin/works/1950/jun/20.htm.

89. Pijl, Kees van der, "Soviet Socialism and Passive Revolution," in Stephen Gill (ed.), *Gramsci. Historical Materialism and International Relations*. Cambridge Studies in International Relations 26. Cambridge: Cambridge University Press 1993, p. 241. See also Robert V. Daniels, "Part I. Marxism and Leninism," in Robert V. Daniels, *The Rise and Fall of Communism in Russia*. New Haven, CT: Yale University Press 2007.

90. Martin, Terry, *The Affirmative Action Empire. Nations and Nationalism in the Soviet Union, 1923–1939*. Ithaca & London: Cornell University Press 2001, p. 15.

91. Gramsci, Antonio, *Selections from the Prison Notebooks* (eds. Q. Hoare and G. N. Smith). London: Lawrence & Wishart 1971. pp. 104–5.

92. Daniels, Robert V., "Stalinist Ideology as False Consciousness," in Robert V. Daniels, *Trotsky, Stalin, and Socialism*. Boulder, CO: Westview Press 1991, quotations p. 176. See also the analysis of the relationship between the English aristocracy and middle classes in Karl Marx and Frederick Engels, *Articles on Britain*. Moscow: Progress 1971.

93. Pijl, Kees van der, "Soviet Socialism and Passive Revolution," in Stephen Gill (ed.), *Gramsci. Historical Materialism and International Relations*. Cambridge Studies in International Relations 26. Cambridge: Cambridge University Press 1993, pp. 246–47.

94. Gramsci, Antonio, *Selections from the Prison Notebooks* (eds. Q. Hoare and G. N. Smith). London: Lawrence & Wishart 1971, p. 106.

95. See S. Frederick Starr, "Tsarist Government: The Imperial Dimension," in Jeremy R. Azrael (ed.), *Soviet Nationality Policies and Practices*. New York: Praeger 1978, pp. 3–38.

96. Raeff, Marc, "The Russian Autocracy and its Officials," *Harvard Slavic Studies*, 4, 1957, p. 59.

97. Anderson, Perry, *Lineages of the Absolutist State*. London: New Left Books 1974; Hintze, Otto, *Historical Essays* (ed. Felix Gilbert). New York: Oxford University Press 1975; Skocpol, Theda, *States and Social Revolutions. A Comparative Analysis of France, Russia, and China*. Cambridge: Cambridge University Press 1978.

98. See Karl Marx, "Preface to *A Contribution to the Critique of Political Economy*," in K. Marx, F. Engels, V. Lenin, *On Historical Materialism. A Collection*. Moscow: Progress 1972, pp. 136–44. For an excellent modern, analytical exposition, see G. A. Cohen, *Karl Marx's Theory of History: A Defence*. Oxford: Clarendon Press 1978.

99. Avrekh, A. in S. D. Skazkin (ed.), Dokumenty sovetsko-italiansko konferentssii istorikov 8–10 aprelja 1968 goda: absoliutizm v Zapadnoĭ Evrope i Rossii: russko-italianskie sviazi vo vtoroĭ polovine XIX veka. Akademiia nauk SSSR, Institut vseobshcheĭ istorii, Institut istorii SSSR. Moscow: Nauka 1970, p. 222. See as well Alexander Gerschenkron, "Soviet Marxism and Absolutism," *Slavic Review*, 30:4, 1971, pp. 853–69; and Arne Kommisrud, Relativ tilbakeliggenhet som problemfelt og forklaringsfaktor i sammenliknende historisk forskning. Magistergradsavhandling i statsvitenskap. Universitetet i Oslo 1982, pp. 251–55.

100. Garushyants, Iurii, "Ob aziatskom sposobe proizvodstva," *Voprosy Istorii*, 2, 1966, pp. 84–100, (p. 99). See also L. V. Danilova, "Disskusia po vaznoi probleme," *Voprosy Filosofii*, 12, 1965. For the fate of the concept during the Stalin era, see Marian Sawer, "The Politics of Historiography: Russian Socialism and the Question of the Asiatic Mode of Production 1906–1931," *Critique*, 10:1, 1979, 15–35.

101. Shapiro, A. L., "Ob absoliutizme v Rossii," *Istoria SSSR*, May 1968, pp. 69–81. The discussion was introduced by A. I. Avrekh's, "Russii absoliutizm i evo rol v utverzhdenie kapitalizma v Rossi," *Istoria SSSR*, February 1968, pp. 82–103. Here he attacked the official Soviet view of Russian absolutism. P. V. Volubuev is here cited following S. D. Skazkin (ed.), *Dokumenty sovetsko-italiansko konferentssii istorikov 8–10 aprelja 1968 goda*. Moscow 1970, p. 196.

102. Shunkov, V. I., et al. (eds.), *Perekhod ot feodalizma k kapitalizmu v Rossii: materialy Vsesoiuzno diskusii*. Moscow: Nauka 1969, pp. 5, 41. See also the contribution of K. N. Tarnovskii in V. V. Adamov, et al. (eds.), *Voprosy istorii kapitalisticheskoi Rossii: problema mnogoukladnosti*. Sverdlovsk: Uralskii gosudarstvennyi universitet 1972.

103. See Raymond Boudon, *The Logic of Social Action. An Introduction to Sociological Analysis*. London: Routledge & Keegan Paul 1981, pp. 132–33.

104. See the two collections of essays Alexander Gerschenkron, *Economic Backwardness in Historical Perspective: A Book of Essays*. Cambridge, MA: Belknap Press 1962; and Alexander Gerschenkron, *Continuity in History and Other Essays*. Cambridge, MA: Belknap Press of Harvard University Press 1968, as well as his four lectures delivered at Cambridge University in 1968 collected in Alexander Gerschenkron, *Europe in the Russian Mirror: Four Lectures in Economic History: Four Lectures in Economic History*. London: Cambridge University Press 1970. See as well Arne Kommisrud, *Relativ tilbakeliggenhet som problemfelt og forklaringsfaktor*

i sammenliknende historisk forskning. Magistergradsavhandling i statsvitenskap. Universitetet i Oslo 1982, pp. 52–54, 261.

105. Personally I have benefited greatly from conversations with my now late colleague at the University of Tromsø, Gunnar Opeide, who was associate professor of Russian culture studies, regarding the view of Alexander Gerschenskron's theories. See also Gunnar Opeide, "Tilbakeliggenhetens problem," *Forum Øst*, 3:3, 1985, pp. 8–30. The exposition is based on those conversations as well as the sources referred above.

106. Quoted in Robert C. Tucker, *Stalin in Power: The Revolution from Above, 1928–1941*. New York: Norton 1990, p. 9.

107. Daniels, Robert V., "Stalin: Revolutionary or Counterrevolutionary?" *Problems of Communism*, September–October 1989, pp. 81–86.

108. Romanovich-Slavatinskii, A., Dvorianstvo v Rossii ot nachala XVIII vieka do otmieny kriepostnogo prava: svod materiala i priugotovitel'nye etiudy dlia istoricheskago izsliedovaniia A. Romanovich-Slavatinskago. St. Petersburg: Tip. Ministerstva vnutrennikh diel, 1870. Issued as *Slavistic Printings and Reprintings no 100*. The Hague: Mouton 1968, pp. 487–88.

109. For a comprehensive view of these offices, see Ivan Adreevskii, *O namestnikakh, voevodakh i gubernatorakh*. St. Petersburg: E: Prats 1864. See also John P. Ledonne, "Russian Governors General, 1775–1825. Territorial or Functional Administration?" *Cahiers du Monde russe*, 42:1, Janvier–Mars 2001, pp. 5–30.

110. Bezkrovnyi, L. G., *Russkaia armiia i flot v XIX veke Moscow: Voen.-èkon. potentsial Rossii*. Akademiia nauk SSSR. Institut istorii SSSR. Moskva: Nauka 1973, pp. 19, 23, 26, 34, 48, 52, 55, 65, 88, 90, 93.

111. Galuzo, P. G., "Kolonialnaia sistema imperialistitcheskoi Rossii," in Akademia Nauk SSSR, Institut istorii, Istoria SSSR c drevneishikh vremen do nashikh dnei, vol 6, *Rossiia v period imperializma 1900–1917 gg*, Moscow: Nauka 1968, pp. 309–12. By the same author, "Das Kolonialsystem des russischen Imperialismus am Vorabend der Oktoberrevolution," *Zeitschrift fur Geschichtswissenschaft* Berlin/GDR 15:6, 1967.

112. Kliuchevskii, Vasilii, *Kurs russkoĭ istorii: sochineniia v deviati tomakh* I. Moscow: Mysl 1987, p. 50.

113. Hodnett, Grey, *Leadership in the Soviet National Republics. A Quantitative Study of Recruitment Policy*. Oakville, Ontario: Mosaic Press 1978, pp. 104ff.

114. See Alfred G. Meyer, "USSR Incorporated," *Slavic Review*, 20, 1961, pp. 366–76; and Alfred G. Meyer, *The Soviet Political System: An Interpretation*. New York: Random House 1965.

115. Strugatskii, Boris, "Zhit interesnee chem pisat," *Literaturnaya Gazeta*, April 10, 1991, p. 9.

116. Voslenskii, Mikhail, *Nomenklatura. Gospodstvuiushchii klass Sovetskogo Soiuza*. London: Overseas Publications Interchange 1984. See also the discussion in Jerry Hough, *The Soviet Prefects: The Local Party Organs in Industrial Decision-making*. Cambridge, MA: Harvard University Press 1969, pp. 114–16, 150–70; and B. Harasymiw, "Die sowjetische Nomenklatur 1," *Osteuropa*, 7, 1977, pp. 583–98; and B. Harasymiw, "Die sowjetische Nomenklatur 2," *Osteuropa*, 8, 1977, pp.

665–81. On the origin of the system, see T. H. Rigby, "Staffing USSR Incorporated: The Origins of the Nomenklatura System," *Soviet Studies*, 40:4, 1988, pp. 523–37. For a discussion of the nomenklatura and Soviet social stratification, see also Alec Nove, "History, Hierarchy and Nationalities," and "Is there a Ruling Class in the USSR," in Alec Nove, *Political Economy and Soviet Socialism*. London: G. Allen & Unwin 1979, pp. 2–26, 195–219.

117. Miliukov, Paul, *Russia and its Crisis*. Chicago: University of Chicago Press, 1905; *History of Russia*. New York: Funk & Wagnalls 1968; Paul Miliukov, *Skizzen Russischer Kulturgeschichte*. Leipzig: Verlag Otto Migand 1898. See as well Thomas M. Bohn, *Russische Geschichtswissenschaft von 1880 bis 1905: Pavel N. Miljukov und die Moskauer Schule*. Beiträge zur Geschichte Osteuropas 25. Köln: Böhlau Verlag 1998.

118. Baron, Samuel H., *Plekhanov; The Father of Russian Marxism*. Stanford: Stanford University Press 1963; Baron, Samuel H., "Plekhanov, Trotsky, and the Development of Soviet Historiography," *Soviet Studies*, 26:3, 1974, pp. 380–95; Georges Plekhanov, *Introduction a l'histoire Sociale de la Russie*. Paris: Editions Bossard 1926; Sawer, Marian, "Plekhanov on Russian History: A Marxist Approach to Historical Pluralism," *Science and Society*, 39:1, 1975, pp. 292–317.

119. Baron, Samuel, "Plekhanov, Trotsky, and the Development of Soviet Historiography," *Soviet Studies*, 26:3, 1974, p. 384.

120. Plekhanov, Georges, *Introduction a l'histoire Sociale de la Russie*. Paris: Editions Bossard 1926, p. 61–62.

121. Ibid., pp. 4–5.

122. Baron, Samuel, "Plekhanov, Trotsky, and the Development of Soviet Historiography," *Soviet Studies*, 26:3, 1974, p. 384.

123. For the details on the etymological history of these concepts, see Ladis Kristof, "The State Idea, the National Idea and the Image of the Fatherland," *Orbis*, 11, Spring 1967.

124. See Boris E. Nolde, *Iurii Samarin i ego vremia*. Paris: Impr. de Navarre 1926, pp. 45, 47–48.

125. See, for example, Marc Raeff, "Patterns of Russian Imperial Policy Toward the Nationalities," in Edward Allworth (ed.), *Soviet Nationality Problems*. New York: Columbia University Press 1971, pp. 22–42.

126. See E. H. Carr, *The History of the Russian Revolution*. London: MacMillan 1978, reprint. The complete 14-volume series. The original editions appeared between 1950 and 1978 and had the distinctions between the concepts realism and utopianism as a main organizing principle.

127. See the discussions in Robert V. Daniels, *Trotsky, Stalin and Socialism*. Boulder: Westview Press 1991.

128. About the parallels between bolshevism and Italian fascism in these matters, see A. James Gregor, *Italian Fascism and Developmental Dictatorship*. Princeton, NJ: Princeton University Press 1979, pp. 162ff, 206ff, 300–334.

129. For the history of this concept see Erwin Oberlander, *Sowjetpatriotismus und Geschichte, Dokumentation*. Cologne: Verlag Wissenschaft und Politik 1964.

130. See Michail Agursky, *The Third Rome. National Bolshevism in the USSR*. Boulder, CO: Westview Press 1987.

131. Nove, Alec, "History, Hierarchy and Nationalities," and "Is there a Ruling Class in the USSR," in Alec Nove, *Political Economy and Soviet Socialism*. London: G. Allen & Unwin 1979, pp. 2–26, 195–219.

132. See Gerhard Simon, "Nationalismus und Nationalitätenpolitik in der Sowjetunion seit Stalin," *Berichte des Bundesinstituts für Ostwissenschaftliche und Internationale Studien*, Köln, 1979.

133. See L. V. Ostapenko and A. A. Susokalov, "Etnosotsialnye osobennosti vosproizvodstva intelligentsia," *Sotsiologicheskie Issledovaniia*, 1, 1983, p 10.

134. See N. A. Petrovichev, *Vazhnyĭ faktor vozrastaniia rukovodiashcheĭ roli KPSS*. Moskva: Politizdat, 1979, p. 71.

135. Miller, John, "Nomenklatura: Check on Localism," in T. H. Rigby and H. Harasymiw (eds.), *Leadership Selection and Patron-Client Relations in the USSR and Yugoslavia*. Selected papers from the second World Congress for Soviet and East European Studies [Garmisch-Partenkirchen, 1980] London: Allen & Unwin 1983, pp. 62–97.

136. For the details of the Habsburg administration, see Adam Wandruszka and Peter Urbanitsch (eds.), *Die Habsburgermonarchie 1848–1918*, vol. 2, Verwaltung und Rechtwesen. Vienna: Verlag der Österreichischen Akademie der Wissenschaften 1975; and Oscar Jaszi, *The Dissolution of the Habsburg Monarchy*. Chicago: University of Chicago Press 1929.

137. Hugelmann, Karl Gottfried (ed.), *Das Nationalitätenrecht des alten Osterreich*. Wien-Leipzig: W. Braumüller, Universitäts-Verlagsbuchhandlung 1934, p. 280; and W. A. Jenks, "Economics, Constitutionalism, Administration and Class Structure," *Austria History Yearbook* 3/1 1967, pp. 53ff.

138. Kann, Robert, *The Multinational Empire: Nationalism and National Reform in the Habsburg Monarchy 1848–1918*, vol. 1. New York: Columbia University Press 1950, pp. 30–31.

139. Kann, Robert, *The Multinational Empire: Nationalism and National Reform in the Habsburg Monarchy 1848–1918*, vol. 1. New York: Columbia University Press 1950, pp. 33ff. (quotation p. 36).

140. Conze, Werner, "Die Strukturkrise des östlichen Mitteleuropas für und nach 1918," *Vierteljahrehäfte für Zeitgeschichte* I, 1953, pp. 319ff; Rothfehls, Hans, "Grundätzliches zum Problem der Nationaliät," *Historische Zeitschrift* 174, 1952; Kann, Robert, *The Multinational Empire: Nationalism and National Reform in the Habsburg Monarchy 1848–1918*, vol. 1. New York: Columbia University Press 1950, p. 33ff.

141. Sutter, Bernhold, "Politische und rechtliche Stellung der deutschen in Österreich 1848–1918," in Adam Wandruszka and Peter Urbanitsch (eds.), *Die Habsburgermonarchie 1848–1918*, vol. 31: Die Völker des Reiches. Vienna: 1980, pp. 215–40. Furor teutonicus: see Solomon Wank, "The Impact of the Dual Alliance on the Germans in Austria and Vice-versa," *East Central Europe*, 7:2, 1980; and Andrew G. Whiteside, *The Socialism of Fools. Georg Ritter von Schönerer and Austrian Pan-Germanism*. Berkeley: University of California Press 1975.

142. Hugelmann, Karl Gottfried (ed.), *Das Nationalitätenrecht des alten Osterreich*. Wien-Leipzig: W. Braumüller, Universitäts-Verlagsbuchhandlung 1934, pp. 90, 124, 125.

143. See Robert Kann, *The Multinational Empire: Nationalism and National Reform in the Habsburg Monarchy 1848–1918*, vols. 1 and 2. New York: Columbia University Press 1950; and also his "Zur Problematik der Nationalitätenfrage in der Habsburgermonarchie 1848–1918," in Adam Wandruszka and Peter Urbanitsch (eds.), *Die Habsburgermonarchie 1848–1918*, vol. 3/2. Vienna: Verlag der Österreichischen Akademie der Wissenschaften 1980, pp. 1321–30.

144. Ibid.

145. See Walker Connor, *The National Questions in Marxist–Leninist Theory and Strategy*. Princeton, NJ: Princeton University Press 1984, pp. 300–322.

146. See Robert A Lewis, Richard H. Rowland, and Ralph S. Clem, *Nationality and Population Change in Russia and the USSR: An Evaluation of Census Data, 1897–1970*. New York: Praeger 1976; and Paul Kolstoe, "The State of Statelessness," and Paul Kolstoe and Andrei Edemsky, "Russia's Policy Towards the Diaspora," in Paul Kolstoe, *Russians in the Former Soviet Republics*. London: Hurst 1995, chaps. 5 and 10.

147. Lewin, Moshe, *The Gorbachev Phenomenon*. Berkeley: University of California Press 1988, p. 1.

148. See the various contributions to *Problems of Communism* 40, November–December 1991, especially "Moscow, August 1991—The Coup de Grace: A Symposium," pp. 1–63.

149. Hroch, Miroslav, "Part I," in Miroslav Hroch, *Social Preconditions of National Revival in Europe. A Comparative Analysis of the Social Composition of Patriotic Groups among the Smaller European Nations*. Cambridge: Cambridge University Press 1986.

150. For a discussion of the concept of cumulative causality in historical sociology, see Stephen Kalberg, "Conjunctural Interaction and the Context of Patterned Action," in Stephen Kalberg, *Max Weber's Comparative Historical Sociology*. Cambridge: Polity Press 1994, pp. 168–77.

151. See Christian Schmidt-Häuer, "Das Imperium schlägt zurück," *Die Zeit*, December 7, 1990.

152. On the former non-existence of such a connection, see Roman Szporluk, "Dilemmas of Russian Nationalism," in Rachel Denber (ed.), *The Soviet Nationality Reader. The Disintegration in Context*. Boulder, CO: Westview Press 1992, pp. 513–17.

153. Duncan, P. J. S., "The Rebirth of Politics in Russia," in Geoffrey A. Hosking, Jonathan Aves, and Peter J. S. Duncan, *The Road to Post-Communism. Independent Political Movements in the Soviet Union 1985–1991*. London: Pinter Publishers 1992, pp. 67–123.

154. A term coined by Roman Szporluk, see his "Dilemmas of Russian Nationalism," in Rachel Denber (ed.), *The Soviet Nationality Reader. The Disintegration in Context*. Boulder, CO: Westview Press 1992.

155. Roeder, Philip G., "Soviet Federalism and Ethnic Mobilization," in Rachel Denber (ed.), *The Soviet Nationality Reader. The Disintegration in Context*. Boulder, CO: Westview Press 1992, pp. 147–78.

156. Hroch, Miroslav, "Old Nationalism or New National Movements," *The Oslo Congress: Minority Protection and Human Rights in the New Europe*. Leangkollen January–February 1991.

157. Aves, Jonathan, "The Evolution of Independent Political Movements After 1988," in Geoffrey A. Hosking, Jonathan Aves, and Peter J. S. Duncan, *The Road to Post-Communism. Independent Political Movements in the Soviet Union 1985–1991*. London: Pinter Publishers 1992, pp. 29–66; Simon, Gerhard, "Bricht die Sowjetunion auseinander?" *Berichte des Bundesinstituts für ostwissenschaftliche und internationale Studien* 18, 1990.

158. Waldenberg, Marek, *Kwestie Narodowe w Europie Srodkowo-Wschodniej: dzieje, idée*. Warszawa: Wydawn, Nauk, PWN, 1992, p. 393.

159. For a discussion of the concept, see K. McRae, "The Principle of Territoriality and the Principle of Personality in Multilingual States," *Linguistics*, 158, 1975, pp. 33–54. See also R. Davison, "Nationalism as an Ottoman Problem and the Ottoman Response," in William W. Haddad and William Ochsenwald (eds.), *Nationalism in a Non-National State: The Dissolution of the Ottoman Empire*. Columbus: Ohio State University Press 1977, pp. 25–56 for a discussion of the millet system.

Chapter Three

East European Development in the Light of Stein Rokkan's European Macro Model

The 1960s and 1970s saw a renaissance for historical–sociological work in, or rather on the periphery of, Western social sciences. As a genre of the social sciences, it could be shown in many ways to continue the classic tradition in sociology and political science. In a field of tension between, on the one hand, specific historical research emphasizing what is characteristic in the development sequences of certain countries and regions and, on the other hand, the generalizing research in social sciences, the discipline made relatively bold comparisons of structures and processes in different societies and historical periods.

However today, the field of historical sociology is said to be in a state of crisis, determined in part by the more overriding crisis characterizing the political project from which its modern reformulation has sprung after the end of the cold war and the attraction of poststructuralism to radical intellectuals. Matters of culture and ideology, meaning and identity are said to be either neglected or inadequately integrated in this subject area, which is afflicted by a general structural—materialistic determinism.[1]

I will here attempt to contribute to that discussion by going into the question of East European development using a long-term perspective. Without rejecting any possible fruitfulness of a poststructuralist approach, I shall do this in the light of some of the principles underlying the construction of Stein Rokkan's European macro model. His contribution may have been somewhat superseded today, but I believe that it is nevertheless suited as a starting point for elaborating the discipline without rejecting the considerable insights gained in the 1970s. Rokkan's four-phase model will be taken as my point of departure.

PHASE 1: THE PROBLEMS OF STATE BUILDING

State Building in the Narrower Sense

The process of political penetration took place in Western Europe through the formation of nonterritorial-based elites in the absolute monarchies. As a offspring of the Parsonian sociological tradition, the starting point for Rokkan's view of state building, in the more restricted sense, had been a Weberian perspective. Max Weber emphasized explicitly that he was mainly interested in dominance only so far as it is manifested through administration, that is, in its instrumental aspects.[2] A major part of Max Weber's analysis is dedicated to the way armies can be organized and held together. It describes the administrative problems military conquerors have to face when trying to integrate a conquered territory, and the factors that determine the size of an army: why the military skeleton of a state tends to be large or small, centralized or decentralized, collegial or hierarchical.

With territorial expansion, a dynamics toward progressive fragmentation takes effect. Transferring more authority to subordinate links makes it increasingly difficult for the prince or commanding leader of the state to maintain personal control of the administration and of subordinates. At the same time, these subordinates start to receive material rewards on a larger scale and on a more permanent basis than before. This increases their social status and consequently their independence from the prince as their supreme overlord.

In the case of the Balkans, Rokkan's city-belt theory seems to justify a simple Weberian analysis as well. Historically, the typical political form in the region had been either the large multiethnic empire, or the fragmented ethnical groups that had not succeeded in establishing their own states. In the 19th century the position of Eastern Europe resembled that of colonial peoples in Asia and Africa, except that the former were dominated by the land, and the latter by maritime powers. The All-Russian Empire, the Habsburg monarchy, Prussia (the German Reich) and the Ottoman Turkish Empire were not able to penetrate the city belt, but more or less conquered the land between the belt and their respective city centers. According to one author, the "triangle of empires" between Byzantium, Vienna and Moscow could have functioned, if we follow Rokkan's way of reasoning, so that they, for centuries to come, emptied the territorial space between them.[3] The strength of the empires was contradictory to the development of a city belt in Eastern Europe, that is, "the state-centralizing efforts prevented other cities from growing and to achieve the kind of dynamic authority characterizing the cities within the belt."[4] The military and fiscal imperatives of the Habsburg and Ottoman empires had not least a retarding effect, demographic as well as socioeconomic, on the Balkan borderlands they shared.

As for the pattern in the southeastern European countries under the Ottoman empire, the Turks' conquest of Balkan resulted in the elimination of the local ethnic nobility, a fact that had great consequences for the region's future development. The most important political consequences were a return to a system based on clan institutions (universal organizations), the *zadruga*, the *bratstvo*, and the *pleme*, particularist traditions, and a notable decline in literacy. The primitive codes of honor, not very different from the culture of the Southern Italian mafiosi, which survived into the modern period, contributed and partly accounted for the repulsive practices that invariably emerged during the Balkan wars. Traditionally, the Orthodox Church supported the secular power. The lack of dualism of church and state continued under the Sultan, himself appointing the patriarch, as the emperors of Byzantium had done before. Church administration was *in toto* adopted as an instrument for secular administration. The bishops became government officials, and by the middle of the 18th century both the Bulgarian and the Serb church had slipped under the control of the ecumenical (i.e., Greek) patriarchate. The Orthodox Church under the Ottoman Turks was mainly concerned with surviving and was, therefore, characterized by a fundamental conservatism.

From a position paradoxically freer than anywhere else in Eastern Europe with Christian rulers at the end of the 16th century, history until the early 20th century, the end of Turkish supremacy, is about the dissolution of the central power and the consolidation of a local landowning class at the expense of the peasants, while the towns lost their commercial and intellectual importance. However, the most prominent feature of agrarian conditions was the breakdown of any fixed, civil system imposed from above.[5]

Indeed, Balkan bandits (*haiduks*), encouraged by the region's mountainous terrain, established a tradition of local insurrection that antedated the wars of independence and social revolutions. One should however be skeptical of ascribing 19th- and 20th-century nationalist feelings to isolated and uncoordinated acts of belligerency, as was done by members of the liberationalist school of Balkan historians. Still, as pointed by Eric Hobsbawn, when the social bandits built an operational support system with the assistance of the peasantry, they constructed an infrastructure that could be of inestimable value in the event of a massive uprising.[6]

John Lampe summarizes the correlation of forces as follows:

> This potential for military, or at least guerilla, action in their upland retreats combined with low density of lowland population to give the Balkan peasantry some leverage in a three-cornered struggle for power between themselves, the Ottoman central government, and the local Moslem military and judicial authorities. The result of this struggle before the nineteenth century was not clear-cut victory for any side but rather another case of "reciprocal exhaustion."[7]

The national movements in the Balkans, among Serbs, Bulgarians and Greeks, assumed the character of mass movements before the emergence of a civil society and constitutional government, leading to armed revolts that drove out the Ottoman occupation from country to country. The salient fact of both Bulgarian and Serbian development is precisely that in both countries the retreat of Turkish rule just before the beginning of the modern era meant the end of traditional rule by the landowners "as the landed elite, which had existed for several centuries, was ejected."

This gave the region a unique agrarian pattern, with expulsion of the landed aristocracy, which distinguished it from both Western and Central Europe. However, while rural recruits comprised the bulk of revolutionary contingents and military regulars, non-village residents virtually monopolized leadership roles and, with a few exceptions, concentrated their energies on the construction of independent national states. "Three competitors vied for control of the new political system. One remained the bureaucracy, a second become the politicians who achieved prominence through party politics, and the third was the prince." Power—as well as wealth—was on the whole, concentrated in the hands of the bureaucratic/military ruling class, while the majority of the population continued to live in great poverty. Subsequent to the birth and growth of a centralized polity, state interests advocating imperial aggrandizement largely ignored peasant concerns seeking social justice and economic change.[8]

Seen in the light of Rokkan's models, the political aspects of the turn of the Balkans toward modernity, where the state itself became the dominant class, which filled the social vacuum, is on the one hand almost outside the definitional categories of Rokkan's so-called critical junctures of splits and alliances. The lack of class power allows the state, captured by a small faction, to become the dominant force in national politics. This situation of "passive revolution," in which where "one stands in relation to the state apparatus makes up the main social datum," on the other hand is easily explained by the Rokkan city-belt theory.[9] When introducing Western European institutions into their own polities pro forma, the functions of comparatively strong autonomous spheres and centers of powers had to be performed by some other agency—the state. Thus from the start the modernizers were involved in the contradictory project of creating a civil society from above. Whenever civil society moved to fulfill the role assigned to it by modernization, initiatives from below were contained and the relationship of rulers–ruled reimposed. "The process of enforced social mobilization formed the basis of the statism often mentioned as the main characteristic of interwar Central and Eastern Europe. And even when the state did succeed in building structures of civil society, it often proved unwilling to relinquish control."[10]

Rokkan's city-belt theory tends to fit in with a view of the region as a *transitional* or *shatter* zone of the European continent, which has often been subject to foreign domination. Due to the relative weakness of East European nations as compared to outside powers, the politics of the area have been governed by the principle of *Primat der Aussenpolitik* over domestic political developments. In modern history most of them only rarely were allowed to have their independent states. This approach also does much to explain the relative backwardness of Eastern Europe as compared with Western Europe. Foreign empires have shown little concern about economic progress in their peripheries (Bohemia, locked in the midst of German lands, being an exception). And the lack of native political institutions did not facilitate the growth of democracy, although nations under German rule, in contrast to the despotic tsarist or Ottoman empires, profited from the concept of the *Rechtsstaat.* The adherents to a geopolitical approach see Communism as basically a new phase of outside intervention in Eastern Europe.

Weaknesses of the Weberian Approach to State Penetration

The "blind spot" of Weberian state theory, however, is its lack of a systematic analysis of social alliances during the state-building process. When turning to the comparison between the Southeastern European and the Central European case, elaborating Rokkan's debt to the neo-Marxist analysis of Barrington Moore Jr. will be of great importance. Barrington Moore Jr.'s model posits four sets of actors in the change from traditional to modern society: the central dynasty and its bureaucracy, the trading and manufacturing bourgeoisie in the cities, the lords of the land, and the peasantry. None of these four sets of actors is strong enough to constitute a center-forming collectivity on its own: the model forces them to enter into coalitions where at least one set of actors will be left outside to form an opposition front against the center-building alliance.[11]

The contrast in the resource bases for political consolidation goes far to explain the differences between the Western and Eastern systems in their internal structure and in the character of their mass politics. This is the thrust of Moore's detailed analysis: the greater the distance between the urban and the landed economies, the greater the likelihood of an unchecked and unbalanced growth of the state, the greater, in fact, the chances for a cumulation of crises in the transition to mass politics.

At the transition from the 15th to the 16th century, when the West began its dramatic and crucial transformation into a modern, capitalist world, Central and Eastern Europe lagged catastrophically behind. Rigid feudal structures were re-created and introduced in areas where they had never existed before, the much discussed second serfdom. In contrast to Western Europe, production in this part of the world was carried out by a large number of serfs working at the landowners' latifundia. The system of serfdom spread in the German, Czech, Hungarian and Russian areas and in the Romanian principalities, where it was introduced just before the French Revolution. Because of differences in their domestic development, these countries could not follow the course initiated by the English Industrial Revolution and the French political revolution, and thus dropped even further behind.

One distinctive feature of the Prussian, Hungarian, Polish and Russian societies was the fact that the aristocracy had "entrenched" itself and survived socially and politically. Whereas Western European structural changes in the economy were followed by changes in the social structure, in Central and Eastern Europe "the structure of society remained far more rigid and more backward than that of the economy. Social organization and the pattern of attitudes and values remained far more traditional than the economy itself. Even if the gross national product per head increased considerably, the heads which owned it did not change to any great degree."[12] In the aristocratic set of values, trade, business and industry were despised and looked down upon as "Jewish" activities. All socially aspiring elements were highly influenced by their retrospective anticapitalist and parasitic lifestyle.

If proper account is taken of the special political framework given by the dissolution of the Polish state, the Poles too fit into the Central European correlation of social forces. Though the legal status of the *szlachta* was annulled in 1795 by the partitioning powers, its ideals lived on. The Polish intelligentsia heavily descended from it and was culturally and mentally anchored to it, thus preserving a uniform code of values and networks of social connections across the borders of the three partitioning empires that divided Poland among them. In this way the *kultura szlachecka*—with its ideas of exclusivity, unanimity, equality, resistance and individualism, which did not at all amount to supporting "bourgeois values," continued to provide the guideline for Polish social and political thought. "It did not pay much attention to the prosaic, down-to-earth concerns of private law and could hardly understand Napoleon's famous dictum that the essence of freedom is a good Civil Code."[13]

The possibility of developing various strategies to combine old social power structures and modern industrial forms explains some of the differences in various European countries' political development in the 19th and 20th centuries, *Explicanda* in Stein Rokkan's model. Many of the problems that democracy experienced in the interwar period are usually ascribed to this fact.[14] The star example is of course Hungary, which was the least democratic country in interwar Central Europe, as the electoral system (with suffrage restricted to less than 30 percent and an open ballot in rural areas) guaranteed the ruling United Party a permanent majority. Here the landed elite in the 19th century had found a way to induce a significant number of a Jewish pariah bourgeoisie into an alliance by raising them to the highest social level. As part of this policy, the government made sure to lay anti-Semitism politically dead among the Magyars for a generation; and there, therefore, also were "few ghettos to inhibit departures from Jewish Orthodoxy."[15] "220 of 336 new Jewish nobles acquired their ranks after 1900, in the last two decades of the Habsburg monarchy's existence, when Hungary's industrial transformation finally became massive" and were the products of that transformation. Of the same "346 Jewish noble families, 202 resided in Budapest at the time of ennoblement, and of these 154 were directly associated with the world of finance, commerce, and industry."[16]

Furthermore, Jewish nobles were not only members of the new capitalist class of turn-of-the century Hungary, but among them were Hungary's capitalist elite. "There is considerable evidence that after they acquired nobility, our Jewish businessmen and their families behaved in a fashion wholly reminiscent of the old nobles."[17] Many of the richest Jewish families therefore allied themselves with the great landowners in maintaining the dominance of the aristocracy over the political process. Hungary's capitalists, the men that might in theory have been a bourgeois challenge to the Magyar nobles, under those circumstances failed to do so. As pointed out by Oscar Jaszi the middle classes not just in Budapest, but also throughout the monarchy became "moral vassals" of the system as well.[18] Although, the right-wing ethos had been deeply rooted in pre-1918 Hungarian history, the experiences of the year 1919 added to the intensity of right-wing sentiment by reinforcing the established pattern.

Hungary ended up on the losing side in the Great War of 1914–1918. On the basis of the Trianon treaty signed on June 4, 1920, Hungary lost 71.4 percent of its territory and 63.6 percent of its population. Nearly one-third of all Magyars found themselves living outside of Hungary, mostly in the new Romanian, Yugoslav and Czechoslovakian states. Romania alone received a larger share of the country's former territory than that which was left to Hungary. Hungary, between the wars, was mentally dominated by the aftermaths of the Trianon treaty, which produced a trauma—a psychological shock upon the country's mind—that in fact determined almost everything in interwar Hungary.[19]

"Thus, the Trianon trap had a tighter grip of the majority of our nation than did the dualistic system [that preceded it]. The most grotesque aspect of this tragic trap was that thereafter [Hungarian] national consciousness found itself bound not to a living, but to a non-existing, to a vanished absolute."[20] The aristocracy tried to prevent the peasants and other disadvantaged groups from demanding economic and political reforms by reminding them of the territories lost in the Peace of Trianon. Between the wars right-wing dominance was at its most complete in Hungary where the conservative Government Party, founded after 1920, won a decisive majority of seats in all elections held during the interwar period except in 1920.

Prime ministers tended to emerge from the administrative elites and then proceeded to "elect" a parliament to serve them. But what was most distinctive about this form of technocracy was that its own legitimacy derived from nationalism. Although Hungarian elections were conducted in a climate of official pressure on the electorate, it appears that the results were not far out of line with popular sentiment. This much may at least be judged from the results of the 1939 election, the last one held before World War II: that election was less affected by government pressures than any since 1920, and yet the results only confirmed the previous right-wing pattern.[21] Right-wing support in Hungary was underscored by the emergence in the late 1930s of the Arrow Cross as the largest fascist movement in Europe outside Germany and Italy; at its peak in the election of 1939, it won 25 percent of the popular vote. Outside the initial months of counterrevolutionary reaction, however, anti-Semitism manifested itself more in polemics than in actual governmental policy, and most of the formal rules of democratic rule could be observed.[22]

However, given the Trianon syndrome and Hungarian revisionism, "following the logic of the situation, Hungary's hope of finding a way out and receiving help with its territorial demands against it neighboring countries lay exclusively with the right-wing dictatorships which aimed at upsetting the peace treaty. . . . In such a framework, the original anti-communist and, anti-liberal and dictatorial character of the system mingled with Nazi-fascist elements, and even attempts to introduce a German-type totalitarian system."[23]

Bohemian Exceptionalism?

The one exception to the Central and East European patterns was Bohemia, where general economic and social development included a number of West European elements that made this region quite different from the rest of East Central Europe, and which had as its political result the existence of a group of middle-class parties that could seize power and introduce a democratic political solution in 1918.

Whereas among the neighboring Poles the ancient *szlachta* lived on through the newly ascendant intelligentsia, among the Czechs the native medieval nobility vanished. The Habsburg reconquest of Bohemia after the Battle of the White Mountain in 1620 was followed by the systematic destruction of the old Czech and German aristocracy of the Bohemian lands, which was provided with a new and foreign nobility of Catholic faith and cosmopolitan origins. The new "Bohemian" aristocracy, for whom no modern state existed to seize, was a court nobility, providing the dominant contingent of cadres to the Habsburg state and thereby becoming the major social basis of the dynasty. The system of elite alliances that followed from this transformation of the landed upper classes made for the result that in the Czech lands alone did anything like a native entrepreneurial class succeed in achieving a political position commensurate with its political strength and creating political structures corresponding roughly to the growing complexity of social life.

Possibly the most interesting examples of large manufactures erected by noblemen on the European continent were to be found in the Czech lands. Some of these works may therefore, with some justification, be considered forerunners of the relatively early industrialization of Bohemia and Moravia.[24] As for political development, Cisleithania acquired a "two-tracked" system of government by virtue of the October Diploma of 1860, the February Patent of 1861, and subsequent legislation during Constitutionalism after 1867. This system divided governmental responsibilities at the provincial, district, and communal levels between imperial officials on one hand and self-governmental bodies elected by highly restrictive suffrage on the other. A District Board of Representatives was established in 1864 in each of the eighty-nine districts of Bohemia as the intermediate body responsible to the Provincial Executive Council for the supervision of all communal self-governmental bodies in its borders.

In the Czech lands, local self-government provided an excellent vehicle for the realization of national ambitions, thereby giving middle-class politicians the possibility of educating themselves politically in democratic behavior. An expanding and prosperous economy provided an adequate tax base. When, after 1861 and even more after 1867, constitutional life was resumed in Austria, Czech middle classes found themselves able to use several institutions of self-administration promoted by the state.

By 1890, the growing power of Czech commercial institutions permeated the whole system of limited self-government. Directly, business interests dominated second- and third-curial elections of delegates to district boards and to provincial diets. Regularly held elections furnished opportunities for the organization of Czech parties in all areas to the Chambers of Commerce and Industry.[25] A close network of national associations came into being, covering all areas of social life and branching into every Czech town and region. Indirectly, commercial institutions provided that fiscal independence from Viennese capital necessary to an autonomous Czech political development and paid many of the direct taxes that made possible the continual expansion and relatively efficient operation of self-governmental bodies.[26] The dissolution of the Habsburg empire and the demise of the centralized Viennese apparatus did therefore "not create a vacuum, but opened the opportunity to a prepared stratum" to impose a solution without substantially changing the basic political pattern.[27]

PHASE 2: CULTURAL STANDARDIZATION

State and Church

Rokkan's cultural standardization phase of the state-building process consists of an attempt from the center to establish a unified religious and linguistic standard. In the West the church was combined with the state and its supranational ties cut off. Latin gradually disappeared as the medium of written communication and gave way to a standardized vernacular language. As the population as a whole was joined to the state center, and lost their local or international cultural symbolic loyalty, nation building was taking place.

In Rokkan's European model, the outcomes of the early struggles between the state and the church determined the structure of national politics in the era of democratization and mass mobilization 300 years later. In northern Europe the opposition to the *ancien regime* was far from indifferent to religious values. The broad left coalitions against the established powers recruited decisive support among Orthodox Protestants in a variety of sectarian movements inside and outside of the national churches. Anticlericalism—defined as an attitude that views the Catholic Church as an authoritarian force and seeks to reduce its influence in the secular realm—was, on the other side, a characteristic stance of 19th-century liberal and socialist parties in most Catholic countries in Europe. In Southern and Central Europe the Counterreformation had consolidated the position of the church and tied its fate to the privileged bodies of the *ancien regime*. The result was a polarization of politics between a national–radical–secular movement and a Catholic-traditionalist one.

"The distinction between these two types of 'Left' alliances against the inherited political structure is fundamental for an understanding of European political development in the age of mass elections."[28] In Southern and Central Europe the bourgeois opposition to the *ancien regime* tended to be indifferent if not hostile to the teachings of the church: the cultural integration of the nation came first and the Church had to find whatever place it could within the new political order. Among the Czechs, furthermore, it seems to have acquired a quality of its own; in its sweep and ardor, it came close to being synonymous with the Czech national movement (more so in Bohemia than in Moravia). As early as the Revolution of 1848–1849, anticlericalism had permeated the Czech national movement and press. At the same time it developed two unusual features: it reached into the ranks of the clergy itself and besides the urban population, it affected large segments of the rural population.

Czech politics were born in 1848 without a major conservative movement (or political counterbalance to liberalism on the right), something that distinguished Czech political culture from that of other Catholic nations of Eastern Europe. This absence was due to the weakness in Czech society of classes or interest groups that became, in other European nations, the bearers of a conservative ideology: the nobility, the church and the army. According to the 1900 census 96.6 percent of the population in Bohemia were Catholics. The Young Czech period (1891–1907) stands out as a rare instance in Catholic Eastern Europe of a people voting a liberal democratic party into power. Although other Catholic nations of the Habsburg monarchy also produced such parties (the main distinguishing mark of democratic liberalism was advocacy of universal male suffrage), these seldom became a major political force, and did not attract a majority of the constituents.[29]

In the Balkans, historic "adherence to the Orthodox and Uniate churches had symbolized the major bulwark of resistance against the Ottoman overlords."[30] In Europe as a whole, agrarian parties were much more likely to occur in Orthodox (and Protestant) societies, than in Catholic areas, since Orthodox (as well as Protestant) churches were less supranationally oriented. Also in the Balkans, however, nationalism based on the struggle between the Cross and the Crescent was gradually to be superseded by historical nationalism supported by the states and based on, and nourished by, historic memories and experiences. The Balkan national movements in the 19th century expressed agrarian as well as clearly defined national trends. In due course, the latter gradually supplanted the former and dominated the political scene. The cultivation of national identity then became an integral part of domestic statecraft and foreign policy of the new Balkan states. "It is precisely this role of the modern state in shaping up national identity and in cultivating national consciousness among Balkan peoples that forms the critical factor in the growth of nationalism in south-eastern Europe to the point of the explosive antagonisms of rival national movements in the late nineteenth and throughout most of the twentieth century."[31]

National Homogenization as a Center–periphery Conflict

Nation building in the Rokkanian European model represents, if seen from below, a transfer of loyalty from smaller primary group-oriented social units (family, kinship, locality, household) to aggregate units of a political and administrative nature. This represents a departure from the earlier patterns of social and political organization, with their old local and particularistic mentality, which follows from a definite tendency to level down and weaken all intermediate structures between state and individual and tie the influential elites to the state's bureaucratic structure. However, in Central and Eastern Europe a state-supporting elitist culture was not the only possible value system by which political loyalty could be reoriented. An important feature of Central and East European development has been the fact that it was uneven and complex, not only economically and politically, but also with regard to national homogenization. Again, the typical political form in the region had been either the large multiethnic empire, or fragmented ethnic groups that had not succeeded in establishing their own state. Typical of the regions in the Habsburg monarchy was the fact that two ethnic groups, which differed from one another in their social structures, coexisted in the same territory. One of these groups represented the bulk of the population, the population masses in the rural districts, and often even the lower strata of the urban population. The other ethnic group (disregarding language islands of an agrarian nature) was made up of the higher strata: the nobility, the urban higher social strata, and often the majority of the towns' inhabitants, the intellectuals, and the new class of officials (for these, an advancement in the social hierarchy also meant national assimilation).

In this picture, then, belongs a division of an ethnic nature between town and country: the peasant population and the rural population, with the exception of the noble lords, belong to the ethnic group that makes up the majority of the population. In the towns the ethnic group of the higher social classes is dominant, and although it is not necessarily numerically predominant, its economic, cultural and social superiority influences the ethnic character of the towns. The cultural life of the regions is characterized by the language of the population majority being the language of popular culture and used, at best, in lower education and popular literature. The language of the higher classes dominates in intermediate and higher education, the theatre and "higher arts." Generally speaking, it is the language of public administration, particularly the internal language of the civil service and the language in which acts and documents are written.

After Otto Bauer's theoretical analysis in *Die Nationalitätenfrage und die Sozialdemokratie,* it has become common in the literature to associate the concept *non-historical nations* with the first of the ethnic categories described, and *historical nations* with the second.[32] Thus far, the concepts of nations with history and nations without history provide a foundation for the classification of the Habsburg monarchy's ethnic groups. If we follow the exposition that Robert Kann uses as the outline basis for his book *The Mul-*

tinational Empire" (1950), then the following ethnic groups were historical nations in the sense assigned to the term by Otto Bauer: Germans, Magyars, Poles, Italians, Croats and Czechs. All social classes here were represented in the same language community. The national languages were the languages of all social classes, and it is reasonable to talk about complete nations.[33]

Bauer's distinction partly overlaps Rokkan's distinction between so-called *genuine* or *enclave peripheries* (ethnic groups without any independent political organization in the Middle Ages) and *failed centers* (which for a time sustained special polities, but were subsequently assimilated into larger territorial units).[34] Where Miroslav Hroch is concerned, this is one of the three criteria he uses to characterize the initial situation of nation building (in Rokkan's narrow sense of the word). The other two are whether a nation "inhabited an administratively defined subunit that matched the extent of their ethnic population"; and whether a nation had "a continuous tradition of cultural production in their own literary language."[35]

Therefore, in Eastern Europe it is necessary to distinguish between two types of nations, or in other words between two types of tradition as the starting point for a national identity, which will represent two different centers of gravity in the nation-building process in the 19th century. The distinction, then, is between nations where the national identity is very much associated with a previous tradition in a separate political framework (such as experiences from opposition against the Habsburg dynasty's centralization efforts, which have later been made the object of hero worship and legends), and the part that claims to be connected with special ethnic characteristics, such as can be said to materialize most markedly in a national literature, in the visual arts and music, and so on.

Here the subject of nationalism (or *patriotism* in the terminology of Miroslav Hroch) comes into the focus. Rokkan did not say much about the phenomenon of nationalism. However, as explained in chapter 1, two perspectives on nationalism are more or less implicated by his models: 1) nationalism as a *longue durée* process in the form of political and cultural center–periphery conflicts that follow from attempts at cultural standardization, that is, the relationship between phase 1 and 2; 2) nationalism created by tensions between relatively advanced and relatively backward regions and countries (the interaction between the industrial and the national revolution), mainly phase 4, but also phase 3.

Nationalizing States and Stability in the Interwar Years

However, and in addition to the factors just mentioned, seen in the light of *phase 3 in Stein Rokkan's model*—the political mobilization and incorporation of the population—a main feature of the Dual Monarchy before 1918 making it even more complicated, its ethnic-topographic structure must be emphasized: it did not primarily consist of complete nations, but of fragments of nations. The majority of the population in six of its eleven nationalities were to be found living outside its borders: the Germans, the Italians, the Romanians, the Ukrainians, the Serbs and the Poles. This was a period of considerable irredentist mobilization. At the same time nationalism was evolving into a mass phenomenon, and democratic currents were undermining the political supremacy of the old social elites. All these factors put together meant that the unity of the monarchy was irretrievably lost. Absolute demands, no longer relative ones, characterized the type of nationalism now flourishing in Cisleithania. These demands were too particular to be weighted against the claims raised by other nations.[36]

Also the political dynamics between the wars reflected the contradictions of state building within empires. Due to the arbitrary character of state borders, the old movements to create nation-states repeated themselves, this time not only on the basis of old empires, but also with their basis in the new nation states themselves. Before 1914, between 100 million and 120 million people lived in the large area between Finland and the Mediterranean, and approximately 50 million of these belonged to minority groups; after 1920 this figure had dropped to 20 million. This decline was the only improvement brought about by the new nation-state organization of the area, from an ethnic point of view. The Peace of Versailles did not untie the old national knots, one nation's right soon became the other's wrong, and a very large number of mines were left in the landscape. The consequence of all this was that the peace in the area remained as threatened by ethnic tensions after 1918–1919 as it had been before.

The existence of socially and ethnically disparate populations had one vital consequence: "The failure of either social and ethnic integration of society into a single relatively homogeneous civil society also represented a failure of these new states to develop a single public opinion that could exercise control over the political sphere."[37] In Czechoslovakia and Yugoslavia the national revolutions created new national movements almost immediately. From these an increasing number of national impulses emanated, creating a soil fertile for fascist movements.[38]

As for political stability, political theory identifies a number of factors that differentiate the so-called moderate pluralism of stable democracies and the extreme pluralism of unstable democracies. These are factors that are easily adapted within Rokkan's overall theory. Giovanni Sartori points to the number of cleavages and the structure of cleavages as important factors influencing the party structure. Also the timing of franchise (the extension of suffrage), the timing of proportional representation and the degree of party organization are of great importance. His observation is that the more conflict dimensions are prevalent in a society, and the more complex they are, the more likely it is that a large number of political parties will be able to find a niche for themselves.[39] Such a framework goes a long way to explain the difficulties for democracy in interwar Central Europe. The constitutions did have few safeguards against extreme multipartyism; the structure of social conflicts was unfavorable. National, ethnic and religious antagonisms are relatively difficult to resolve in a democratic framework, and exactly those conflict dimensions were both heated and at the top of the political agenda.

"Party formation," as pointed out by Berglund, Ekman and Aarebrot, "in immediate post-independence Central and Eastern Europe was co-determined by ethnicity, class, ideology and religion, but . . . ethnicity was the defining cleavage, to which other cleavages—including left/right—were subordinated."[40] A typical feature connected with the multinational character of the majority states was the existence of separate minority parties along national lines, that is, in Czechoslovakia, Poland, Yugoslavia and Romania. In Austria, Bulgaria, and Hungary, where the nationality composition of the population was more uniform, such minority parties did not exist. The most numerous minority groups, the Germans in Poland and Czechoslovakia, the Ukrainians and White Russians in Poland, created their own parties of the right and left. In Western Byelorussia and Western Ukraine separate Communist Parties were created on a territorial basis without regard to national allegiance. In an ideological ethnic matrix there were three main groupings—socialists, nationalists and agrarians—but all spawned with a bewildering array of regional parties and factions, largely a result of the fact that they had emerged in triplicate during partition.

Quite apart from its ethnic problems, Poland, like many other Eastern European countries, was imperfectly integrated. In 1918 both Galicia and Cracow strenuously opposed the establishment of a centralized governmental system directed from Warsaw. Despite their desire to secede from Germany, the Poles in Poznan held serious reservations about joining Poland and for a short while even erected a tariff barrier between it and other Polish provinces. This kind of action inhibited the ability of the Polish agrarian parties to expand beyond their original geographical bases: they failed to win any significant support in the western provinces.

Between the wars Czechoslovakia was even more multinational than Poland. Czechs and Slovaks constituted (according to the 1931 census) jointly 66.9 percent of the population; the Czechs over 50 percent, the Slovaks over 16 percent. The Germans with 23 percent came, in fact, second after the Czechs; the Hungarians amounted to some 5 percent and the Ukrainians to about 3.8 percent. The Jews constituted 4.8 percent in Slovakia, and in

Carpatho-Ukraine around 12 percent. Only about half of all people of Judaic faith defined themselves as being of Jewish nationality. This represented 1.3 percent of the total population of Czechoslovakia. In Bohemia and Moravia the figures were much smaller—0.2 and 0.6 percent—because many persons of Jewish faith regarded themselves as Czechs or Germans.[41]

Statewide, the basic fragmentation was two dimensional: economic and ethnic. Class voting was the prevalent pattern for voters of Czech ethnicity; the only significant exception was the appeal generated by Catholic Populists. For most major Czech parties, there were rough German counterparts, neatly mirroring the political alignments of the dominant national grouping. For the Slovaks and the Hungarians, however, the two-dimensional structure of party politics was neither fully compartmentalized nor uniform. Unlike the Czechs and the Germans, neither of the more easterly ethnicities sustained a range of class-based parties. Rather, the major Czechoslovak organizations contested elections with two major local groupings, the Hlinka Slovak Populists and the German–Magyar Christian Socialists.[42]

The linguistic and regional cleavages of Yugoslavia exerted a dominant influence upon both the party system and governments. In Serbia the agrarians found their way barred by the radicals. The latter had (for the Balkans) an effective organization in both town and countryside through which they were able to appeal successfully to the peasantry. At least until the end of the 1920s the radicals were identified by the peasants as the party most suitably expressing their prejudices against the other nationalities of Yugoslavia, especially the Croats.

All governments were Serbian-oriented, and all tended to be directed by the Serbian radicals. Despite this orientation, however, the small Serbian Agrarian Party never participated in government. The Croat Peasant Party was normally in opposition, a stance that most suited its political style. It did enter a government with the Serbian radicals on three occasions in 1925 and 1926. Despite pressing agricultural problems, the increasingly urban and intellectual leadership of the party seemed to ignore everything in their struggle for independence and autonomy.

The failure of the League of Nations pushed the nations of the Balkans into the arms of big powers in the search for security. Fragile at the outset because of their national minorities, and weakened by unresolved national ambitions, the governments began courting powerful neighbors, no matter whether despised or considered friendly. This endeavor to find allies at all costs weakened regional alliances and often fragmented these nations internally. It is interesting to note that even the irreconcilable fractions in these states reproduced their governments' frantic pursuit of foreign allies. While both the Macedonian and the Croatian liberation movements originally had a patriotic goal, "by the 1930s they had become playballs of foreign interests," knowing as they must that their foreign provider would extort a high price from them if they were victorious (like Italy in Croatia).[43]

The interwar period was a virtually continuous period of social crises, which was in turn aggravated by the economic world crisis of 1929. It was also a crisis in terms of relations between rulers and ruled. Neither a ruling strategy based on hegemony and consensus, nor a strategy transforming the state into a means of social development itself seemed to work. According to Antonio Gramsci, a crisis of ideological hegemony occurs when social classes became detached from their party representatives, that is, the breaking of the representational ties between the dominant classes and fractions and their political parties, and the organizational weakness of these parties. "Left to themselves the classes and fractions at the level of political domination are not only exhausted by internal conflicts but, more often than not, founder in contradictions which make them incapable of governing politically . . . their impact is all-important . . . they create . . . a permanently unstable situation at the political level."[44] Anything can happen and violent solutions are possible. Traditional political leaders are in a pitiable political situation, unable to impose the necessary leadership and political organization to integrate the state system, therefore "where there is a crisis a hegemony and/or growing disunity within the state system, the state is vulnerable to particularistic degeneration."[45] The ethnic–national fragmentation of the party system must be mentioned as one of the contributing causes of the hegemonic crisis, as well as the deepened conflict between the urban bureaucracies and the overwhelming agrarian population. Moreover, as I will argue later, a tendential fragmentation and loss of unity of the state, or its *internal feudalization*, must be expected to take place where *sector bureaucrats* form *clintela* coalitions, or *segments* will compete for influence and resources and make coordination of state activities difficult. This makes a strategy based on passive revolution and *transformismo* difficult as well. In Gramscian terms, the use of "force, fraud and corruption" as a means of social control can be considered as a transitional form between "passive revolution" and "war of maneuver." "Between consent and force stands corruption and fraud (which is characteristic of certain situations when it is hard to exercise the hegemonic function, and when the use of force is too risky)."[46] Corruption and fraud are tactical weapons in a rear-guard struggle to preserve power, and temporary surrogates of power. They are therefore not the expression of power, but of a failure of power.[47] All in all, a non-fascist solution to the crisis would, as Gramsci stressed, require the fusion of the competing organizations into a single party of the bourgeoisie. In East Central Europe the answer, however, was to link the national idea with various types of right-wing dictatorships.

As a rule, in Central and Eastern Europe, stability could result only if *one* elite was securely in control of all or most positions of influence.[48] Poland can serve as a prototype: the rise of the civilian elite and the concomitant decline in the fortunes of the military, not surprisingly, created strong resentment among the latter, who eventually united under Josef Pilsudski in May 1926 to overthrow Poland's constitutional government. Following Pilsudski's resumption of power, decision making was simply transferred from the faction-ridden legislature to the inner councils of the regime. As was true in other armies around the world, the Polish military between the wars was characterized by the presence of a powerful *affinity group* or faction known as the *legionnaires.* They were a collection of individuals joined together by a kind of ethos or *esprit de corps* going back to their World War I experiences. Most members of the "colonels clique" were born in the former Russian or Austrian parts of the country.

They soon occupied all leading positions, not only in the military but also in the civilian political, economic, and social areas. In many respects the system introduced by the Polish *Sanacja* resembled the one earlier introduced in Hungary. Pilsudski's system never relied on a mass party. The formation of the Non-Party Bloc for Cooperation with the Government (BBWR) indicated a growing hostility toward the traditional parties. The core of the BBWR consisted of Pilsudski's ex-Legionary paladins, who were intellectually reinforced and "modernized" by the sponsors and practitioners of the new cult of technocracy. To this inner group were assimilated converts from all the earlier political orientations in Poland, even from ethnic minorities. This great variety of membership could be accommodated on only one political ground: the appeal of strong executive government after a decade of confused parliamentary instability.[49] Everywhere, writes Stein Berglund, Joachim Ekman and Frank Aarebrot, "the influence of informal 'old boys' network[s]—such as the Polish and Czech Legionnaires, the Estonian Freedom Fighters, the Lithuanian Light Infantry Association, the IMRO in Bulgaria and Macedonia—sometimes resembling secret societies, marked the clientelistic nature of political loyalties and encouraged opportunistic defections and sudden shifts in coalitions."[50]

The drift of the national revolutions toward the extreme right was an almost general tendency in the region when "the success of the national revolution did not provide the panacea for social, political and economic backwardness."[51] This drift permeated the originally democratic-nationalist movements, although, as Eric Hobsbawn points out, "it was rhetoric that identified every turn to the antidemocratic right in Europe between the war with fascism."[52] The major difference between fascist and non-fascist right was that fascism existed by mobilizing masses from below. Rightist-radical mobilizations emerged in an increasing number of countries, sometimes only as minority movements, but its effects penetrated the regimes, which adopted elements of the programs of the extreme right in order to keep the fascist movements out. The only route to power available to fascists passes through cooperation with conservative elites. The most important variables are, therefore, the degree to which conservative elites are willing to cooperate with the fascists (along with a reciprocal flexibility on the part of the fascist leaders), and the degree to which the crisis is deep and comprehensive enough to induce them to cooperate. Stanley Payne, among others, considers authoritarian military dictatorships the most effective barrier against the fascist acquisition of power. He points out that without conditions of at least relative freedom—even if not the purest constitutional democracy—a fascist leader could not expect to be able to take power: "Once this was barred by a preemptive nonfascist authoritarian regime, as in Austria and the various countries of eastern and southern Europe, they could only come to power (like Communist in Eastern Europe after 1945) by outside military intervention."[53] One-party regimes or *national fronts* arose, where various conservative and extreme rightist political forces joined "national socialists" in a united power block with dictatorial and hypernationalist programs, although in most countries party activities continued after the abrogation of unhindered political life. However, politics essentially involved a confrontation between two blocs of parties, one supporting and the other opposed to the new authoritarian development.[54]

In the 1930s the strategy of technocratic adjustment had strong proponents in nearly all East European states. The mobilizing states were now seen as the bearers of the moral projects of their nations, and were supposed to be able to achieve late development. In his works of economic development Romanian Finance Minister Mihail Manoilescu (later a fascist) had written that poor, agrarian nations were condemned to permanent poverty unless they closed themselves off from the world capitalist market. His ideas were publicized globally through his writings. He advocated policies of import-substitution industrialization, a model of social corporatism, and a strong, centralized state in which class-based divisions had to be overcome by national solidarity. Nationalism and corporatism were thus ideally suited and progressive.[55] Manoilescu's ideas gained widespread popularity in his own time and were put into practice in part or as a whole by most East European governments.

How then to account for the one and only instance where political democracy survived in East Central Europe between the wars? This was due in part to the rise of an extraconstitutional organ, which prevented unbridled strife among parties. Shortly after the adoption of the constitution in 1920, the heads of the five parties then forming the government coalition began the practice of meeting in private and deciding issues before they reached the floor of the parliament. The institution of the "Five" (*Petka*), which drew its name from the original five participating parties, the National Democratic, Populist, Agrarian National Socialist, and Social Democratic, became a peculiar feature of Czechoslovak politics, and lasted, with short interruptions, as long as the First Republic. The acceptance of continued cooperation among the central parties was a conflict-reducing mechanism; it assured that the coalition-building process would not have to begin from scratch in the wake of each election or political crisis.[56]

The connections between the parties and their constituencies and the substantive nature of this relationship, rather than the formal structure and dimensions of party competition, is suggested as an indicator of democratic consolidation. In the case of Czechoslovakia, the Republican Party of Smallholders and Farmers, popularly known as the Agrarians, played a leading role. Except for a brief interregnum in 1926 every Czechoslovak premier between 1922 and 1938 came from Agrarian ranks. Underneath a facade of continuous turnover lay a core of "perpetual ministers" who moved in and out of government, or from one post to another.

The Republican Party of Smallholders and Farmers was undoubtedly the Agrarian Party that proved the most successful in mobilizing its own electorate, as well as attracting significant urban support (it won 17 percent of the vote in Prague in 1925). The Republicans were able to move beyond the interest groups that were their primary constituency. Lack of this ability has been seen as fatal to the highly articulated party system in Weimar, Germany. "In Weimar, although, the parties had hammered out elaborate political programmes that were recognized by each other and most of the electorate . . . Programmatic party competition in a weakly commoditized post-imperial democracy ensured that programmes articulated quite narrow interests—which were nonetheless in each case identified with those of the nation as a whole."[57]

Czechoslovakia followed a course that was strikingly similar to that which eventuated in the social democratic political economies of Scandinavia.[58] In response to the depression, as in Scandinavia, a Red–Green coalition broke decisively with deflationary orthodoxy in a bargain aimed at aiding both peasants and industrial workers. During the crisis period of the 1930s, Gregory Luebbert argues, "the minimum conclusion that is confirmed by Czechoslovakia is that democratic stabilization of an aliberal society that lacked a hegemonic clerical movement (as in Belgium and Netherlands) required a coalition of the urban working classes and the family peasantry."[59] The Agrarians and the Social Democrats in Czechoslovakia used large fiscal deficits to stimulate a recovery, and the state assumed a determining role in the labor market.

As for the Germans, from 1926 until 1938 there were always at least two Sudeten German Parties in every coalition, and on measures of particular interests there was international cooperation between the Czechoslovak and Sudeten German agrarian, Catholic and Socialist parties. Yet there was also concern among the Czechoslovak parties that no government be dependent on Sudeten Germans for its parliamentary majority. Most government majorities were therefore oversized; that is, each contained more ministerial parties than were necessary to control a minimum majority vote. "The inner circle of Czechoslovak parties held together both because of the attractions of sharing political power and the national dangers if they did not."[60]

Seen from a nationalist point of view, however, the Czechoslovak system was far from perfect. As pointed out by Carol Skalnik Leff, the nationalist parties of the cleavage structure were largely ignored: "Neither German, Hungarian, nor Slovak nationalist groupings were deemed fit coalition partners. Coupled with the slighting of left and right economic extremists, this exclusionary pattern streamlined the process of governing. Such a pattern was feasible because a respectable number of Slovaks always voted for the statewide Czechoslovak parties, while many Germans (until 1935) voted for German equivalents of the statewide parties."[61] However "the central government accepted exclusion of much of the electorate in Slovakia from a voice in policy making in exchange for a vast simplification in bargaining; for governmental purposes, with this backing, governments could get along without the disruptive nationalist parties."[62] The minorities therefore participated in the processes of the country's political system, but realizing that they were not admitted to the inner circles of power, they had little reason for building up more genuine patriotic loyalties to the Czechoslovakian state.

When comparing Czechoslovakia with neighboring Poland, it is furthermore, almost impossible to imagine the functioning of the cumbersome Czechoslovakian system without the tutelary presence of the President–Liberator Masaryk as a guiding force, both because of the aura of legitimacy and dignity he lent to government and because of his backstage involvement in political decision making:

> The 'Castle group' that clustered around Masaryk and the 'Nonparty Bloc for Support of the Government' that Pilsudski founded was similar in that both attempted to cut across party lines. The situation in Czechoslovakia made it possible for Masaryk to establish executive authority through his involvement in the political process and thereby to give direction to the state's constitutional development.

Unlike Pilsudski he did not feel himself forced to violate the constitution. But his purpose, like Pilsudski's was to give the state stable and efficient government.[63] As a major scholar of the period, F. Gregory Campbell, therefore sees interwar Czechoslovakia as a presidentially directed democracy, and this is an essential key to a complex political situation. "In practice Czechoslovakia enjoyed a presidential democracy—and therefore greater political stability than its neighbours."

PHASE 3: POLITICAL MOBILIZATION

The East European Context

The elites dominating the premodern, political systems in Eastern Europe were, nonetheless, very attracted by English liberalism and French rationalism. Their development illustrates the problem of political learning, as latecomers may have specific political institutions, corresponding not only to their economic backwardness (i.e., the need for the state in capital formation), but also to the impact of the political institutions of the pioneers. In the Balkans, with its relatively egalitarian or little differentiated social structure, Greece in as early as 1877 changed the broad suffrage of 1864 into a general male franchise. The petty notables who formed the constituent assembly of independent Bulgaria refused the advice of their Russian helpers and installed universal male suffrage in the 1879 constitution of Tirnovo. Serbia established in its 1899 constitution a low threshold for voting rights. The Russian Revolution in 1905 made for internal democracy in Finland, and more indirectly contributed to the final breakthrough of male suffrage to the Austrian part of Austria–Hungary, largely as an imperial means of blunting the edge of the fighting liberal nationalists of various ethnicities but also as a response to wide popular demands.

The Eastern states of landed aristocracy or autocracy made some concessions to elective principles, but not that many. The 1905 revolution brought forth a three-class electoral system in Russia. Romania had something similar, and Hungary gained a broader system of tax and education thresholds. However, what took place during the 19th century, such as the abolition of serfdom, can be seen as attempts to respond to the West European challenge.[64]

Then in 1919 Central European powers were dismantled and a whole series of new nation-states were created in the ensuing political vacuum. The dominant tendency was the program of state building. The Franco–British-dominated international regime pressured the lesser nations of East Central Europe to modify constitutions, and for the first time in history, to extend citizens' rights to ethnic and religious minorities. The successor states in Central and Eastern Europe—(Weimar) Germany, Poland, Austria, Hungary, Czechoslovakia, Finland, Estonia, Latvia, Lithuania, Yugoslavia—all adopted essentially liberal democratic forms of government. Wilsonian ideals of democracy—often instrumentalized by nationalist politicians in order to gain Allied support at the peace conferences for statehood for their national group—and the concept of popular national sovereignty triumphed when the major authoritarian dynastic states collapsed in the final stages of the war. The League of Nations was publicly proclaimed by its author, U.S. President Woodrow Wilson, as designed to extend to international relations that system of parliamentary democracy that had become the accepted form of national governments in all of the great powers except Russia. The basic assumption upon which the League of Nations was founded was that democracy itself was a prescription for peace. That assumption, in turn, had its origin in the contemporary liberal interpretation of the world war.

Wilson did not see any basic distinction between domestic and foreign politics. To prevent a repetition of the catastrophe of 1914–1918, it was necessary to substitute for the Habsburgs and Hohenzollerns the system of parliamentary democracy prevailing among the victorious Western Allies. New constitutions were passed in Austria in 1920, in Czechoslovakia 1920, in Yugoslavia in 1921, in Poland in 1921, and in Romania in 1923. In Hungary, there was no single unified constitutional law, just as in Great Britain, although most of the constitutional laws mainly were based on the constitution of 1867. The monarchies (Bulgaria, Yugoslavia, Romania and Hungary) and republics all declared themselves parliamentary states.[65]

The international system and foreign policies of the East European states exerted a great impact on their domestic evolution and vice versa. "It would therefore be hard to explain the rise of liberal constitutionalism in Eastern Europe in the 19th century or the extension of suffrage in the 1920s, without taking into consideration the larger international milieu."[66]

However, the general problem concerning the ability to turn one's own backwardness to one's advantage, through borrowing and learning, is the following: How can one learn from other people's development, or, if relevant, copy other people's achievements, without having to undergo the same processes that produced them, and thereby attain the same background for oneself? What are the connections between a country's own historical conditions and its adaptability and social receptiveness to foreign elements? When do one's own experiences become cultural barriers or structural constraints on the realization of borrowing and learning as successful strategies? In the case of Eastern Europe the political borrowing and learning processes were forced to emerge from above and from outside. This problem had its effect on the development in the region. In the words of Edward Carr, "When the theories of liberal democracy were transplanted, by a purely intellectual process, to a period and to countries whose stage of development and whose practical needs were utterly different from those of Western Europe in the nineteenth century, sterility and disillusionment were the inevitable sequel."[67]

The collapse of the old empires and the establishment of independent nation-states removed the imperial context that had so heavily conditioned politics in these societies. Between the World Wars, domestic conflicts assumed a more decisive role in shaping the political economies of Eastern and Central Europe. Those countries, however, although varying a great deal in population and history, in outlook and structure, had one essential factor common to them all: their peasant–agrarian character. After the First World War, a radical expropriation of property and large estates, however, occurred in all the old empires' successor states except Poland, Hungary and Austria. The reforms had been portrayed as nationalist measures. Before 1918 much of the land in large estates had been held by ethnic minorities: Phanariots in Moldavia and Wallachia, Magyars in Transylvania and Slovakia, Germans in Bohemia, Moravia and the Baltic provinces of Russia. In Romania, Yugoslavia and Czechoslovakia, the Hungarian- or German-owned estates were divided among the peasants. In Poland a fairly liberal land reform program was planned, but the land reform itself was postponed for political reasons and was not completed during the interwar era. By far the least significant land reform was undertaken in Hungary where the old, land-owning aristocracy retained its political power and clung with every available means to their lands.[68] These reforms gave some peasants access to land and to some extent reduced large landholdings, particularly of foreign owners.

The reforms had little to do with matters of farming; they were never enacted as agricultural reforms but simply as matters for dividing the land.[69] Behind this phenomenon hides the basic dilemma of that region in the interwar period. Thwarted in their drive to industrialization, its people also found their agrarian export markets closing against them, so that a rapidly rising population was driven back on its land, where in the face of rising productivity, a "surplus population" remained bottled up after closing of overseas emigration. The surplus population began to increase steadily around 1920. This surplus population was somewhere between 25 and 35 percent of the population, or around 9 million to 10 million people.[70] A League of Nations study in 1945 estimated that the countries of Poland, Romania, Bulgaria, Albania, and Yugoslavia needed under 50 percent of the available agricultural workers.[71] Rural–urban migration could not offer major outlets until the possibilities of urban employment grew rapidly. In much of Eastern Europe the flow to the towns did not take place until the rapid growth of the manufacturing industry and secondary employment under Communist Party rule.

"Politics in these societies was strongly sculptured by an accentuated cleavage between urban bureaucracies and agrarian peasantism."[72] The town–country cleavage was especially deep in southeastern Europe, which intensified the tensions caused by ethnic differences. The peasants were heavily exploited, and the remarkably large unproductive class of bureaucrats, lawyers and intelligentsia was kept artificially alive by the peasants' taxes (in Bulgaria the Ministry of Education had at its disposal one-third of the national budget), which also left the capitalist economic sector to the Jews. In Eastern Europe between the wars "the neglected, village, with its vegetating, unemployable, undernourished, disease-ridden, semiliterate, surplus population, presented a more refractory and more explosive problem than did the urban slum."[73]

Peasant Politics and Peasant Mobilization

After the war, more important than the economic consequences of reform was the fact that the peasantry now for the first time emerged as a class with its own political and economic interests and programs. Accordingly to Stein Rokkan, typically agrarian parties appear to have emerged in countries or provinces:

- where the cities and the industrial centers were still numerically weak at the time of the decisive extensions of the suffrage;
- where the bulk of the agricultural populations were active in family-size farming and either owned their farms themselves or were legally protected lease holders largely independent of socially superior landowners;
- where there were important cultural barriers between the countryside and the cities and much resistance to the incorporation of farm production in the capitalist economy of the cities; and
- where the Catholic Church was without significant influence.[74]

He concluded,

> We can clearly identify three major agencies of rural mobilization before the breakthrough of the socialist parties in the wake of the decisive extensions of suffrage: the large-scale estate, the cultural and economic organizations of freehold family farmers, the Catholic Church. The Roman Catholic movements have throughout continental Europe proved able to cross-cut the cleavage between rural and urban economic interests generated by the Industrial Revolution: distinctly agrarian parties have rarely if ever emerged in countries or regions with strong Catholic parties. Ireland is a very interesting case just from this point of view: in the only Catholic country *without* a distinctive Catholic party, sizeable groups of farmers have found it to their advantage to put up their own candidates and organise for separate political action.[75]

Lasting agrarian parties emerged in those countries where only a large minority of the population is employed in agriculture, if two additional factors are present: 1) where properties and holdings are the "freehold family farm" size type, and 2) the family holdings primarily produce for the market. Czechoslovakia comes in this category, especially if we consider the Czech areas where extensive commercial agriculture existed and where the Republican Party had most of its voter support. Between its inception in 1896 and the expansion of suffrage in 1906 it was specifically a party of landowners and large farmers. After 1918 the necessity to present a united national front led it initially to cooperate with the strong Social Democrats. This, plus the land reforms, gave it a more progressive image that it never entirely lost throughout the interwar period. By the 1930s the Social Democratic Party had become a protagonist of numerous agricultural industries, state monopolies, financial interests, and huge cartels in several industrial fields, all of which inevitably pushed it in a conservative direction. The more commercially oriented character of Czech agriculture, more prosperous farmers and high rural levels of education, all enabled the party to discard a peasantist orientation. In its behavior the party became in many ways a broker party that appealed to several groups. The party failed to surmount the country's ethnic cleavages. The large German and the small Magyar and Jewish minorities developed autonomous party systems, in which an agrarian party was prominent. The *Bund der Landwirte* was particularly successful in mobilizing the German farmers of the Sudetenland. From 1924, it cooperated closely in government with the Czech Republicans.

While singling out "the principal distinctions between Eastern and Western Europe in the level of organization and institutionalization of rural life, and the degree of market penetration into the countryside,"[76] Derek Urwin stresses the following factors as contributing to successful party formation: Agrarian parties are more likely to arise in countries having traditional peasant cultures, where agriculture is considered a form of life and the cultural affiliation with the land is intense, "in countries which possessed a more traditional peasant society, where land-hunger was strong, enterprise were small and domestic-oriented, and where there was a powerful parochial nexus of social and cultural traditions." Where such cultures exist the urban–rural conflict will be strong. Pressures from the center, for instance a desire for speedy industrialization, the emergence of an ambitious urban middle class and the need for efficient government administration may cause a political reaction among peasants. The various aspects of this situation include economic policy favoring industry through taxation of rural areas, and an inadequate national financial basis, a cultural challenge to the peasant population. In such societies the introduction of political rights of participation occurred at the same time as redistribution of land: agrarian parties had "something to defend and the means to do so." Such egalitarian conditions in rural areas are found in southeast Europe (the Balkans) and to a lesser extent in Czechoslovakia. The formation of political cleavages from such social conditions sometimes resulted in more than one agrarian party, due to religious and ethnic differences or internal economic differences among the peasants themselves.[77]

The existence of multiethnic empires in Eastern Europe up until 1918 contributed to preserving the considerable gap between town and country. Landowners and public officials often belonged to another ethnic group than the peasant masses in the rural districts, especially in the Ottoman Empire (like the Phanariots in Wallachia, the landowners in Bosnia converted to Islam). The imperial power also brought two factors that prevented the urban contagion from reaching the rural districts: the education gap remained wide between town and country, and the elite languages of the administrators was different from the language of the peasants. The urban middle classes supported land reform mainly because it enabled them to emerge as leaders of a mass movement. As John H. Kautsky pointed out, the urban intelligentsia "press for land not because of what it will do *for* the peasant, but because of what it will do *to* the aristocracy. The latter is the intellectual's only powerful domestic enemy, and land reform strikes at the very heart of its economic and social position."[78] On the other hand the peasants could be mobilized by urban groups in the struggle for national independence only in exchange for a promise of agrarian reform. From one point of view, therefore, it is interesting that land reform as an integral part of the national revolution failed in just those two countries, Poland and Hungary, in which the native aristocracy had survived to take the leadership in the 19th-century struggle for national independence.

The potential power given to the peasants by universal suffrage was everywhere in Eastern Europe held in check by the quick emergence of a political ruling class of bureaucrats, allied with and recruited from an artificially large intelligentsia. Both the civilian and military branches of the government administration were recruited from the so-called intelligentsia, which in turn could be identified from their diplomas.[79]

This intelligentsia was recruited from several sources, from the aristocracy, from among peasants, and from what bourgeoisie existed. The means of climbing the social ladder was not that of enterprise, but rather what is today called "rent-seeking," by following the Turkish pattern and taking advantage of one's position in the state apparatus to gain wealth: open corruption and speculation.[80] Rent-seeking behavior, conceptualized as corruption and unbridled individual maximization, is not only detrimental to developmental performance but also undermines trust and *social capital* among the sectors of civil society that are connected to the state.[81] "The exchange relation between incumbents and supporters is the essence of state actions. To survive, incumbents require political supporters, and these in turn must be provided with incentives sufficient to prevent their shifting support to other potential officeholders."[82] Instead of reinforcing the associations of civil society and expanding their scope, it encourages the primacy of individual ties to particular bureaucrats and undercuts associational life. The result is that many agencies may be effectively captured by elite groups and used for rent-seeking purposes. Personalistic patron–client relations remain central features of state organization, and these are closely hooked into networks with the dominant class.

The historical conditions for these patterns can be clarified by means of the Weberian concept of "bureaucratic patrimonialism," which contrasts feudal societies (decentralized through fiefdoms and tenure), with highly centralized bureaucracies connected through payment for services (that is benefices or prebends), such as the Ottoman Empire.[83] In bureaucratic patrimonial societies there was no clear distinction between the center and periphery, a relatively low symbolic and institutional division of labor, and a narrow status association.[84] This was a premodern form of social organization, where authority was anchored to the person rather than to the officeholder. Weber argued that patrimonialism was characterized by an undeveloped market, a small entrepreneurial middle class, and an undifferentiated bureaucracy. Patrimonial administration "is alien to and distrustful of capitalist development, which revolutionizes the given social conditions."[85]

This sheds some light on the constraints on political development in Eastern Europe, although at first "the overthrow of the foreign rule and the achievement of political independence came to be seen as *conditio sine qua non* of progress" and there likewise was an "unqualified admiration for the West."[86] Particularly in the Balkans centuries of indirect rule had created a mercenary and calculating attitude toward public office. In such systems "incumbents may either distribute resources directly to supporters—through subsidies, loans, contracts, or the provision of services—or use their rule-making authority to create rents for favoured groups by restricting the ability for market forces to operate."[87] Intermediaries between rulers (Byzants, the Osmans) and the population had spent the earnings from their exercise of public positions to cover their own expenses and pay back political debts to their local supporters. The peasants' "hunger for land" had its counterpart in the "hunger for public office" in intellectual groups, as has been claimed. A continuing overproduction of legal candidates created growing academic unemployment, which was channeled into political activity.

With the collapse of the empires, the way was open for small groups of middle-class individuals to dominate the national political scenes: In most instances the leadership of the Balkan agrarian parties was overwhelmingly urban, mainly professionals and intelligentsia, that is, urban lawyers. A 1936 publication contained a list of prominent politicians with their party affiliation and occupation. Of the 195 individuals who belonged to the National Peasants, 85 (43.6 percent) were lawyers and 70 (35.9 percent) belonged to other urban groups, mainly the educational intelligentsia, while only 11 (5.6 percent) were employed in agriculture.[88] Agrarian parties had been formed already before 1914: the Czech Republican party in 1896, the Agrarian Union in Bulgaria in 1899 and the Croatian Agrarian Party in 1904. With the exception of Bulgaria, where the Agrarian Union gained 14.4 percent of the votes in 1911, these parties had no real significance until after 1918. The Bulgarian party first emerged as a protest against the government's proposal to introduce a tithe on the farmers' crops.

The peasant parties of Eastern Europe, however, did not appear as significant political forces until after the land reforms: they were at first agents for carrying out and defending land redistribution. The lack of urban–rural integration, of the penetration of urban culture into the countryside, and the weakening of rural stratification explain the failure of urban-based political movements to mobilize the countryside under their own banners. Peasantism therefore develops into a separate ideology:

Peasantism emerged as an East European variant of populist politics, characterized by a romanticization of the peasant community. The town–country conflict was regarded as a struggle between the good and the evil—distrust of all political systems and an idealization of "the great charismatic leader figure." In populist mythology, shared by most peasantists, "the people" are seen as the sustainers of integral social culture, the relationships based on the feeling of solidarity, on social harmony and moral traditions that hold society together.

The populist considers the apologetics of the national cultural heritage as something to counterbalance the destructive effect of capitalism and as a kind of ideological and psychological compensation for it. Populists were certain that capitalism would destroy what was exceptional and genuine in their own way of life. Taken by itself there was nothing new in this attitude; it was its combination with other elements that gave a special Eastern European flavor to it. Here the peasantry constituted the structuring element of "the people" as a whole. The peasantry were seen not as "farmers in the British sense, not just a set of human beings engaged in agriculture. Peasants form the foundation of the nation itself, and give specific and distinct features to the whole national life."[89] Thus, the pioneer of the Hungarian trend at the end of World War I was Dezsö Szabó, who presented a cohesive program in the form of a 1919 novel titled *Az elsodort falu* (A Village is Swept Away), in which the village is seen as a symbol of national purity against a corrupting town. High-level consumption, polished needs and urban models in leisure were regarded with suspicion.

In almost every respect the Peasantist parties differed from traditional Western European interest-group parties, in their antagonism to the cities and to urban interests, in their uncrystalized organizational pattern, in the mixing of their rude ideologies with other elements such as nationalism, ethnic defense, and embryonic fascism. The traditionalist declarations by the populists are closely tied to their modernistic orientations; conversely, modernism is intertwined with traditionalist elements. "Slogans of the type 'Eastern ethics, Western technology' are more or less characteristic of all the main ideological varieties of populism."[90] Populism's economic strategy attempts to solve a dual task: to effect modernization and technical progress in a backward society and, at same the time, to ensure that the changes take on such forms as are less painful for the broad masses of the population and alleviate its unfolding marginalization. This was put plainly in the program of the Polish People's Party of December 1933: "With the object of attaching the people to the land, of adjusting the country's social structure and cultural level, new industrial enterprises should as far as possible be transferred to rural centers."[91]

The Peasantists' most original contribution to Romanian social thought was perhaps a systematic elaboration of the doctrine of agrarianism as a third world situated between the capitalist individualism to the West and socialist collectivism to the East. This doctrine, in turn, rested on two fundamental assumptions: first, that the family holding was a distinct mode of production and formed the foundation of the national economy, and second, that the "peasant state, a political entity administered by and responsible to the majority of the population, must replace the existing order. The Romanian Peasant Party's programme of the 1920s declared class struggle to be a decisive force in the evolution of society, and acknowledged the party as the representative of the peasant class."[92]

"Besides 'the people' a society includes 'the friends of the people, and 'the enemies of the people," writes V. Khoros. "The 'enemies of the people' are defined in conjunction with 'the people' and 'the friends of the people.' They include, above all, the big bourgeoisie (primarily foreign), the pre-capitalist exploiters and the top bureaucracy."[93] Here one must add that, more often than not, the Jews were included among "the enemies of the people." Populist social criticism was directed against the system of large estates where it still existed, as in Hungary, and everywhere against big capitalism. Anti-semitism was part of the reaction against modern life. The features shared with the fascist movements (i.e., the Iron Guard in Romania, the Arrow Cross movement in Hungary, the Hlinka movement in Slovakia, the Ustasha movement in Croatia) were an anti-intellectualist and anti-establishment attitude.[94]

While the phenomenon of *populism*, in the the particular meaning modeled on the Russian *narodnichestvo*, was essentially an urban (and mostly peculiarly Russian) movement; *peasantism* was a reaction not only to Western capitalism, but also to Russian *narodnichestvo*. The *narodnikis* aimed at forming Russian socialism from the traditional village communities and evoked only a limited response among the peasantry. Peasantists, on their side, stressed their adherence to the principles of private property and their hostility toward Marxism.[95] Historical circumstances connected with the multinational character of the region had played a part here: "When it occurred, peasant mobilization in Eastern Europe was stimulated by nationalist aspirations rather than by agrarian socialism: the former held a promise of land reform and individual peasant proprietorship, while the latter possessed collectivist implications."[96] However, by exchanging the earlier ideas of the folk for those of the ethnic community organized in the form of states many East European populists crossed the borderline between the Left and Right.[97] As for the peasants themselves, "[as] their relative deprivation and exclusion from the general progress in Europe were ever more clearly exposed, large parts of the peasantry chose to identify groups outside 'the peasant life' as their enemy."[98] Grassroots anti-semitism gave those East-European fascist movements that obtained a mass base—particularly the Romanian Iron Guard and the Hungarian Arrow Cross—their foundation.

The first appeal of a premature fascist movement was an appeal against intruders: in the words of Codreanu, the Romanian populist fascist leader, there was a Jewish conspiracy that was "effected against Romania according to a well-established plan. The great Judaic council probably intends to establish a new Palestine on a section of land extending from the Baltic Sea down through parts of Poland and Czechoslovakia, then covering half of Romania to the Black Sea."[99] Fascism's rejection of the modern world disguised as anti-capitalism was the rejection of the Spirit of 1789. "The populist rebellion prepared the ground for the different nazi movements, and brought into existence those pre-fascist ideological systems whose realisation those movements fought for."[100] Of the new states in Eastern Europe, only in Czechoslovakia, Yugoslavia, Estonia and Latvia did the agrarian parties succeed in resisting the fascist nationalist challenge. In the Baltic states the agrarian parties "averted" the threat by seizing dictatorial powers themselves.

The East European workers could hardly constitute a foundation for working-class politics as it had developed in the West and, indeed, left-wing parties were marginal after the initial upsurge of the post-1918 era, whose dynamics, however, was dependent on peasant radicalism and war weariness. Radicalism on the left was confined to a few geographically or occupationally distinct sectors.

Peasantism, Populism and the Approach to Political Cleavage Structures

All this at least meant two things: 1) the cleavage between town and country was looming, overshadowing all others, except perhaps those along nationality lines, and 2) the party systems were to a lesser degree organized in a direct way around political cleavages, rather than around other incentives that bind people to a party. Traditional clientelistic politics or *transformismo* of the Mediterranean, South European type had, however, difficulties in taking root. Political parties "frequently had only the appearance of modern organizational structure: underneath most were merely personal coteries fiercely fighting each other for power."[101] Political parties were "more often a matter of personal following than of program and organizational or educational endeavor. . . . Personal magnetism and demagogic skill brought more than . . . one unemployed intellectual forward as the leader of a successful . . . political group."[102]

Populism is often described as an authentic political culture and is closely related to charismatic politics. According to Edward Shills it is distinguished by two salient features: 1) the priority given to the "will of the people" over any other political slogan, and 2) the desire of the leaders to establish "direct contact" with the people without the mediation of any political institutions (which is typical also of any charismatic tendency). This seems to be to the point when describing Eastern Europe between the wars.

However, a leader was also supported because of the power, influence and the positions he was able to distribute. Charismatic authority is unstable not only because it stands and falls with a unique personality, but also because leaders sooner or later have to provide nontrivial benefits to their constituencies. At that point they are compelled to embark on the trajectory of organization building and begin to produce selective incentives that tend to result in clientelistic parties.

Herbert Kitschelt has therefore argued that political cleavages and related programmatic divisions cannot explain the emergence of new parties or the affiliations of newly enfranchised voters, as in Eastern Europe between the wars. When voters choose *new* parties, according to Kitchelt, one of three considerations is the key: 1) sympathy with the personality of a party's candidates, 2) expected personal and selective tangible and intangible advantages derived from the victory of a party, or 3) the production of indirect advantages in the form of collective goods if the party of choice wins the election.[103] Other incentives that bind people to a party, such as the attraction of a charismatic personality or clientelistic favors, rather than programmatic cleavages, must then be used to account for party politics in interwar Eastern Europe.

Clientelistic parties advertise the provision of collective goods in their official programs, but voters know that all the parties will deliver are personal services and benefits to their loyal following. Clientelistic parties work around rather than through the stated rules of democratic competition. "Typically, when a party or coalition left the government there was either strong business approaches to the new government for favors or a considerable turnover of government contracts, the state everywhere being the largest capitalist enterprise."[104]

Between the wars this kind of patronage system was present in the economically advanced Czech regions as well: Government membership was important, the parties were job providers on a large scale, not only in the state administration but also in industry, the banks, unions and associations which prospered around each party. Ministries tended to be staffed almost entirely by officials belonging to one party and to remain in the hands of the same party from government to government. [105]

Nonetheless, in my opinion, Kitschelt's theoretical framework amounts to abstracting from the contextual embedment of party politics to too large a degree: "the rural obsession" of Central Eastern European politics, connected with the cleavage between the countryside and the bureaucracy, made it very difficult, if not impossible, for urban parties to penetrate into the countryside. It constituted, so to speak, the "rhetorical soundboard" to all kinds of political mobilization, without which it is inexplicable. Politics in Eastern Europe therefore, had, as pointed out by Henry Lithgow Roberts, to be "the art of taking advantage of the amorphous character of the peasantry."[106] The low degree of political institutionalization, with the degree of clarity in the formulation of political goals as an empirical indicator, seems to be an intermediary variable explaining the incidence of charismatic–clientelistic politics. On the other hand, the fact that the leaderships seemingly used the organization to advance their own careers, and rank and file members saw in peasant organizations a means of attaining solutions to their own problems, seems to have strengthened this lack of institutionalization. In the words of Derek Urwin,

> Whereas many of the pre-1914 populist movements had been reluctant to identify with specific class interest, many of the new agrarian parties made representation and social elevation of the peasant class their sole ideological *raison d'etre*. The urban leadership of these agrarian parties did nothing to diminish the salience of this political dimension, while simultaneously weakening both the likelihood of a specific urban-rural confrontation and the chances of an agrarian victory.[107]

Conditions in Bulgaria appeared to be more favorable for the establishment of a large agrarian party: it possessed a highly egalitarian structure and was homogeneous in terms of both religion and race. The Agrarian Union had reached significant electoral proportions before 1914. But under the leadership of Alexander Stamboliski it dominated Bulgarian politics for a few years after 1918, with a membership of over 120,000 by 1922.

The party's leader, Stamboliski, argued that mechanization was not the most satisfactory way of organizing agriculture, that Bulgaria should possess only secondary industries of direct value to the countryside, and that industrial workers should be placed under the direct political control of the Agrarian Union and its paramilitary arm, the Orange Guard. The left-wing populist regime sought to liquidate the "parasitic" merchant class and bureaucracy. The political activity of lawyers was restricted and intellectuals excluded from the party. Progressive taxation was introduced according to class principles and a state monopoly on grain trading was introduced to eliminate private traders.

In 1920 Stamboliski had, without hesitation, ordered troops into action to end a strike by railway workers. By driving city and countryside into total opposition to each other, he had sealed his own fate. The Bulgarian regime of Stamboliski was overwhelmed by a counterrevolution, in which the military and the endangered elite of the old order joined hands with the Macedonian terrorist organization, IMRO, and the Communist Party of Bulgaria on the day the *putch* took place adopted a platform of neutrality. Bulgarian politics then became the same as elsewhere—a factional struggle to share in the spoils.[108]

The Cultural Basis of Agrarian Parties: Agrarian Mobilization and Religion in Eastern Europe

Agrarian parties arose in the Catholic areas of East Europe, such as Czechoslovakia and Croatia. This contradicts Rokkan's thesis of the unlikelihood of agrarian parties in Catholic countries. Slovenia and Slovakia do not offer particular problems. Although Slovakia was essentially rural (61 percent of the population was dependent on agriculture, compared with 33 percent in Czechoslovakia as a whole), the Czechoslovakian agrarian party, the Republican Party of Farmers and Smallholders, found it difficult to compete with the particularistic, clerically led Slovakian People's Party.

The strength of the Republicans in Slovakia was due to a merger in 1920 with the Slovakian National Peasants' Party, which had its support primarily from the Protestant minority (18 percent of the Slovakian population). In Slovenia the People's Party, formed in 1890 by Catholic priests, was similar to the Christian Democratic parties of West Europe. The People's Party was able to resist the challenge from a Slovenian Peasants' Party in 1920 (which it quickly absorbed) and later a Republican Peasants' Party that gained 11 percent of the votes in Slovenia at the *Skupstina* election before it suddenly vanished.

It seems to be more difficult to explain the existence of the prominent agrarian parties in Catholic Czechoslovakia and Croatia, which during the first decades of their existence were non-religious, and tended to be anti-clerical, in their attitudes. In the case of Czechoslovakia the best explanation is perhaps the special historical circumstances in the Czech provinces. The nationalistic agitation toward the end of the Habsburg monarchy was strongest in Bohemia and Moravia. It even led to an unsuccessful attempt at creating an independent Czech Catholic Church. There exists a strong historical association between the Protestant Hussite kingdom, destroyed by the Habsburgs in the battle of the White Mountain in 1620, and the emergence of Czech nationalism in the late 19th century. Despite the forced introduction of Catholicism, Bohemia "in spirit" remained very much a Protestant country. In addition, the few Protestants had considerable influence on political life. It was in Bohemia that the Czech agrarian party, the Republicans, had their greatest support. The Czech People's Party (the Catholic party) under clerical leadership had its strength among smallholders and laborers in Moravia–Silesia. In Slovakia, religion coupled with efforts to achieve autonomy prevented a strong agrarian party.

Nationalism also played an important part in the case of Croatia: the formation of the Croatian Peasants' Party took place in 1904, when Croatia was ruled by Hungary. Like its Czech counterpart, it tended to be anticlerical in its leaning and developed the most extensive peasant ideology apart from the Agrarian Union in Bulgaria. After 1918 Croatian opposition to what was seen as Greater Serbia caused the Croatian Peasants' Party to accept drawing closer to the church and to claim to represent interests other than the purely agrarian.

Poland is an interesting case, where numerically important but politically weak Catholic *and* peasant parties emerged. The most important determinants in the Polish party system were the different levels of development and institutional characteristics in the various regions. Apart from the Ukrainian and Jewish party systems, different party systems emerged in the three regions previously ruled by Germany, the Habsburg monarchy and Tsarist Russia. Catholic parties were strong in the former German Poland. Bismarck's *Kulturkampf* had been especially rigorously forced on the Polish parts of the *Reich* (for instance a ban on the Polish language in government administration and in schools). These areas were consequently strengthened in their Catholicism and nationalism. In Poznan the National Democrats were the biggest party. The Christian Democrats were chiefly concentrated in the industrial population in Silesia, originally mobilized by the German *Zentrum.*

The agrarian parties had little success here. The peasants obeyed the Polish aristocrats and big landowners, as they had done prior to 1914. The biggest agrarian party, *Piast*, was formed in Austrian Galicia, where there were many medium-sized freehold farms. The Poles had been a privileged group under the Habsburg dynasty, which favored the Poles at the expense of the Ukrainian peasant masses. *Piast* remained strong in Galicia, but failed to repeat the success elsewhere. The poor Congress Poland, for its part, was the scene of a more radical agrarian movement, *Wyzwolenie,* which advocated a radical agrarian reform, albeit in the framework of private ownership.

Social Structure and Support of Agrarian Parties: The Case of Yugoslavia

The absence of national integration in Yugoslavia prevented any party from mobilizing across the regions (the exception was of course the Communist Party). Even within each region agrarian parties had difficulty mobilizing all peasants. It is therefore not surprising that, for instance, only one-tenth of the members of the *Skupstina* in 1927 were peasants or laborers. Within each nationality a dominant party grew up around a strong leader in defense of their own cultural and national characteristics. In Serbia, this party was the Radical Party under Nikola Pasic, which the Serbian Peasants' Union was unable to beat in elections. Similarly, the Slovenian People's Party dominated in Catholic Slovenia, while the Yugoslav Muslim Organization was the dominant party in Bosnia–Hercegovina. The only regional peasant party that had majority status in its nation was the Croatian Peasants' Party. However, this party owed its success more to its defense of Croation autonomy against Serbian nationalism than to the fact that it was an agrarian party. As it gained support in the towns, it threw the original peasant ideology overboard and at the same time renounced its anticlerical position.

SOME CONCLUDING REMARKS

This chapter discusses East and Central European history in light of the European macro model of the Norwegian political scientist and sociologist Stein Rokkan. This involves a geographical extension of the model's range as well as a highlighting of some possibilities for a theoretical modification. The following aspects of the model have been examined and discussed comparatively: Rokkan's city-belt theory, problems associated with alliance formation in state building, cultural standardization of heterogeneous populations (center–periphery conflicts) and political mobilization. The focus is empirical and the discussion *longue durée*, from the Middle Ages until the Second World War. Nationalism, a phenomenon largely ignored by Stein Rokkan, has been discussed in light of Otto Bauer's analyses in the classically Marxian tradition and contemporary theories, and has been followed through the interwar period, not least with regard to the significance of the question of nationality for the stability of democratic regimes established in the wake of the peace at Versailles. Political mobilization has been discussed empirically with special regard to the significance of the agrarian mobilization (peasantism, populism) and religion for the political-cleavage structures. Rokkan himself attempted to apply both diachronic and synchronic variables in his models, with both historical and structural explanatory factors. The problem for the historical analysis is the fact that Eastern Europe was not at the center of his scientific interest. However, there is nothing that prevents us from specifying and extending that interest empirically so as to include even the dynamics of Eastern Europe's political development down to the interwar period.

When approaching the question of today's postcommunist nation-building processes, however, a greater problem is nevertheless the structural: the fact that today we are not dealing with the same societies as then, but societies that have undergone extensive restructuring of their entire social and economic order, and that contain social groups and potential agents that are different from those of the interwar period, and also from the social-democratic and liberal systems of today's Western Europe. They must be analyzed on the background of the state Socialist experience and Rokkan's models must be supplemented here by other analytical instruments.

NOTES

1. See Daniel Chirot's review of Theda Skocpol's "Social Revolutions in the Modern World," *Social Forces*, 75:3, 1997, 1121–26.

2. Weber, Max, *Economy and Society. An Outline of Interpretative Sociology*, vol. 2. Berkeley: University of California Press 1978, p. 948.

3. Ugelvik Larsen, Stein, "The Logic of Stein Rokkans Overall Model of Europe." Paper presented at the XVI World Congress of the International Political Science Association, Berlin, August 21–25, 1994, p. 11.

4. Ibid.

5. McGowan, Bruce, *Economic Life in Ottoman Europe. Taxation, Trade and the Struggle for Land, 1600–1800*. Cambridge & New York: Cambridge University Press 1981; Vucinich, W. S., "The Yugoslav Lands in the Ottoman Period: Post-War Marxist Interpretations of Indigenous and Ottoman Institutions," *Journal of Modern History*, 27:3, 1955, pp. 287–305; Barkey, Karen, *Bandits and Bureaucrats: The Ottoman Route of State Centralization*. Ithaca, NY: Cornell UP 1994. See also the

contributions and discussions in Daniel Chirot (ed.), *The Origins of Backwardness in Eastern Europe. Economics & Politics from the Middle Ages until the Early Twentieth Century.* Berkeley: University of California Press 1989.

6. Cvetkova, Bistra, "The Bulgarian Haiduk Movement in the 15th–18th Centuries," in Gunther Rosenberg, Bela Kiraly, and Peter Sugar (eds.), *East Central European Society and War in Pre-Revolutionary Eighteenth Century.* New York: Columbia University Press 1982, pp. 327–29; Hobsbawn, Eric, *Bandits.* Harmondsworth: Penguin 1969, pp. 70–71; Sugar, Peter, *Southeastern Europe under Ottoman Rule, 1354–1804.* Seattle: University of Washington Press 1977, 242–44.

7. Lampe, John, "Imperial Borderlands or Capitalist Periphery? 1520–1914," in Daniel Chirot (ed.), *The Origins of Backwardness in Eastern Europe. Economics & Politics from the Middle Ages until the Early Twentieth Century.* Berkeley: University of California Press 1989, p. 190.

8. In my discussion of the Balkan (and Romanian) development I have relied much on Gale Stokes fine piece of comparative analysis, "The Social Origins of East European Politics," in Daniel Chirot (ed.), *The Origins of Backwardness in Eastern Europe.* Berkeley: University of California Press 1989, citations, pp. 234, 236. See also Charles and Barbara Jelavich, *The Establishment of the Balkan National States, 1804–1920.* Seattle: University of Washington Press 1977; and Joseph Rothschild, *East Central Europe between the Two World Wars.* Seattle: University of Washington Press 1988.

9. Stokes, Gale. "The Social Origins of East European Politics." In Daniel Chirot (ed.), *The Origins of Backwardness in Eastern Europe. Economics & Politics from the Middle Ages until the Early Twentieth Century.* Berkeley: University of California Press 1989, p. 244.

10. Berglund, Stein, Joakim Ekman, and Frank Aarebrot, "The Challenge of History in Central Europe," in *The Handbook of Eastern Europe*, 2nd ed. Cheltenham: Edward Elard 2004, p. 23.

11. Rokkan, Stein, with Angus Campbell, Per Torsvik, and Henry Valen, *Citizens, Elections, Parties; Approaches to the Comparative Study of the Processes of Development.* Oslo: Universitetsforlaget/New York: McKay 1970, p. 54.

12. See Ivan T. Berend, *The Crisis Zone of Europe: An Interpretation of East-Central European History in the First Half of the Twentieth Century.* Cambridge: Cambridge University Press 1986, citation p. 14.

13. Walicki, Andrzej, "The Three Traditions in Polish Patriotism," in Stanislaw Gomulka and Antony Polonsky (eds.), *Polish Paradoxes.* London: Routledge 1990, pp. 27–28.

14. See Gale Stokes, "The Social Origins of East European Politics," in Daniel Chirot, *The Origins of Backwardness in Eastern Europe. Economics & Politics from the Middle Ages until the Early Twentieth Century.* Berkeley: University of California Press 1989; and the various contributions in Stein Ugelvik Larsen, Bernt Hagtvet, and Jan Petter Myklebust (eds.), *Who Were the Fascists.* Oslo & Bergen: Universitetsforlaget 1980.

15. McCagg Jr., William, "Hungary's 'Feudalized' Bourgeoisie," *Journal of Modern History*, 44:1, 1972, p. 66.

16. Ibid., pp. 74, 67.

17. Ibid., p. 75.

18. Jaszi, Oscar, *Dissolution of the Habsburg Monarchy*. Chicago: University of Chicago Press 1961, p. 153.

19. Macartney, C. A, *Hungary and Her Successors; The Treaty of Trianon and Its Consequences 1919–1937*. London & New York: Oxford University Press 1937; Kiraly, Bela, and Laszlo Veszpremy (eds.), *Trianon and East Central Europe*. Boulder, CO: Social Science Monographs 1995; R. W. Seton-Watson, *Treaty Revision and the Hungarian Frontiers*. London: Eyre & Spottiswoode 1934.

20. Peter Hanak cited in Steven B. Vardy, "The Impact of Trianon upon Hungary and the Hungarian Mind: The Nature of Interwar Hungarian Irredentism," *Hungarian Studies Review*, 10:1, 1983, pp. 24–25.

21. Vago, Bela, and George L. Mosse (eds.), *Jews and Non-Jews in Eastern Europe, 1918–45*. New York: Wiley 1974.

22. Berglund, Stein, Joakim Ekman, and Frank Aarebrot, "The Challenge of History in Central Europe," in *The Handbook of Eastern Europe*, 2nd ed. Cheltenham: Edward Elard 2004, p. 24.

23. Berend, Ivan T., *The Crisis Zone of Europe. An Interpretation of East-Central European History in the First Half of the Twentieth Century*. Cambridge: Cambridge University Press 1986, p. 66.

24. Pollard, Sidney, *Peaceful Conquest. The Industrialization of Europe 1760–1970*. Oxford: Oxford University Press 1981, p. 80.

25. Koralka, Jiri, "The Czechs," in Andreas Kappeler, Fikret Adanir, and Alan O'Day (eds.), *The Formation of National Elites. Comparative Studies on Governments and Non-Dominant Ethnic Groups in Europe, 1850–1940*, vol. 6. Dartmouth: European Science Foundation/New York University Press 1992.

26. A significant number of Czech members of the Bohemian diet were lawyers—mostly self-employed; a similar phenomenon can be seen in other parliamentary bodies in 19th-century Europe. The percentage of lawyers reached its peak in Bohemia in 1878 (33 percent) and in Moravia in 1878 (almost 42 percent). In the beginning the circle of politically active Czech lawyers was rather limited in both diets; by the end of the 19th century their predominance was challenged by peasant representatives, mostly elected in rural constituencies. Up to 1884 a temporary decrease in the number of peasant members appeared in Moravia because as a rule it was only in rural constituencies that Czech candidates had an assurance of being elected. The peasants, therefore, elected recognized leaders of the Czech national party. In Bohemia also the authority of the Old Czech and Young Czech leaders was undiminished among the rural population. See Jiri Koralka, "The Czechs," in Andreas Kappeler, Fikret Adanir, and Alan O'Day (eds.), *The Formation of National Elites. Comparative Studies on Governments and Non-Dominant Ethnic Groups in Europe, 1850–1940*, vol. 6. Dartmouth: European Science Foundation/New York University Press 1992, pp. 91, 92, tables 4.3 and 4.4.

27. This is also Gale Stoke's conclusion in her "The Social Origins of East European Politics," in Daniel Chirot, *The Origins of Backwardness in Eastern Europe. Economics & Politics from the Middle Ages until the Early Twentieth Century*. Berkeley: University of California Press 1989, citation pp. 218–19.

28. Lipset, Seymor Martin, and Stein Rokkan (eds.), *Party Systems and Voter Alignment: Cross-National Perspectives*. New York: Free Press 1967, pp. 38–39.

29. Pech, Stanley Z., "Political Parties in Eastern Europe 1848–1939: Comparisons and Continuities," *East Central Europe*, 5:1, 1978, pp. 1–38.

30. Urwin, Derek W., *From Ploughshare to Ballotbox. The Politic of Agrarian Defence in Europe*. Bergen: Universitetsforlaget 1980, 89.

31. Kitromilides, Paschalis M., "Imagined Communities' and the Origins of the National Question in the Balkans," *East European Quarterly*, 19, 1989, pp. 149–94 (p. 160).

32. Bauer, Otto, *Die Nationalitätenfrage und die Sozialdemokratie*. Vienna: Wiener Volksbuchhandlung 1924 (1907).

33. Kann, Robert, *The Multinational Empire*, vol. 1–2. New York: Colombia University Press 1950.

34. Rokkan, Stein, "Territories, Centers, and Peripheries: Toward a Geoethnic–Geoeconomic–Geopolitical Model of Differentiation Within Western Europe," in Jean Gottmann (ed.), *Center and Periphery. Spatial Variation in Politics*. Beverly Hills & London: Sage 1980, pp. 174–78.

35. Hroch, Miroslav, "How Much Does Nation Formation Depend on Nationalism?" *East European Politics and Societies*, 4:1, 1990, p. 109.

36. Kann, Robert, *The Multinational Empire*, vol. 1–2. New York: Colombia University Press 1950.

37. Scöpflin, George, "The Political Traditions of Eastern Europe," *Dædalus*, 119:1, 1990, p. 69.

38. See the excellent interpretation of Ivan Berend, *The Crisis Zone of Europe. An Interpretation of East-Central European History in the First Half of the Twentieth Century*. Cambridge: Cambridge University Press 1986; and Peter Sugar (ed.), *Native Fascism in the Successor States, 1918–1945*. Santa Barbara, CA: ABC-Clio 1971; Joseph Rothschild, *East Central Europe between the two World Wars*. Seattle: University of Washington Press 1988; Stein Ugelvik Larsen, Bernt Hagtvet, and Jan Petter Myklebust, *Who Were the Fascists*, Part 4. "Fascism in Eastern Europe." Oslo & Bergen: Universitetsforlaget 1980.

39. Sartori, Giovanni, "European Political Parties: The Case of Polarized Pluralism," in Joseph La Palombara and Myron Weiner (eds.), *Political Parties and Political Development*. Princeton, NJ: Princeton University Press 1966.

40. Berglund, Stein, Joakim Ekman, and Frank Aarebrot, "The Challenge of History in Central Europe," in *The Handbook of Eastern Europe*, 2nd ed. Cheltenham: Edward Elard 2004, p. 20.

41. Wandycz, P., *The Price of Freedom. A History of East Central Europe from the Middle Ages to the Present*. London: Routledge 1992, pp. 206–14.

42. See Carol Skalnik Leff, *National Conflict in Czechoslovakia. The Making and Remaking of a State, 1918–1987*. Princeton, NJ: Princeton UP 1988, chap. 2.

43. Laqueur, Walter, *Terrorism*. Boston: Little, Brown & Co. 1977, p. 76.

44. Poulantzas, Nicos, *Political Power and Social Classes*. London: Verso 1982, p. 298.

45. Jessop, Bob, *State Theory. Putting the Capitalist State in its Place*. Oxford: Polity Press 1990, p. 163.

46. Gramsci, Antonio, *Selections from the Prison Notebooks* (ed. and trans. Quintin Hoare and Geoffrey Nowell Smith). London: Lawrence & Wishart 1971, p. 80, n. 48.

47. Jessop, Bob, *State Theory. Putting the Capitalist State in its Place*. Oxford: Polity Press 1990, p. 163.

48. See Frank Aarebrot and Sten Berglund, "Statehood, Secularization, Cooptation: Explaining Democratic Survival in Inter-War Europe—Stein Rokkan's Conceptual Map Revisited," *Historical Social Research*, 20:2, 1995, p. 220.

49. Korbonski, Andrzey, "Civil–Military Relations in Poland Between the Wars: 1918–1939," *Armed Forces and Society*, 14: 2, 1988, pp. 161–90.

50. Berglund, Stein, Joakim Ekman, and Frank Aarebrot, "The Challenge of History in Central Europe," in *The Handbook of Eastern Europe*, 2nd ed. Cheltenham: Edward Elard 2004, p. 24.

51. Berend, Ivan T., *The Crisis Zone of Europe. An Interpretation of East-Central European History in the First Half of the Twentieth Century*. Cambridge: Cambridge University Press 1986, p. 64.

52. Hobsbawn, Eric, *The Age of Catastrophe. The Short Twentieth Century*. London: Michael Joseph, 1995, p. 127.

53. Payne, Stanley, *A History of Fascism, 1914–1945*. London: UCL Press 1995, pp. 492, 252.

54. Berend, Ivan T., "Different Modes of Social Revolt after World War I," in Ivan T. Berend, *The Crisis Zone of Europe. An Interpretation of East-Central European History in the First Half of the Twentieth Century*. Cambridge: Cambridge University Press 1986, chap. 3.

55. Manoilescu, Mihail, *The Theory of Protectionism and of International Trade*. London: King & Son 1931; Manoilescu, Mihail, *Le siècle du corporatisme: doctrine du corpoaratisme integral et pur*. Paris: Felix Alcan 1934. See also Philippe Schmitter, "Reflections on Mihail Manoilescu and the Political Consequences of Delayed-Development on the Periphery of Western Nations," in Kenneth Jowitt (ed.), *Social Change in Romania, 1860–1940: A Debate on Development in a European Nation*. Berkeley: Institute of International Studies at the University of California 1978.

56. Carol Leff, *National Conflict in Czechoslovakia. The Making and Remaking of a State, 1918–1987*. Princeton, NJ: Princeton UP 1988, pp. 60–61, 63.

57. Hanson, Stephen E., and Jeffrey S. Kopstein, "The Weimar/Russia Comparison," *Post-Soviet Affairs*, 13:3, 1997, p. 261.

58. See Gregory Luebbert, *Liberalism, Fascism, or Social Democracy. Social Classes and the Political Origins of Regimes in Interwar Europe*. New York & Oxford: Oxford University Press 1991, 291–95.

59. Ibid., p. 293.

60. Campbell, F. Gregory, "Central Europe's Bastion of Democracy," *East European Quarterly*, 11:2, 1977, pp. 155–76 (p. 165).

61. Leff, Carol, *National Conflict in Czechoslovakia. The Making and Remaking of a State, 1918–1987*. Princeton, NJ: Princeton UP 1988, p. 74.

62. Ibid.

63. Campbell, F. Gregory, "Central Europe's Bastion of Democracy," *East European Quarterly*, 11:2, 1977, pp. 155–76; Stein Ugelvik Larsen, "The Logic of Stein Rokkan's Overall Model of Europe," *East European Quarterly*, 11:2, 1977, p. 170.

64. See again the contributions in Daniel Chirot, *The Origins of Backwardness in Eastern Europe*. Berkeley: University of California Press 1989; Alexander Gerschenkron, *Economic Backwardness in Historical Perspective*. Cambridge: Belknap Press of Harvard University Press 1962; Ivan T. Berend and György Ranky, *Economic Development in East-Central Europe in the 19th and 20th Centuries*. New York: Columbia University Press 1974.

65. Balcerak, Wieslaw, "The Disintegration of the Versailles System in Central-Eastern Europe, 1919–1939," *Acta Poloniae Historica*, 26, 1972, pp. 47–72; Carr, Edward Hallett, *The Twenty Years Crisis*. London: Macmillan 1958; Knock, Thomas J., *To End All Wars: Woodrow Wilson and the Quest for a New World Order*. New York: Oxford University Press 1992; MacMillan, Margareth, *Paris 1919: Six Months That Changed the World*. New York: Random House 2002; Schmitt, Bernadotte E., "The Peace Treaties of 1919–1920," *Proceedings of the American Philosophical Society*, 104:1, 1960, pp. 101–10.

66. Janos, Andrew, "Continuity and Change in Eastern Europe: Strategies of Post-Communist Politics," in Beverly Crawford (ed.), *Markets, States, and Democracy. The Political Economy of Post-Communist Transformation*. Boulder, CO: Westview Press 1995, pp. 150–74 (p. 159).

67. Carr, Edward Hallett, *The Twenty Years Crisis*. London: Macmillan 1958, p. 27.

68. Evans, Ifor L., *The Agrarian Revolutions in Roumania*. Cambridge: Cambridge University Press 1924.

69. Mitrany, David, *Marx Against the Peasant. A Study in Social Dogmatism*. New York: Collier Books 1961, p. 115.

70. Rosenstein-Rodan, Paul N., "Problems of Industrialization of Eastern and South-Eastern Europe," *Economic Journal*, 53, June–September 1943, pp. 202–11.

71. Moore, Wilbert E., *Economic Demography of Eastern and Southern Europe*. Geneva: League of Nations; reprint New York: Arno Press 1972, pp. 65–66.

72. Urwin, Derek W., *From Ploughshare to Ballotbox. The Politic of Agrarian Defence in Europe*. Bergen: Universitetsforlaget 1980, p. 184. All Rokkanian, and indeed all comparative, research on peasant politics is indebted to Derek Urwin's work.

73. Rothschild, Joseph, *East Central Europe between the two World Wars*. Seattle: University of Washington Press 1988, p. 210.

74. Flora, Peter, Stein Kuhnle, and Derek Urwin (eds.), *State Formation, Nation-Building and Mass Politics in Europe. The Theory of Stein Rokkan*. Oxford: Oxford University Press 1999, p. 322.

75. Ibid., pp. 333–34.

76. Urwin, Derek W., *From Ploughshare to Ballotbox. The Politic of Agrarian Defence in Europe*. Bergen: Universitetsforlaget 1980, p. 206.

77. Urwin, Derek W., *From Ploughshare to Ballotbox. The Politic of Agrarian Defence in Europe*. Bergen: Universitetsforlaget 1980, pp. 170–72, citations p. 172.

78. Kautsky, John H. (ed.), *Political Change in Underdeveloped Countries: Nationalism and Communism*. New York: John Wiley 1962, p. 47.

79. Rothschild, Joseph, *East Central Europe between the Two World Wars*. Seattle: University of Washington Press 1988, pp. 17–19.

80. Janos, Andrew C., "The Politics of Backwardness in Continental Europe, 1780–1945," *World Politics*, 41:3, 1989, p. 336.

81. Peter Evans combines a Weberian and institutional perspective on development with more recent development theories. He identifies useful insights provided by the neo-utilitarians. They focus, like the Weberians and to some degree the Marxists as well, on the state as an actor and thereby bury the neoclassical economists' vision of the state as a neutral arbiter, partially recapturing Marx's insights into the biases that characterize state policy. See Peter Evans, *Embedded Autonomy. States and Industrial Transformation*. Princeton, NJ: Princeton University Press 1995, chaps. 1 and 2.

82. Evans, Peter, *Embedded Autonomy. States and Industrial Transformation*. Princeton, NJ: Princeton University Press 1995, p. 23.

83. Turner, Bryan, *For Weber: Essays in the Sociology of Fate*. London: Routledge & Kegan Paul 1981, p. 245.

84. Eisenstadt, Shmuel Noah, "Comparative Analysis of State Formation in Historical Context," *International Social Science Journal*, 32:4; Weber, Max, *Economy and Society. An Outline of Interpretative Sociology*, vol. 2. Berkeley: University of California Press 1978, pp. 1006–69.

85. Weber, Max, *Economy and Society. An Outline of Interpretative Sociology* (eds. Guenther Roth and Claus Wittich). Berkeley: University of California Press 1978, pp. 1108–109.

86. Daskalov, Roumen, "Ideas about, and Reactions to Modernization in the Balkans," *East European Quarterly*, 31:2, 1997, pp. 142, 171.

87. Evans, Peter, *Embedded Autonomy. States and Industrial Transformation*. Princeton, NJ: Princeton University Press 1995, p. 23.

88. Urwin, Derek W., *From Ploughshare to Ballotbox. The Politic of Agrarian Defence in Europe*. Bergen: Universitetsforlaget 1980, p. 226.

89. Krnjevic, Juraj, "Peasants Movements in Eastern Europe," *Contemporary Review*, 174, July/December 1948, p. 112.

90. Khoros, V., *Populism: Its Past, Present and Future*. Moscow: Progress 1984, 79.

91. Mitrany, David, *Marx Against the Peasant. A Study in Social Dogmatism*. New York: Collier Books 1961, p. 246, n. 27.

92. See Keith Hitchins, *Rumania: 1867–1947*. Oxford: Clarendon Press 1994.

93. Khoros, V. *Populism: Its Past, Present and Future*. Moscow: Progress 1984, p. 83.

94. See the contributions in Ghita Ionescu and Ernest Gellner (eds.), *Populism; Its Meaning and National Characteristics*. New York: Macmillan 1969; David Mitrany, *Marx Against the Peasant. A Study in Social Dogmatism*. New York: Collier Books 1961; and also Joseph Rothschild, *East Central Europe between the two World Wars*. Seattle: University of Washington Press 1988.

95. Urwin, Derek W., *From Ploughshare to Ballotbox. The Politic of Agrarian Defence in Europe*. Bergen: Universitetsforlaget 1980, p. 178.

96. Urwin, Derek W., *From Ploughshare to Ballotbox. The Politic of Agrarian Defence in Europe*. Bergen: Universitetsforlaget 1980, p. 89.

97. See Umberto Eco, "Ur-Fascism," *New York Review of Books*, June 22, 1995.

98. Berglund, Stein, Joakim Ekman, and Frank Aarebrot, "The Challenge of History in Central Europe," in *The Handbook of Eastern Europe*, 2nd ed. Cheltenham: Edward Elard 2004, p. 28.

99. Codreanu, Corneliu Zelea, *For My Legionaire: The Iron Guard*. Madrid: Editura "Libertatea" 1976, p, 105.

100. Berend, Ivan T., *The Crisis Zone of Europe. An Interpretation of East-Central European History in the First Half of the Twentieth Century*. Cambridge: Cambridge University Press 1986, p. 30.

101. Urwin, Derek W., *From Ploughshare to Ballotbox. The Politic of Agrarian Defence in Europe*. Bergen; Universitetsforlaget 1980, p. 245.

102. Wolff, Robert Lee, *The Balkans in Our Time*. Cambridge, MA: Harvard University Press 1956, p. 102.

103. Kitchelt, Herbert, "Formation of Party Cleavages in Post-Communist Democracies—Theoretical Propositions," *Party Politics*, 1:4, 1995, pp. 447–72.

104. Stoianovich, R., "The Social Foundations of Balkan Politics 1750–1941," in Charles and Barbara Jelavich (eds.), *The Balkans in Transition. Essays on the Development of Balkan Life and Politics Since the Eighteenth Century*. Berkeley: University of California Press 1963, p. 336.

105. See Carol Skalnik Leff, *National Conflict in Czechoslovakia. The Making and Remaking of a State, 1918–1987*. Princeton, NJ: Princeton UP 1988, p. 48–50.

106. Roberts, Henry L., *Rumania. Political Problems of an Agrarian State*. New Haven, CT: Yale University Press 1951, pp. 90–91.

107. Urwin, Derek W., *From Ploughshare to Ballotbox. The Politic of Agrarian Defence in Europe*. Bergen: Universitetsforlaget 1980, p. 251.

108. Bell, John D., *Peasants in Power: Alexander Stamboliski and the Bulgarian Agrarian National Union, 1899–1923*. Princeton, NJ: Princeton University Press 1977.

Bibliography

Aarebrot, Frank, and Sten Berglund. "Statehood, Secularization, Cooptation: Explaining Democratic Survival in Inter-War Europe—Stein Rokkan's Conceptual Map Revisited," *Historical Social Research* 20:2, 1995. pp. 210–25.

Abrams, Philip. *Historical Sociology*. Somerset, England: Open Books 1982.

Adamov, V. V., et al. (eds.). *Voprosy istorii kapitalisticheskoi Rossii: problema mnogoukladnosti*. Sverdlovsk: Uralskii gosudarstvennyi universitet 1972.

Adreevskii, Ivan. *O namestnikakh, voevodakh i gubernatorakh*. St Petersburg: Prats 1864.

Agursky, Michail. *The Third Rome. National Bolshevism in the USSR*. Boulder, CO: Westview Press 1987.

Allardt, Erik, and Henry Valen. "Stein Rokkan. An intellectual Profile," in Per Torsvik (ed.), *Mobilization, Center-Periphery Structures and Nation-Building*. Bergen: Universitetsforlaget 1981.

Allworth, Edward (ed.). *Soviet Nationality Problems*. New York: Columbia University Press 1971.

Amburger, Erik. *Geschichte der Behördenorganisation von Peter Grossen bis 1917*. Studien zur Geschichte Osteuropas 10. Leiden: E. J. Brill 1966.

Anderson, Benedict. *Imagined Communities. Reflections on the Origin and Spread of Nationalism*. London: Verso 1986.

Anderson, Perry. *Lineages of the Absolutist State*. London: New Left Books 1974.

Andreevskii, I. E. (ed). *Entsiklopedicheskii Slovar* 13. Saint Petersburg: Izd. F. A. Brokgauz & Efron 1894.

Arutiunian, Iurii. "Izmenenie sotsialnoi struktury sovetskikh natsii," *Istoriia SSSR*, 4, 1972, pp. 3–20.

Aves, Jonathan. "The Evolution of Independent Political Movements After 1988," in Geoffrey A. Hosking, Jonathan Aves, and Peter J. S. Duncan. *The Road to Post-Communism. Independent Political Movements in the Soviet Union 1985–1991*. London: Pinter Publishers 1992, pp. 29–66.

Avrekh, A. I. "Russii absoliutizm i evo rol v utverzhdenie kapitalizma v Rossi," *Istoria SSSR*, February 1968, pp. 82–103.

Balcerak, Wieslaw, "The Disintegration of the Versailles System in Central-Eastern Europe, 1919–1939," *Acta Poloniae Historica* 26: 1972, pp. 47–72.

Baranova, T. J. "Iz istorii prepodavaniia russkovo iazyka v nerusskikh shkolakh SSSR," *Sovetskaia pedagogiga* 12, 1977, pp. 115–23.

Barany, George. "Hungary: The Uncompromising Compromise." *Austria History Yearbook*, III:1, 1967, pp. 234–59.

Barkey, Karen. *Bandits and Bureaucrats: The Ottoman route of State Centralization*. Ithaca, NY: Cornell UP 1994.

Baron, Samuel H. *Plekhanov; The Father of Russian Marxism*. Stanford, CA: Stanford University Press 1963.

———. "Plekhanov, Trotsky, and the Development of Soviet Historiography." *Soviet Studies* 26:3, pp. 380–83.

Bauer, Otto. *Die Nationalitätenfrage und die Sozialdemokratie*. Vienna: Wiener Volksbuchhandlung 1924 (1907).

———. "Schlusswort zur Minoritätenfrage." *Der Kampf. Sozialdemokratische Monatschrift*. Vienna 1911, 4, pp. 201–9.

Beales, Derek. *Enlightenment and Reform in Eighteenth-Century Europe*. London & New York: I. B. Tauris 2005.

Bell, John D. *Peasants in Power: Alexander Stamboliski and the Bulgarian Agrarian National Union, 1899–1923*. Princeton, NJ: Princeton University Press 1977.

Bendix, Reinhard. "Backwardness and Intellectual Mobilization." In Reinhard Bendix, *Force, Fate, and Freedom. On Historical Sociology*. Berkeley: University of California Press 1984.

Bennigsen, Aleksandre, and Chantal Lemercier-Quelquejay. *Islam in the Soviet Union*. London: Pall Mall Press 1967.

Berend, Ivan T. "Besondere Characterzüge der Industrierevolution in österreichisc-hungarischer Monarchie," *Zeitgeschichte*, 1:11–12, 1974, pp. 222–38.

———. *The Crisis Zone of Europe: An Interpretation of East-Central European History in the First Half of the Twentieth Century*. Cambridge: Cambridge University Press.

Berend, Ivan T., and György Ranky. *Economic Development in East-Central Europe in the 19th and 20th Centuries*. New York & London: Columbia University Press 1974.

———. "Economic Factors in Nationalism. The Example of Hungary at the Beginning of the Twentieth Century." *Austria History Yearbook* 3:3, 1967, pp. 163–86.

———. *Hungary: A Century of Development*. Newton Abbot: David & Charles 1974.

———. "Ungarns wirtschaftliche Entwicklung 1848–1918," in Adam Wandruszka and Peter Urbanitsch (eds.), *Die Habsburgermonarchie 1848–1918*, vol. 1. *Die Wirtschaftliche Entwicklung*. Vienna: Verlag der Österreichischen Akademie der Wissenschaften 1973.

Berglund, Stein, Joakim Ekman, and Frank Aarebrot. *The Handbook of Eastern Europe*. 2nd ed. Cheltenham: Edward Elard 2004.

Berntzen, Einar, and Per Selle. "Struktur og aktør i Stein Rokkans forskning," *Norsk statsvitenskapelig tidsskrift*, 1988, no. 3.

Bezkrovnyi, L. G. *Russkaia armiia i flot v XIX veke Moscow: Voen.-e'kon. potentsial Rossii*. Akademiia nauk SSSR. Institut istorii SSSR Moskva: Nauka 1973.

Bilinsky, Yaroslav. "Expanding the Use of Russian or Russification? Some Critical Thoughts on Russian as a Lingua Franca and the 'Language of Friendship and Cooperation of the Peoples of the USSR,'" *Russian Review* 40:3, 1981, pp. 317–32.

Bohn, Thomas M. *Russische Geschichtswissenschaft von 1880 bis 1905: Pavel N. Miljukov und die Moskauer Schule*. Beiträge zur Geschichte Osteuropas: Bd. 25. Köln: Böhlau Verlag, 1998.

Boudon, Raymond. *The Logic of Social Action. An Introduction to Sociological Analysis*. London: Routledge & Keegan Paul 1981.

——. *Theories of Social Change*. Cambridge: Polity Press 1986.

Brenner, Rober. "The Origins of Capitalist Development. A Critique of Neo-Smithian Marxism," *New Left Review* 104, 1977.

Bromlei, Iu. *Sovremennye etnicheskie protsessy v SSSR*. Moscow: Nauka 1977.

Buci-Glucksmann, Christine. *Gramsci and the State*. London: Lawrence & Wishart 1980.

Bugge, Peter. "Habsburgmonarkiets tysk-østerrikere, " *Den Jyske Historiker* 57, 1991.

Campbell, F. Gregory. "Central Europe's Bastion of Democracy," *East European Quarterly* 11:2, 1977, pp. 155–76.

Carr, Edward Hallett. *The Twenty Years Crisis*. London: Macmillan 1958.

Cherniavsky, Michael. "Russia," in Orest Ranum, *National Consciousness, History, and Political Culture in Early-Modern Europe*. Baltimore: Johns Hopkins University Press 1975.

——. *Tsar and People. Studies in Russian Myths*. New Haven, CT: Yale University Press 1961.

Chirot, Daniel (ed.). *The Origins of Backwardness in Eastern Europe. Economics & Politics from the Middle Ages until the Early Twentieth Century*. Berkeley: University of California Press 1989.

——. "Review of Theda Skocpol's Social Revolutions in the Modern World," *Social Forces* 75:3, 1997, pp. 1121–26.

Clem, Ralph S. "The Changing Geography of Soviet Nationalities Socioeconomic and Demographic Correlates," Peter J. Potichnyj and Jane Shapiro Zacek (eds.), *Politics and Participation Under Communist Rule. Selected Papers From the Second World Congress for Soviet and East European Studies*. New York: Praeger 1983.

Codreanu, Corneliu Zelea. *For My Legionaire: The Iron Guard*. Madrid: Editura "Libertatea" 1976.

Cohen, G. A. *Karl Marx's Theory of History: A Defence*. Oxford: Clarendon Press 1978.

Connor, Walker. *The National Questions in Marxist-Leninist Theory and Strategy.* Princeton, NJ: Princeton University Press 1984.

Conquest, Robert. *The Great Terror: Stalin's Purge of the Thirties.* London: Macmillan 1968.

Conze, Werner, "Die Strukturkrise des östlichen Mitteleuropas für und nach 1919," *Vierteljahrehäfte für Zeitgeschichte* 1:4, 1953, pp. 319–38.

Cvetkova, Bistra. "The Bulgarian Haiduk Movement in the 15th–18th Centuries," in Gunther Rosenberg, Bela Kiraly, and Peter Sugar (eds.), *East Central European Society and War in Pre-Revolutionary Eighteenth Century.* New York: Columbia University Press 1982, pp. 327–29.

Daniels, Robert V. "Marxism and Leninism." Part 1 in Robert V. Daniels, *The Rise and Fall of Communism in Russia.* New Haven, CT: Yale University Press 2007.

———. "Stalin: Revolutionary or Counterrevolutionary?" *Problems of Communism* September–October 1989, pp. 81–86.

———. "Stalinist Ideology as False Consciousness," in Robert V. Daniels, *Trotsky, Stalin, and Socialism.* Boulder, CO: Westview Press 1991.

Danilova, L. V. "Disskusia po vaznoi probleme," *Voprosy Filosofii* 12, 1965.

Dann, Otto (ed.). *Nationalizmus in vorindustrieller Zeit.* Munich: R. Oldenbourg 1986.

Daskalov, Roumen. "Ideas About, and Reactions to Modernization in the Balkans," *East European Quarterly* 31:2, 1997, pp. 141–80.

Davies, R. W. *The Development of the Soviet Budgetary System.* Cambridge: Cambridge University Press 1958.

Davison, R. "Nationalism as an Ottoman Problem and the Ottoman Response," in William W. Haddad and William Ochsenwald (eds.). *Nationalism in a Non-National State: The Dissolution of the Ottoman Empire.* Columbus: Ohio State University Press 1977, pp. 25–25.

Denber, Rachel (ed.). *The Soviet Nationality Reader. The Disintegration in Context.* Boulder, CO: Westview Press 1992.

Desheriev, Iu. D. "Bytovaia kultura i ee otrashenie v iazyke," in Iu. D. Desheriev, *Natsionalnyi iazyk i kultura.* Moscow: Nauka 1978.

Deutsch, Karl. *Nationalism and Social Communication.* Cambridge, MA: MIT Press 1966.

Dolgorukov, Peter Vladimirovich. *Rossiiskaia rodoslovnaia kniga, izdavaemaia kniazem Petrom Dolgorukovym.* St. Petersburg: V tipografii Karla Vingebera 1855.

Duncan, P. J. S. "The Rebirth of Politics in Russia," in Geoffrey A. Hosking, Jonathan Aves, and Peter J. S. Duncan, *The Road to Post-Communism. Independent Political Movements in the Soviet Union 1985–1991.* London: Pinter Publishers 1992, pp. 67–123.

Dvornik, Francis. *The Slavs in European History and Civilization.* New Brunswick, NJ: Rutgers University Press 1962.

Eco, Umberto. "Ur-Fascism," *New York Review of Books,* June 22, 1995.

Eisenstadt, S. N. "Comparative Analysis of State Formation in Historical Context," *International Social Science Journal* 32:4; 1980, pp. 624–54.

Eisenstadt, S. N., and Stein Rokkan (eds.). *Building States and Nations.* Beverly Hills: Sage 1973.

Elster, Jon. "The Theory of Combined and Uneven Development: A Critique," in John Roemer (ed.), *Analytical Marxism*. Cambridge: Cambridge University Press 1986.

Evans, Ifor L. *The Agrarian Revolutions in Roumania*. Cambridge: Cambridge University Press 1924.

Evans, Peter. *Embedded Autonomy. States and Industrial Transformation*. Princeton, NJ: Princeton University Press 1995.

Evans, R. J. W. "Joseph II and Nationality in the Habsburg Lands," in H. M. Scott (ed.), *Enlightened Absolutism: Reform and Reformers in Later Eighteenth-Century Europe*. Houndmills, Basingstoke, Hampshire: Macmillan 1990.

Flora, Peter. "Introduction and Interpretation," in Peter Flora, Stein Kuhnle, and Derek Urwin (eds.), *State Formation, Nation-Building and Mass Politics in Europe. The Theory of Stein Rokkan*. Oxford & New York: Oxford University Press 1999.

———. "Stein Rokkans Makromodell der politische Entwicklung Europas. Ein Rekonstruktionsversuch," *Kölner Zeitschrift für Soziologie und Sozialpsykologie* 33:3, 1981, pp. 475–98.

Flora, Peter, Stein Kuhnle, and Derek Urwin (eds.), *State Formation, Nation-Building and Mass Politics in Europe. The Theory of Stein Rokkan*. Oxford & New York: Oxford University Press 1999.

Galuzo, P. G. "Das Kolonialsystem des russischen Imperialismus am Vorabend der Oktoberrevolution," *Zeitschrift fur Geschichtswissenschaft* Berlin/GDR 15:6. 1967, pp. 997–1014.

———. "Kolonialnaia sistema imperialistitcheskoi Rossii," in *Akademia Nauk SSSR, Institut istorii, Istoria SSSR c drevneishikh vremen do nashikh dnei*, vol. 6, *Rossiia v period imperializma 1900–1917 gg*. Moscow: Nauka 1968.

Garushyants, Iurii. "Ob aziatskom sposobe proizvodstva," *Voprosy Istorii* 2, 1966, pp. 84–100.

Geertz, Clifford. "Thick Description Toward an Interpretive Theory of Culture," in Clifford Geertz, *The Interpretaion of Cultures*. New York: Basic Books 1973.

Gellner, Ernest. *Nations and Nationalism*. Oxford: Blackwell 1983.

Gerschenkron, Alexander. *Continuity in History and Other Essays*. Cambridge, MA: Belknap Press of Harvard University 1968.

———. *Economic Backwardness in Historical Perspective*. Cambridge, MA: Belknap Press of Harvard University 1962.

———. *Europe in the Russian Mirror: Four Lectures in Economic History*. London: Cambridge University Press 1970.

———. "Soviet Marxism and Absolutism," *Slavic Review* 30:4, 1971, pp 853–69.

Glaser, B. G., and A. L. Strauss. *The Discovery of Grounded Theory*. New York: Aldine de Gruyter 1967.

Good, David. "Modern Economic Growth in the Habsburg Monarchy," *East Central Europe* 7:2 1980, pp. 248–68.

Gourevitch, Peter. "The International System and Regime Formation. A Review of Anderson and Wallerstein," *Comparative Politics* 10:3, 1978.

———. *The Political Response to an International Trade Crisis: Comparative Responses to the Great Depression of 1873–1896*. Paper presented to the Canadian Political Science Association, Edmonton, Alberta, June 1–5, 1975.

Gramsci, Antonio. *Selections from the Prison Notebooks* (eds. Quintin Hoare and Geoffrey Nowell Smith). London: Lawrence & Wishart 1971.

Granberg, Aleksander G. *Optimzatsiia territorialnykh proportsii narodnogo khoziaistva*. Moscow: Ekonomika 1973.

Gregor, A. James. *Italian Fascism and Developmental Dictatorship*. Princeton, NJ: Princeton University Press 1979.

Guboglo, M. N. "Razvitie mnogonatsionalnoi sovetskoi pechati v 1917–1940 gg," *Istoriia SSSR* 6, 1972, pp. 121–32.

Haddad, William W., and William Ochsenwald (eds.). *Nationalism in a Non-National State: The Dissolution of the Ottoman Empire*. Columbus: Ohio State University Press 1977.

Hanak, Peter (ed.). *Die Nationalitätenfrage in der Österreichisch-ungarischen Monarchie 1900–1918*. Budapest: Akadémiai Kado/Verlag der Ungarischen Akademie der Wissenschaften 1966.

———. "Verbürgerlichung und Assimilation," and "Ungarns Gesellschaft am Anfang des 20. Jahrhundert," in Peter Hanak, *Ungarn in der Donaumonarchie. Probleme der bürgerlichen Umgestaltung eines Vielvölkerstaates*. Schriftenreihe des Osterreichischen Ost-und Sudosteuropa-Instituts 10. Vienna: Verlag fur Geschichte un Politik 1984.

Harasymiw, B. "Die sowjetische Nomenklatur 1," *Osteuropa* 7, 1977, pp. 583–98.

———. "Die sowjetische Nomenklatur 2," *Osteuropa* 8, 1977, pp. 665–81.

Hechter, Michael. *Internal Colonialism. The Celtic Fringe in the British National Development, 1536–1966*. London: Routledge & Kegan Paul 1975.

Hellmann, Manfred. *Grundzüge der Geschichte Litauens und des litauischen Volkes*. Darmstadt: Wissenschaftliche Buchgesellschaft 1966.

Herz, Friedrich. *The Economic Problems of the Danubian States. A Study in Economic Nationalism*. London: Gollancz 1947.

Hintze, Otto. *Historical Essays* (ed. Felix Gilbert). New York: Oxford University Press 1975.

———. *Staat und Verfassung*. Leipzig: Koehler und Amelang 1941.

Hirschmann, Albert. *Exit, Voice and Loyalty*. Cambridge, MA: Harvard University Press 1970.

Hobsbawn, Eric. *The Age of Extremes. The Short Twentieth Century*. London: Michael Joseph 1995.

———. *Bandits*. Harmondsworth: Penguin 1969.

———. *Nations and Nationalism, Programme, Myth, Reality*. Cambridge: Cambridge University Press 1990.

Hodnett, Grey. *Leadership in the Soviet National Republics. An Quantitative Study of Recruitment Policy*. Oakville, Ontario: Mosaic Press 1978.

Hosking, Geoffrey A., Jonathan Aves, and Peter J. S. Duncan. *The Road to Post-Communism. Independent Political Movements in the Soviet Union 1985–1991*. London: Pinter Publishers 1992.

———. *Russia: People and Empire*. Cambridge, MA: Harvard University Press 1997.

Hough, Jerry. *The Soviet Prefects: the Local Party Organs in Industrial Decision-making*. Cambridge, MA: Harvard University Press 1969.

Hroch, Miroslav. "From National Movement to the Fully-formed Nation. The nation-building process in Europe," *New Left Review* 198, 1993.
———. "How Much Does Nation Formation Depend on Nationalism?" *East European Politics and Societies* 4:1, 1990.
———. *Linguistic Conflicts in Eastern Europe and Their Historical Parallels.* Prague: Charles University 1990. Unpublished.
———. "Old Nationalism or New National Movements." *The Oslo Congress: Minority Protection and Human Rights in the New Europe.* Leangkollen January–February 1991.
———. *Social Preconditions of National Revival in Europe. A Comparative Analysis of the Social Composition of Patriotic Groups among the Smaller European Nations.* Cambridge: Cambridge University Press 1986.
Hroch, Miroslav, and Luda Klusakova (eds.). *Criteria and Indicators of Backwardness. Essays on Uneven Development in European History.* Prague: Faculty of Arts 1996.
Hugelmann, Karl Gottfried (ed.). *Das Nationalitätenrecht des alten Osterreich.* Wien-Leipzig: W. Braumüller, Universitäts-Verlagsbuchhandlung 1934.
Ionescu, Ghita, and Ernest Gellner (eds.). *Populism, Its Meaning and National Characteristics.* New York: Macmillan 1969.
Isaev, M. I. *Iazykovoe stroitelstvo v SSSR.* Moscow: Nauka 1979.
———. "Natsiia i iazyk," *Voprosii istorii* 2, 1968.
Janos, Andrew C. "Continuity and Change in Eastern Europe: Strategies of Post-Communist Politics," in Beverly Crawford (ed.), *Markets, States, and Democracy. The Political Economy of Post-Communist Transformation.* Boulder, CO: Westview Press 1995.
———. "The Politics of Backwardness in Continental Europe, 1780–1945," *World Politics* 41:3, 1989, pp. 325–58.
———. *The Politics of Backwardness in Hungary: 1815–1945.* Princeton, NJ: Princeton University Press 1982.
Jaszi, Oscar. *The Dissolution of the Habsburg Monarchy.* Chicago: University of Chicago Press 1929.
Jelavich, Charles, and Barbara Jelavich. *The Establishment of the Balkan National States, 1804–1920.* Seattle: University of Washington Press 1977.
Jenks, W. A. "Economics, Constitutionalism, Administration and Class Structure," *Austria History Yearbook* 3:1, 1967, pp. 32–62.
Jessop, Bob. *Putting the Capitalist State in its Place.* Oxford: Polity Press 1990.
Kalberg, Stephen. *Max Weber's Comparative Historical Sociology.* Cambridge: Polity Press 1994.
Kann, Robert. *The Multinational Empire: Nationalism and National Reform in the Habsburg Monarchy 1848–1918*, vols. 1 and 2. New York: Columbia University Press 1950.
———. "Zur Problematik der Nationalitätenfrage in der Habsburgermonarchie 1848–1918," in Adam Wandruszka and Peter Urbanitsch (eds.), *Die Habsburgermonarchie 1848–1918* 3/2. *Die Völker des Reiches.* Vienna: Verlag der Österreichischen Akademie der Wissenschaften 1980.

Kappeler, Andreas. "The Ambiguities of Russification." *Kritika: Explorations in Russian and Eurasian History* 5:2, 2004, pp. 291–97.

——. "Czarist Policy toward the Muslims of the Russian Empire," in Andreas Kappeler, Gerhard Simon, and George Brunner (eds.), *Muslim Communities Reemerge. Historical Perspectives on Nationality, Politics, and Opposition in the Former Soviet Union and Yugoslavia*. Durham & London: Duke University Press 1994.

——. *The Russian Empire. A Multiethnic History*. Harlow: Pearson 2001.

Karklins, Rasma. "Ethnic Politics and Access to Higher Education: The Soviet Case," *Comparative Politics* 16:3, 1983–84, pp. 277–94.

Katus, Laszlo. "Die Madiaren," in Adam Wandruszka and Peter Urbanitsch (eds.), *Die Habsburgermonarchie 1848–1918* 3/1. *Die Völker des Reiches*. Vienna: Verlag der Österreichischen Akademie der Wissenschaften 1980.

——. "Über die wirtschaftlichen Grundlagen der Nationalitätenfrage in Ungarn vor dem ersten Weltkrieg," in Peter Hanak (ed.), *Die Nationalitätenfrage in der Österreichisch-ungarischen Monarchie 1900–1918*. Budapest: Akadémiai Kado/Verlag der Ungarischen Akademie der Wissenschaften 1966, pp. 149–217.

Kautsky, John H. (ed.), *Political Change in Underdeveloped Countries: Nationalism and Communism*. New York: John Wiley 1962.

Khansuvarov, I. *Latinizatsiia-orudie Leninskoi natsionalnoi politiki*. Moscow, 1932.

Khoros, V. *Populism: Its Past, Present and Future*. Moscow: Progress 1984.

Khrushchev, Nikita S. *Khrushchev Remembers*. Boston: Little, Brown & Co 1970.

Kiraly, Bela, and Laszlo Veszpremy (eds.), *Trianon and East Central Europe*. Boulder, CO: Social Science Monographs 1995.

Kitchelt, Herbert. "Formation of Party Cleavages in Post-Communist Democracies–Theoretical Propositions," *Party Politics* 1:4, 1995, pp. 447–72.

Kitromilides, Paschalis M. "Imagined Communities' and the Origins of the National Question in the Balkans," *East European Quarterly* 19, 1989, pp. 149–94.

Kliuchevskii, Vasilii. *Kurs russkoĭ istorii: sochineniia v deviati tomakh* I. Moscow: Mysl 1987.

Knei-Paz, Baruch. *The Social and Political Thought of Leon Trotsky*. Cambridge: Cambridge University Press 1978.

Knock, Thomas J. *To End All Wars: Woodrow Wilson and the Quest for a New World Order*. New York: Oxford University Press 1992.

Kolstoe, Paul. *Russians in the Former Soviet Republics*. London: Hurst 1995.

Kommisrud, Arne. *Relativ tilbakeliggenhet som problemfelt og forklaringsfaktor i sammenliknende historisk forskning*. Magistergradsavhandling i statsvitenskap Universitetet i Oslo 1982.

——. *Stat, nasjon, imperium. Habsburgmonarkiet, Tsar-Russland-et historisk-sosiologisk perspektiv*. Oslo: Spartacus 1996.

——. *Verdier og konflikt. Forklaringer i Max Webers historiske sosiologi*. Oslo: Spartacus 1995.

Koralka, Jiri. "The Czechs," in Andreas Kappeler, Fikret Adanir, and Alan O'Day (eds.), *The Formation of National Elites. Comparative Studies on Governments and Non-Dominant Ethnic Groups in Europe, 1850–1940*, vol. 6. Dartmouth: European Science Foundation/New York University Press 1992.

Korbonski, Andrzey. "Civil-Military Relations in Poland Between the Wars: 1918–1939," *Armed Forces and Society* 14:2, 1988, pp. 161–90.

Koropeckyj, I. S. "A Century of Moscow-Ukraine Relations: An Interpretation," *Harvard Ukrainian Studies* 3:4, 1981, pp. 467–96.

Kossior, S. V., and P. P. Postyshev. *Der bolschewistisiche Sieg in der Ukraine. Reden auf dem Vereinigten Plenum des Zk und ZKK der Kommunistischen Partei der Ukraine (Bolschewiki) in November 1933.* Moscow/Leningrad: Verlagsgenossenschaft ausländischer Arbeiter in der UdSSR 1934.

Kramer, Hans. *Die Italiener unter der österreichisch-ungarischen Monarchie.* Wiener historischer Studien Band 2. Vienna: Herold 1954.

Krnjevic, Juraj. "Peasants Movements in Eastern Europe," *Contemporary Review* 174, July/December 1948, pp. 111–14.

Kula, Witold. *An Economic Theory of the Feudal System.* London: New Left Books 1976.

Ladis Kristof. "The State Idea, the National Idea and the Image of the Fatherland," *Orbis* 11, Spring 1967.

Lampe, John. "Imperial Borderlands or Capitalist Periphery? 1520–1914," in Daniel Chirot (ed.), *The Origins of Backwardness in Eastern Europe. Economics & Politics from the Middle Ages until the Early Twentieth Century.* Berkeley: University of California Press 1989.

Larsen, Stein Ugelvik, B. Hagtvet, and J. P. Myklebust (eds.), "The Logic of Stein Rokkan's Overall Model of Europe." Paper presented at the XVI World Congress of the International Political Science Association, Berlin August 21–25, 1994.

——. *Who Were the Fascists: Social Roots of European Fascism.* Bergen: Universitetsforlaget 1980.

Lavrov, V. V., and K. N. Plotnikov (eds.). *Gosudarstvennyj biudzhet SSSR.* Moscow: Finansy 1975.

Ledonne, John P. "Russian Governors General, 1775–1825. Territorial or Functional Administration?" *Cahiers du Monde russe* 42:1, Janvier–Mars 2001, pp. 5–30.

Leff, Carol Skalnik. *National Conflict in Czechoslovakia. The Making and Remaking of a State, 1918–1987.* Princeton, NJ: Princeton UP 1988.

Lewin, Moshe. *The Gorbachev Phenomenon.* Berkeley: University of California Press 1988.

Lewis, Robert A., Richard H. Rowland, and Ralph S. Clem. *Nationality and Population Change in Russia and the USSR: an Evaluation of Census Data, 1897–1970.* New York: Praeger 1976.

Likhachov, Dmitrii S. *Natsionalnoe samosoznanie Drevnei Rusi. Ocherki iz oblasti russkoi literatury* XI–XVII vv. Moscow-Leningrad: Izdatelstvo Akademiia Nauk SSSR 1945.

——. *Velikoe Nasledie. Klassicheskie proizvedeniia literatury Drevnei Rusi.* Moscow: Sovremennik 1979.

Loit, Alexander. "Socio-Ethnic Structures and National Movements in the Late Russian Empire: The Baltic Countries." University of Stockholm, 1990/Paper World Congress of Soviet and Eastern European Studies, Harrogate 1990.

Luebbert, Gregory. *Liberalism, Fascism, or Social Democracy. Social Classes and the Political Origins of Regimes in Interwar Europe.* New York & Oxford: Oxford University Press 1991.

Macartney, C. A. *Hungary and Her Successors; The Treaty of Trianon and its Consequences 1919–1937.* London & New York: Oxford University Press 1937.

MacMillan, Margareth. *Paris 1919: Six Months that Changed the World.* New York: Random House 2002.

Magris, Claudio. *Donau.* Oslo: Cappelen 1991.

Manoilescu, Mihail. *Le siècle du corporatisme: doctrine du corporatisme integral et pur.* Paris: Felix Alcan 1934.

——. *The Theory of Protectionism and of International Trade.* London: King & Son 1931.

Mann, Michael. "State and Society 1130–1815. An Analysis of English State Finances," in Maurice Zeitlin (ed.), *Political Power and Social Theory,* vol. 1. Greenwich, CY: Jai Press 1980.

Martin, Terry. *The Affirmative Action Empire. Nations and Nationalism in the Soviet Union, 1923–1939.* Ithaca & London: Cornell University Press 2001.

Marx, Karl, and Frederick Engels. *Articles on Britain.* Moscow: Progress 1971.

Mãrz, Eduard, and Karl Socher. "Währung und Banken in Cisleithanien," in Adam Wandruschka and Peter Urbanitsch (eds.), *Die Habsburgermonarchie 1848–1918,* vol 1, *Die wirtschaftliche Entwicklung.* Vienna: Verlag der Österreichischen Akademie der Wissenschaften 1973.

McAuley, Alastair, "Economic Development and Political Nationalism in Uzbekistan," *Central Asian Survey* 5:3–4, 1986, pp. 161–82.

McCagg Jr., William. "Hungary's 'Feudalized' Bourgeoisie," *Journal of Modern History* 44:1, March 1972, pp. 65–78.

McGowan, Bruce. *Economic Life in Ottoman Europe. Taxation, Trade and the Struggle for Land, 1600–180.* Cambridge: Cambridge University Press 1981.

McRae, K. "The Principle of Territoriality and the Principle of Personality in Multilingual States," *Linguistics* 158, 1975, pp. 33–54.

Medvedev, Roy. *Let History Judge: The Origins and Consequences of Stalinism.* New York: Vintage 1973.

Meyer, Alfred G. "USSR, Incorporated," *Slavic Review* 20:3, 1961, pp. 369–76.

——. *The Soviet Political System: An Interpretation.* New York: Random House 1965.

Miliukov, Paul. *History of Russia.* New York: Funk & Wagnalls 1968.

——. *Russia and Its Crisis.* Chicago: University of Chicago Press 1905.

——. *Skizzen Russischer Kulturgeschichte.* Leipzig: Verlag Otto Migand 1898.

Miller, John. "Nomenklatura: Check on Localism," in T. H. Rigby and H. Harasymiw (eds.), *Leadership Selection and Patron-Client Relations in the USSR and Yugoslavia.* Selected papers from the second World Congress for Soviet and East European Studies [Garmisch-Partenkirchen, 1980] London: Allen & Unwin 1983, pp. 62–97.

Mitchell, Jeremy C. "Velgerskaren og den hemmelige valghandlingen," in Bernt Hagtvet (ed.), *Politikk mellom økonomi og kultur. Stein Rokkan som politisk sosiolog og forskningsinspirator.* Oslo: Ad Notam Gyldendal 1992, pp. 207–16.

Mitrany, David. *Marx Against the Peasant. A Study in Social Dogmatism.* New York: Collier Books 1961.

Mjøset, Lars. "Can Grounded Theory Solve the Problems of Its Critics," *Sosiologisk Tidsskrift* 13, 2005, pp. 379–408.

——. "Er positivismekritikken den eneste kritikk som det er mulig å reise mot norsk sosiologi?" *Sosiologi i dag* 2:2, 1981.

——. "No Fear of Comparisons or Context: On the Foundations of Historical Sociology," *Comparative Education* 42, 2006, pp. 337–62.

——. "Stein Rokkan's Thick Comparisons," *Acta Sociologica* 43, 2000.

——. *Transition to Capitalism: Escalation of Rationalization.* PRIO Working Paper 4/1982. International Peace Institute of Oslo 1982.

Moore, Wilbert E. *Economic Demography of Eastern and Southern Europe.* Geneva: League of Nations. Reprint New York: Arno Press 1972.

Moore Jr., Barrington. *Social Origins of Dictatorship and Democracy. Lord and Peasant in the Making of the Modern World.* Boston: Beacon Press 1966.

"Moscow, August 1991—The Coup de Grace: A Symposium," *Problems of Communism* 41 November–December 1991, pp. 1–63.

Niederhauser, Emile. *The Rise of Nationalism in Eastern Europe.* Budapest: Corvina Kiado 1982.

Nolde, Boris E. *Iurii Samarin i ego vremia.* Paris: Impr. de Navarre 1926.

Nove, Alec. "History, Hierarchy and Nationalities," in Alec Nove, *Political Economy and Soviet Socialism.* London: G. Allen & Unwin 1979.

——. "Is There a Ruling Class in the USSR?" in Alec Nove, *Political Economy and Soviet Socialism.* London: G. Allen & Unwin 1979.

Oberlander, Erwin. *Sowjetpatriotismus und Geschichte. Dokumentation.* Cologne: Verlag Wissenschaft und Politik 1964.

Offergeld, Wilhelm. *Grundlagen und Ursachen der industrielle Entwicklung Ungarns.* Jena: G. Fischer 1914.

Opeide, Gunnar. "Tilbakeliggenhetens problem," *Forum Øst* 3:3, 1985, pp. 8–30.

Ostapenko, L. V., and A. Susokolov. "Etnosotsialnye osobennosti vosproisvodstva intelligentsii," *Sotsiologicheskie issledovaniia* 1, 1983.

Payne, Stanley. *A History of Fascism, 1914–1945.* London: UCL Press 1995.

Pearson, Raymond. "Privileges, Rights and Russification," in Olga Crisp and Linda Edmondson (eds.), *Civil Rights in Imperial Russia.* Oxford: Clarendon 1983, pp. 83–102.

Pech, Stanley Z. "Political Parties in Eastern Europe 1848–1939: Comparisons and Continuities," *East Central Europe* 5:1, 1978, pp. 1–38.

Penkaitis, Norbert. *Der Finanzausgleich in der Sowjetunion und seine Bedeutung fur die Wirtschaftsentwicklung der Unionsrepublikken.* Giessener Abhandlungen zur Agrar- und Wirtschaftsforschung des europäischen Ostens 89. Berlin Dunker und Humblot 1977.

Petrovichev, N. A. *Vazhnyı̆ faktor vozrastaniia rukovodiashcheı̆ roli KPSS.* Moskva: Politizdat 1979.

Pijl, Kees Van der. "Soviet Socialism and Passive Revolution," in Stephen Gill (ed.), *Gramsci. Historical Materialism and International Relations.* Cambridge

Studies in International Relations 26. Cambridge: Cambridge University Press 1993.

Plekhanov, Georges. *Introduction a l'histoire Sociale de la Russie*. Paris: Editions Bossard 1926.

Plotnikov, N. "Transformation of the Uzbek republic," in E. Robinson (ed.), *Backward Areas in Advanced Countries: Proceedings of a Conference Held by the International Economic Association*. London: Macmillan 1969.

Pollard, Sidney. *Peaceful Conquest. The Industrialization of Europe 1760–1970*. Oxford: Oxford University Press 1981.

Poulantzas, Nicos. *Political Power and Social Classes*. London: Verso 1982.

Raeff, Marc. "Patterns of Russian Imperial Policy Toward the Nationalities," in Edward Allworth (ed.), *Soviet Nationality Problems*. New York: Columbia University Press 1971, pp. 22–42.

——. "The Russian Autocracy and its Officials," *Harvard Slavic Studies* 4: 1957, pp 77–91.

Rigby, T. H. *Communist Party Membership in the USSR 1917–1967*. Princeton, NJ: Princeton University Press 1968.

——. "Staffing USSR Incorporated: The Origins of the Nomenklatura System," *Soviet Studies* 40:4, 1988, pp. 523–37.

Roberts, Henry L. *Rumania. Political Problems of an Agrarian State*. New Haven, CT: Yale University Press 1951.

Roeder, Philip G. "Soviet Federalism and Ethnic Mobilization," in Rachel Denber (ed.), *The Soviet Nationality Reader. The Disintegration in Context*. Boulder, CO: Westview Press 1992, pp. 147–78.

Rogger, Hans. "Nationalism and the State: A Russian Dilemma," *Comparative Studies in History and Society* 4:3, 1961.

Rokkan, Stein. "Cities, States, and Nations: A Dimensional Model for the Study of Contrasts in Development," in S. N. Eisenstadt and Stein Rokkan (eds.), *Building States and Nations*, vol. 1. Beverly Hills, CA: Sage 1973.

——. "Dimensions of State Formation and Nation Building: A Possible Paradigm for Research on Variations within Europe," in Charles Tilly (ed.), *The Formation of National States in Western Europe*. Princeton, NJ: Princeton University Press 1975, pp. 562–600.

——. "Eine Familie von Modellen für die Vergleichende Geschichte Europas," *Zeitschrift für Soziologie* April 1980, pp. 118–28.

——. "Entries, Voices, Exits: Towards a Possible Generalization of the Hirschmann Model," *Social Science Information* 13:1, 1974, pp. 39–53.

——. "Mass Suffrage, Secret Voting and Political Participation," *Archives Européennes de Sociologie* 2:1, 1961, pp. 132–52.

——. "Nation-Building, Cleavage Formation and the Structuring of Mass Politics," in Stein Rokkan, with Angus Campbell, Per Torsvik, and Henry Valen, *Citizens, Elections, Parties; Approaches to the Comparative Study of the Processes of Development*. Oslo: Universitetsforlaget/New York: McKay 1970.

——. *Stat, nasjon, klasse* (ed. Bernt Hagtvet). Oslo: Universitetsforlaget 1987.

——. "The Structuring of Mass Politics in the Smaller European Democracies: A Developmental Typology," *Comparative Studies in Society and History* 10:2, 1968, pp. 26–65.

——. "The Survival of Distinctiveness," in Stein Rokkan et al. (eds.), *Economy, Territory, Identity: The Politics of European Peripheries*. Beverly Hills, CA: Sage 1983.

——. "Territories, Centers and Peripheries: Toward a Geoethnic–Geoeconomic–Geopolitical Model of Differentiation within Western Europe," in Jean Gottmann (ed.), *Center and Periphery. Spatial Variation in Politics*. Beverly Hills, CA: Sage 1980.

——. "Territories, Nations, Parties: Toward a Geoconomic–Geopolitical Model for the Explanation of Variations within Western Europe," in Richard L. Merritt and Bruce M. Russett (eds.), *From National Development to Global Community. Essays in Honor of Karl W. Deutsch*. London: George Allen & Unwin 1981, pp. 70–95.

Rokkan, Stein, with Angus Campbell, Per Torsvik, and Henry Valen. *Citizens, Elections, Parties: Approaches to the Comparative Study of the Processes of Development*. Oslo: Universitetsforlaget/New York: McKay 1970.

Rokkan, Stein, and Bernt Hagtvet. "The Conditions of Fascist Victory," in S. Ugelvik Larsen, B. Hagtvet, and J. P. Myklebust (eds.), *Who Were the Fascists: Social Roots of European Fascism*. Bergen: Universitetsforlaget 1980, pp. 131–53.

Rokkan, Stein, Derek Urwin, Frank H. Aarebrot, Pamela Malaba, Terje Sande. *Center-Periphery Structures in Europe. An ISSC Workbook in Comparative Analysis*. Frankfurt: Campus 1987.

Romanovich-Slavatinskii, A. Dvorianstvo v Rossii ot nachala XVIII vieka do otmieny kriepostnogo prava: svod materiala i priugotovitel'nye etiudy dlia istoricheskago izsliedovaniia A. Romanovich-Slavatinskago. St. Petersburg: Tip. Ministerstva vnutrennikh diel, 1870. Also issued as Slavistic Printings and Reprintings no 100, The Hague: Mouton 1968.

Rosenberg, Bela Kiraly, and Peter Sugar (eds.). *East Central European Society and War in Pre-Revolutionay Eighteenth Century*. New York: Columbia University Press 1982.

Rosenberg, Hans. *Grosse Depression und Bismarckzeit. Wirtschaftablauf, Gesellschaft und Politik in Mittel-Europa*. Veröffentlichungen der historischen Kommision zu Berlin beim Friedrich-Meinecke-Institut der freien Universität 24. Berlin 1967.

——. "Political Consequences of the Great Depression," in Hans Rosenberg, *Machteliten und Wirtschaftkonjunkturen: Studien zur neueren deutschen Sozial- und Wirtschaftsgeschichte*. Kritische Studien zur Geschichtswissenschaft 31. Göttingen: Vandenhoeck & Ruprecht 1978.

——. "Wirtschaftskonjunktur, Gesellschaft und Politik in Mitteleuropa," in Hans Rosenberg, *Machteliten und Wirtschaftkonjunkturen: Studien zur neueren deutschen Sozial- und Wirtschaftsgeschichte*. Kritische Studien zur Geschichtswissenschaft 31, Göttingen: Vandenhoeck & Ruprecht 1978.

Rosenstein-Rodan, Paul N. "Problems of Industrialization of Eastern and South-Eastern Europe," *Economic Journal* 53, June–September 1943, pp. 202–11.

Rothfehls, Hans. "Grundsätzliches zum Problem der Nationalität," *Historische Zeitschrift* 174, 1952, pp. 339–58.

Rotschild, Joseph. *East Central Europe between the two World Wars*. Seattle: University of Washington Press 1988.

Rowley, David G. "Imperial versus National Discourse: The Case of Russia," *Nations and Nationalism* 6:1, 2000.

Rudolph, Richard L., and David Good (eds.). *Nationalism and Empire. The Habsburg Empire and the Soviet Union*. New York: St. Martin's Press 1992.

Safran, William. "Language, Ideology, and State-Building: A Comparison of Policies in France, Israel, and the Soviet Union," *International Political Science Review* 13:4, 1992, pp. 397–414.

Sak, L. M., and M. I. Isaev. "Problemy pismennosti narodov SSSR v kulturnoi revoliutsii," *Voprosy istorii* 2, 1966.

Sartori, Giovanni. "European Political Parties: The Case of Polarized Pluralism," in Joseph La Palombara and Myron Weiner (eds.), *Political Parties and Political Development*. Princeton, NJ: Princeton University Press 1966.

Sawer, Marian. "Plekhanov on Russian History: A Marxist Approach to Historical Pluralism," *Science and Society* 39:1, 1975, pp. 292–317.

Schmidt-Häuer, Christian. "Das Imperium schlägt zurück," *Die Zeit* December 7, 1990.

Schmitt, Bernadotte E. "The Peace Treaties of 1919–1920," *Proceedings of the American Philosophical Society* 104:1, 1960, pp. 101–10.

Schmitter, Philippe. "Reflections on Mihail Manoilescu and the Political Consequences of Delayed-Development on the Periphery of Western Nations," in Kenneth Jowitt (ed.), *Social Change in Romania, 1860–1940: A Debate on Development in a European Nation*. Berkeley: Institute of International Studies at the University of California 1978.

Schroeder, Gertrude. "Regional Differences in Incomes and Levels of Living in the USSR," in V. N. Bandera and Z. L. Melnyk (eds.), *The Soviet Economy in Regional Perspective*. New York: Praeger 1973.

———. "Soviet living standards: Achievements and Prospects," in 97th Cong., 2nd sess., joint committee print, "December 31, 1982," vol. 2, *Selected Papers Submitted to the Joint Economic Committee, Congress of the U.S.: Soviet Economy in the 1980's: Problems and Prospects*. Washington: USGPO 1983.

Schöpflin, George. "The Political Traditions of Eastern Europe," *Dædalus. Journal of the American Academy of Arts and Sciences* 119:1, Winter 1990, pp. 59–93.

Sejersted, Francis. "Norsk historisk forskning ved inngangen til 1990-årene. Et oppgjør med den metodologiske individualisme," *Historisk tidsskrift* 4, 1989.

Seton-Watson, R. W. *Treaty Revision and the Hungarian Frontiers*. London: Eyre & Spottiswoode 1934.

Shapiro, A. L. "Ob absoliutizme v Rossii," *Istoria SSSR* May 1968, pp. 69–81.

Shunkov, V. I., et al. (eds.). *Perekhod ot feodalizma k kapitalizmu v Rossii: materialy Vsesoiuzno diskusii*. Moscow: Nauka 1969.

Simon, Gerhard. "Bricht die Sowjetunion auseinander? Perestrojka und die nationale Frage," *Berichte des Bundesinstituts für ostwissenschaftliche und internationale Studien* 18, 1990.

——. *Nationalismus und Nationalitätenpolitik in der Sowjetunion. Von der totalitären Diktatur zur nachstalinschen Gesellschaft.* Baden-Baden: Nomos Verlagsgesellschaft 1986.

——. "Nationalismus und Nationalitätenpolitik in der Sowjetunion seit Stalin," *Berichte des Bundesinstituts für Ostwissenschaftliche und Internationale Studien* 34, 1979.

Skazkin, S. D. (ed.). *Dokumenty sovetsko-italiansko konferentssii istorikov 8–10 aprelja 1968 goda: absoliutizm v Zapadno Evrope i Rossii: russko-italianskie sviazi vo vtoro polovine XIX veka. Akademiia nauk SSSR, Institut vseobshche istorii, Institut istorii SSSR.* Moscow: Nauka 1970.

Skocpol, Theda. *States and Social Revolutions.* Cambridge: Cambridge University Press 1978.

Skocpol, Theda, and Margareth Somers. "The Uses of History in Macrosocial Inquiry," *Comparative Studies in Society and History* 22:2, 1980, pp. 87–93.

Slocum, John W. "Who, and When, Were the Inorodtsy? The Evolution of the Category of 'Aliens' in Imperial Russia," *Russian Review* 57, 1998, pp. 173–90.

Smith, Anthony D. *The Ethnic Origins of Nations.* London: Basil Blackwell 1986.

——. *The Ethnic Revival.* Cambridge: Cambridge UP 1981.

——. *Theories of Nationalism.* London: Duckworth 1971.

Springer, Rudolf (Karl Renner). *Der Kampf der österreichischen Nationen um den Staat.* Leipzig: Deuticke 1902.

Stalin, Joseph. "Extract from the Report on the Work of the Central Committee of the CPSU Delivered at the Seventeenth Party Congress, January 26, 1934," in Joseph Stalin, *Marxism and the National and Colonial Questions.* New York: International Publishers 1935.

——. "Marxism and Problems of Linguistics." Published in the June 20, July 4, and August 2, 1950, issues of *Pravda.* Stalin Reference Archive marxists.org 2000: http://www2.cddc.vt.edu/marxists/reference/archive/stalin/works/1950/jun/20.htm.

——. "Political Report of the Central Committee to the Sixteenth Congress of the CPSU b June 27, 1930," *Pravda* 177, June 1930; Stalin Reference Archive marxists.org 2000: http://www2.cddc.vt.edu/marxists/reference/archive/stalin/works/1930/aug/27 htm.

Starr, S. Frederick. "Tsarist Government: The Imperial Dimension," in Jeremy R. Azrael (ed.), *Soviet Nationality Policies and Practices.* New York: Praeger 1978, pp. 3–38.

Stoianovich, R. "The Social Foundations of Balkan Politics 1750–1941," in Charles Jelavich and Barbara Jelavich (eds.), *The Balkans in Transition. Essays on the Development of Balkan Life and Politics Since the Eighteenth Century.* Berkeley: University of California Press 1963.

Strauss, A. L. "Discovering New Theory from Previous Theory," in T. Shibutani (ed.), *Human Nature and Collective Behavior. Papers in Honor of Herbert Blumer.* Englewood Cliffs, NJ: Prentice Hall 1970, 46–53.

Stokes, Gale. "The Social Origins of East European Politics," in Daniel Chirot (ed.), *The Origins of Backwardness in Eastern Europe. Economics & Politics from the Middle Ages until the Early Twentieth Century*. Berkeley: University of California Press 1989.

Stone, Norman. "Constitutional Crisis in Hungary 1903–1906," *Slavonic Review* 45:104, 1967, pp. 163–82.

Stourzh, Gerald. "Die Gleichberechtigung der Volksstämme als Vervassungsprinzip 1848–1918," in Adam Wandruszka and Peter Urbanitsch (eds.), *Die Habsburgermonarchie 1848–1918* 3/1. *Die Völker des Reiches*. Vienna: Verlag der Österreichischen Akademie der Wissenschaften 1980.

Strugatskii, Boris. "Zhit interesnee chem pisat," *Literaturnaya Gazeta* April 10, 1991, p. 9.

Sugar, Peter (ed.). *Native Fascism in the Successor States* 1918–1945. Santa Barbara, CA: ABC-Clio 1971.

———. *Southeastern Europe under Ottoman Rule 1354–1804*. Seattle: University of Washington Press 1977.

Suny, Ronald Grigor. "Georgia and Soviet Nationality Policy," in Stephen F. Cohen, Alexander Rabinowitz, and Robert Sharlets (eds.), *The Soviet Union since Stalin*. Bloomington: Indiana University Press 1980.

———. "Nationalities in the Russian Empire," *Russian Review* 59, 2000.

Sutter, Bernhold. "Politische und rechtliche Stellung der deutschen in Österreich 1848–1918," in Adam Wandruszka and Peter Urbanitsch (eds.), *Die Habsburgermonarchie 1848–1918* 3/1 *Die Völker des Reiches*. Vienna: Verlag der Österreichischen Akademie der Wissenschaften 1980.

Szporluk, Roman. "Dilemmas of Russian Nationalism," in Rachel Denber (ed.), *The Soviet Nationality Reader. The Disintegration in Context*. Boulder, CO: Westview Press 1992.

Tilly, Charles. *Big Structures, Large Processes, Huge Comparisons*. New York: Sage 1984.

———. (ed.). *The Formation of National States in Western Europe*. Princeton, NJ: Princeton University Press 1975.

———. "Reflections on the History of European Statemaking," in Charles Tilly (ed.), *The Formation of National States in Western Europe*. Princeton, NJ: Princeton University Press 1975.

———. "Sinews of War," in Per Torsvik (ed.), *Mobilization. Center-Periphery Structures and Nation-Building*. Bergen: Universitetsforlaget 1981.

———. "Stein Rokkans begrepsmessige kart over Europa," in Bernt Hagtvet (ed.), *Politikk mellom økonomi og kultur. Stein Rokkan som politisk sosiolog og forskningsinspirator*. Oslo: Ad Notam/Gyldendal 1992.

Topolski, Jerzy. "The Manorial Serf-Economy in Central and Eastern Europe in the 16th and 17th Centuries," *Agricultural History* 48, 1974, pp. 341–52.

Trotsky, Leon. *The History of Russian Revolution*. London: Pluto Press 1977.

———. *1905*. Harmondworth: Penguin 1972.

Tucker, Robert C. *Stalin in Power: The Revolution from Above, 1928–1941*. New York: Norton 1990.

Turner, Bryan. *For Weber: Essays in the Sociology of fate.* London: Routledge & Kegan Paul 1981.

Urbanitsch, Peter. "Die deutschen in Österreich," in Adam Wandruszka and Peter Urbanitsch (eds.), *Die Habsburgermonarchie 1848–1918* 3/1. *Die Völker des Reiches.* Vienna: Verlag der Österreichischen Akademie der Wissenschaften 1980.

Urwin, Derek W. *From Ploughshare to Ballotbox. The Politic of Agrarian Defence in Europe.* Bergen: Universitetsforlaget 1980.

Vago, Bela, and George L. Mosse (eds.). *Jews and non-Jews in Eastern Europe, 1918–45.* New York: Wiley 1974.

Vardy, Steven B. "The Impact of Trianon upon Hungary and the Hungarian Mind: The Nature of Interwar Hungarian Irredentism," *Hungarian Studies Review* 10:1, 1983, pp. 21–42.

Veblen, Thorstein. *Imperial Germany.* New York: Augustus M. Kelley 1964.

Voslenskii, Mikhail. *Nomenklatura. Gospodstvuiushchii klass Sovetskogo Soiuza.* London: Overseas Publications Interchange 1984.

Vucinich, W. S. "The Yugoslav Lands in the Ottoman Period: Post-War Marxist Interpretations of Indigenous and Ottoman Institutions," *Journal of Modern History* 27:3, 1955, pp. 287–305.

Waldenberg, Marek. *Kwestie Narodowe w Europie Srodkowo-Wschodniej: dzieje, idée.* Warszawa: Wydawn, Nauk, PWN 1992.

Walicki, Andrzej. "The Three Traditions in Polish Patriotism," in Stanislaw Gomulka and Antony Polonsky (ed.), *Polish Paradoxes.* London: Routledge 1990.

Wandruszka, Adam, and Peter Urbanitsch (eds.). *Die Habsburgermonarchie 1848–1918*, vol. 1, *Die wirtschaftliche Entwicklung.* Vienna: Verlag der Österreichischen Akademie der Wissenschaften 1973.

——. (eds.). *Die Habsburgermonarchie 1848–1918*, vol. 2. *Verwaltung und Rechtwesen.* Vienna: Verlag der Österreichischen Akademie der Wissenschaften 1975.

——. (eds.). *Die Habsburgermonarchie 1848–1918*, vols. 3/1 and 3/2. *Die Völker des Reiches.* Vienna: Verlag der Österreichischen Akademie der Wissenschaften 1980.

Wandycz, P. *The Price of Freedom. A History of East Central Europe from the Middle Ages to the Present.* London: Routledge 1992.

Wank, Solomon. "Foreign Policy and the Nationality Problem in Austria-Hungary, 1867–1914," *Austria History Yearbook* 3:3, 1967, pp. 37–56.

——. "The Impact of the Dual Alliance on the Germans in Austria and Vice-versa," *East Central Europe* 7:2, 1980, pp. 288–310.

Weber, Max. *The Protestant Ethic and the Spirit of Capitalism.* London & New York Routledge 1990.

Wessely, Kurt. "Österreich-Ungarns Wirtschaft vor dem ersten Weltkrieg," *Donauraum* 12, 1967, pp. 13–40.

Whiteside, Andrew G. *The Socialism of Fools. Georg Ritter von Schönerer and Austrian Pan-Germanism.* Berkeley: University of California Press 1975.

Wilber, C. K. *The Soviet Model and the Underdeveloped Countries.* Chapel Hill: University of North Carolina Press.

Wittraum, Reinhart. *Baltische Geschichte. Die Ostseelände Livland, Estland, Kurland 1180–1918.* Munich: R. Oldenbourg 1954.

Wolff, Robert Lee. *The Balkans in Our Time*. Cambridge, MA: Harvard University Press 1956.

Wysocki, Josef. *Infrastruktur und wachsende Staatsausgaben. Das Fallbeispiel österreich 1868–1913. Forschungen zur Sozial und Wirtschaftsgeschichte*, 20, Stuttgart: G. Fischer 1975.

Zaslavsky, Victor. "The Evolution of Separatism in Soviet society Under Gorbachev," in Gail W. Lapidus, Victor Zaslavsky, with Phillips Goldman (eds.), *From Union to Commonwealth. Nationalism and Separatism in the Soviet Republics*. Cambridge: Cambridge University Press 1993.

Ziegler, Charles E. "Nationalism, Religion and Equality among Ethnic Minorities: Some Observations on the Soviet Case," *Journal of Ethnic Studies* 13, 1985, pp. 9–32.

Zwitter, Fran. *Les Problemes nationaux dans la Monarchie des Habsbourg*. Belgrade: Comité national yougoslave des sciences historiques 1960.

———. "Nationale Probleme und gesellschaftliche Struktur in der Habsburgermonarchie," *Österreichische Osthefte* 13:3, 1977, pp. 147–60.

Østerud, Øyvind. "Absolutismen som statsbygging," in Øyvind Østerud, *Det moderne statssystem og andre politisk-historiske studier*. Oslo: Gyldendal 1987.

———. *Det moderne statssystem og andre politisk-historiske studier*. Oslo: Gyldendal 1987.

———. "Nasjonalitetsprinsipp og nasjonsbygging," in Øyvind Østerud, *Det moderne statssystem og andre politisk-historiske studier*. Oslo: Gyldendal 1987.

———. "Utvikling gjennom tilbakeliggenhet," in Øyvind Østerud, *Det moderne statssystem og andre politisk-historiske studier*. Oslo: Gyldendal 1987, pp. 125–44.

———. "Wallersteins varldssystemanalys. En kommentar," in G. Behre and Birgitta Oden (eds.), *Historievetenskap och Historiedidaktikk*. Lund: Liber/Oslo: Universitetsforlaget 1982.

Index

About the Author

Arne Kommisrud is a Norwegian political scientist working at the Department of Political Science and Sociology at the University of Tromsø, Northern Norway, where he has been since 1998. He received his Master's Degree and Ph.D. from the University of Oslo. He is the author of two books and a number of articles in the field of Comparative Historical Sociology in Norwegian. He is currently working on a project analyzing the history of basic political sociological concepts.

www.ingramcontent.com/pod-product-compliance
Ingram Content Group UK Ltd.
Pitfield, Milton Keynes, MK11 3LW, UK
UKHW012040150926
475560UK00001B/109

9 780739 128718